For Glenn

Third edition published 2011
by Routledge
711 Third Avenue, New York, NY 10017

Simultaneously published in the UK
by Routledge
2 Park Square, Milton Park, Abingdon, Oxon OX14 4RN

Routledge is an imprint of the Taylor & Francis Group, an informa business

First edition published by Kogan Page 2000

Second edition published by Routledge Falmer 2003

Library of Congress Cataloging in Publication Data
Salmon, Gilly.
    E-moderating: the key to online teaching and learning/
    Gilly Salmon. – 3rd ed.
        p. cm.
      Includes bibliographical references and index.
    1. Teaching – Computer network resources.
    2. Computer-assisted instruction.   3. Distance
    education.   I. Title.
    LB1044.87.S249 2011
    371.33′4 – dc22   2010052320

ISBN13: 978–0-415–88173–9 (hbk)
ISBN13: 978–0-415–88174–6 (pbk)
ISBN13: 978–0-203–81668–4 (ebk)

Typeset in Bembo and Gill Sans by
Florence Production Ltd, Stoodleigh, Devon

Printed and bound by TJ International Ltd, Padstow, Cornwall

E-moderating

Professor Gilly Salmon has achieved continuity and illumination of the seminal five-stage model, together with new research-based developments, in her much-awaited third edition of *E-moderating* – the most quoted and successful guide for e-learning practitioners.

Never content to offer superficial revisions or simple 'solutions' against the pace of technological advances, the expanding interest and requirements for online learning, and the changes they have wrought, *E-moderating, 3rd edition* offers a richness of applied topics that will directly impact learners and teachers of all kinds. The book is carefully crafted and supported with evidence, examples and resources for practical guidelines, making it potentially transformational for all practitioners.

E-moderating, 3rd edition includes:

- Updates of literature, key terms, case studies and projects
- Fresh examples of the use of the five-stage model around the world, at different levels of education and across disciplines
- Guidelines for moderating for podcasting and virtual worlds
- Illustrations from the latest All Things in Moderation development programmes (www.atimod.com)
- New resources for practitioners

Gilly Salmon spent six years as head of the Beyond Distance Research Alliance and the Media Zoos at the University of Leicester (www.le.ac.uk/mediazoo).

She is now Professor of Learning Futures and Executive Director of the Australian Digital Futures Institute at the University of Southern Queensland, Australia (www.usq.edu.au/adfi).

E-moderating

The Key to Teaching and Learning Online

Third Edition

GILLY SALMON

Routledge
Taylor & Francis Group

NEW YORK AND LONDON

Contents

Preface

E-moderators are the new generation of teachers and trainers who work with learners online. Earlier editions of this book have 'struck a spark' and helped make the online world a creative, happy, productive and relevant place for successful learning. In this expanded and revised third edition my aim is to bring readers up to date with recent exciting changes in that world, and our growing knowledge and excellent online practice.

Human use of computing is vast and growing. Networked technologies such as the internet and the World Wide Web have been called 'transformational' because of their wide-ranging impact. Electronic networking creates communications across terrestrial boundaries, across cultures and on a global scale. Concepts of space and time are changing, and of how and with whom people can collaborate, discover communities, explore resources and ideas and learn.

Computer Mediated Communication and its collaborative sister, Computer Mediated Conferencing (CMC), actually arrived before the internet and the World Wide Web became widely available. CMC encouraged teachers to challenge perceived and received wisdom and practice about learning online and to reflect on their experiences. Computer mediation has become so much part of our everyday lives now, that in this book I just call it a place 'Online'.

In this book, I call attention to the mediator, or e-moderator, in online learning processes. Successful online learning depends on teachers and trainers acquiring new competencies, on their becoming aware of its potential and on their inspiring the learners, rather than on mastering the technology.

Investigating the use of online has many facets and aspects. Web utopians once predicted virtual schools, colleges and universities with very low-cost learning and truly effective 'any time, any place' student interaction. They said that the need for expensive campus buildings or large corporate training facilities will disappear along with the requirement for learners to physically congregate. The 'web-phobes' were very worried that the benefits of learning together might be lost and that it will be a bad day for knowledge, for feelings, for the joys of gatherings and groups.

Meanwhile, many people got on with creating the future – as each year has unfolded the potential for learning online has become greater along with the complexity of identifying the most viable and desirable ways forward. Small factions of teachers, researchers and trainers have led the way. Like all pioneers, they have a tough time. For them, and for the thousands of online teachers that will follow, I hope this book will be of interest and of use. It's time to start the wagon train again but this time with somewhat stronger pathways of understandings to follow.

There are many definitions of an online course. At one end of the spectrum of 'online-ness', these include classroom-based teaching supplemented by lecture notes posted on a website or by electronic communication such as e-mail. At the other end of the spectrum, materials may be made available and interactions occur exclusively through networked technologies. This book is concerned with more or less the full spectrum (and not-yet-created combinations), but the key issue is that the teacher, instructor, tutor or facilitator – the e-moderator – is operating in the electronic environment along with his or her students, the participants.

I have drawn on my own experience of online learning, as well as that of many other people. I have selected case studies and experiences where the storyteller is the academic, teacher or e-moderator involved, where implementation occurred within the regular learning and teaching situation, and where there was some evaluation or at least serious reflection on practice.

For some twenty years, I have been able to study and practise the art of e-moderating, particularly within the Open University (OU). I began learning online in 1988, when I was a student on the first OU course to use online conferencing on a large scale. The software and systems we had at that time were primitive, although they felt revolutionary to me! I was excited by the experience and by the potential. In 1988, we used a system called 'CoSy' (short for Conferencing System) that worked on commands from the keyboard. Offline readers, point and click mouse commands, graphics and ever-increasing sophistication of functions followed as software systems developed. Each new function seemed like a great step forward at the time. When I joined the OU Business School (OUBS) as a lecturer in 1989, I was able to experiment with online conferencing for teaching management courses at a distance. Later I was responsible for training hundreds of e-moderators for the school.

You will appreciate the irony of writing a book about something I strongly believe needs to be experienced in the electronic environment itself. So when

I first put the book together, I thought of you, the readers, as potential collaborators in an online experience. I still think of you as:

● academics, teachers, course managers, teaching assistants, tutors, instructors, moderators and trainers of any discipline at post-secondary level in any country or training department, who are planning to move from conventional teaching to teaching online or who are working in open and distance learning;
● staff developers and academic developers of all kinds;
● developers of corporate learning, training departments of large companies, brokers of and agents for online training.

I believe there may be some 'lurkers' or 'browsers', too. They are likely to be:

● software designers who are working on education and training projects;
● developers considering the use of learning technologies in educational programmes;
● teachers working in primary and secondary schools;
● staff in community programmes or local government departments dealing with health and social welfare who are planning to deploy online for building communities or for democratic purposes;
● managers and academics responsible for assessment of trainees' and teachers' performance.

In this third edition, I have added two new chapters, but the book is still in two parts. In Part 1, Chapter 1 explains what I see as e-moderating and explores it. Chapters 2 and 3 offer a research-based model for understanding training and development for online conferencing and interaction and apply it in discussion boards and other new technologies for collaborative learning. Chapter 4 explores the roles and competencies of e-moderators, with examples. Chapters 5 and 6 explore key issues in training e-moderators at, respectively, the OU and All Things In Moderation Ltd. Chapter 7 looks at the learners' experiences. No book of this kind can resist a peek at the future, which you'll find in Chapter 8.

Part 2 changes tack and offers an updated set of practical resources largely based on my own practice as an e-moderator. I also reflect research and acknowledge the research and development teams I have worked within over the past six years. I hope you will find them useful for meeting this exciting challenge.

This book will provide you with support in thinking through your online teaching, for your topic, your subject, your organization, your programme, your teaching practice and your learners. This is the way to take part and *shape* the future of teaching and learning online – through the actions of the e-moderators.

Drivers in education are many and complex. Borders and boundaries between physical locations, disciplines and levels are reducing and sometimes disappearing. The use of information and communication technologies (ICT) to support easy access to learning or flexibility of all kinds is often a central tenet of educational missions. Some countries, such as Australia, forged ahead using leaders and champions to show direction. In others, such as the UK, government initiatives have promoted new institutional forms or technological systems approaches. Until recently, the allure of the technology has received the lion's share of attention. Although the ideas of increasing access, participation, skills and competencies for new forms of societies of the twenty-first century are at the heart of many intentions, the investment in the role of human intervention and support to harness the technology into the service of teaching and learning has been meagre by comparison.

One notable development in the last few years is the increasing exploration around the nature of teaching and learning itself, which has been fed, stimulated and challenged by the increasing use of computing in most educational arenas. Many educationalists are excited that networked technologies provide a new kind of window on the world of information, but feel uncomfortable that they also may serve to reduce the social and collaborative aspects of learning. The debate about how to engage students online continues, and about what kinds of technologies, provided by whom, create the right kind of environments for what! My book *E-tivities* attempts to address some of these.

Since I wrote the first edition of *E-moderating*, there is less reason to convince the world that we need support for online teachers, trainers and facilitators (from a happy and successful band of e-moderators) to make e-learning work well. Thinking has moved on from believing that technology may do away with teachers and towards how they can be trained and supported to work online. Researchers have stopped making spurious comparisons between online and face-to-face, and explored instead when and what we need to do to make online really worthwhile. We still need to find ways of scaling up the e-moderating task force without consuming huge amounts of diminishing resources.

By the time you read these pages I will be working at the University of Southern Queensland as Professor of Learning Futures. I am certain that despite all these changes, e-moderating will remain the key to successful learning and teaching online.

Gilly Salmon
Leicester
October 2010

Acknowledgements for the third edition

The research for this, the third edition of *E-moderating*, has spanned six very happy and productive years for me as Professor of E-learning and Learning Technologies and Head of the Beyond Distance Research Alliance at the University of Leicester in the UK. It's been one of the most exciting times in my career, a time when I've had the privilege and joy to work in a forward-looking, knowledge-constructing team, within an innovative and student-centred university. No, I really mean it! I'm moving now to be Professor of Learning Futures at the University of Southern Queensland, so this book is my Leicester swansong.

Beyond Distance (www.le.ac.uk/beyonddistance) is an alliance of teachers and researchers willing to create a productive future for learning online, rather than simply watch it unfold. Hundreds and hundreds of people, in the university and elsewhere, have touched this future. Whether named here or not, they have had an impact on this book, and I thank them for their inspiration, encouragement, comments, sources, help, experiences and challenges. The alliance team has worked with almost every academic department at Leicester, with fantastic people who tell us how it really, really IS!

The idea of a research and development unit in a higher education institution is still unusual and my thanks go to the senior management team at Leicester for the faith they've put into Beyond Distance – Vice Chancellor Professor Sir Bob Burgess, PVCs John Fothergill and Christine Fyfe, and Registrar

Dave Hall. And to Professor Annette Cashmore for her unending encouragement. I thank them for their strong acknowledgement and for opening so many doors.

Outside the university, my thanks go to the Association of Learning Technology (http://www.alt.ac.uk/), a wonderful community, constantly impacting on learning. And to all the people who asked me to talk at their conferences, seminars and meetings and who came to see us at Leicester. I'm sure we learnt more from them than they did from us. My special thanks go to those who contributed case studies and examples to this book – and to their online participants – truly a cast of thousands. Hundreds more participants in the All Things in Moderation Ltd. (www.atimod.com) courses have advanced our understanding of how to prepare people to e-moderate – there's more about them in Chapter 6, with the latest 2010 example. Thanks to David Shepherd and Ken Giles as always for their keenness and contributions.

I hope you'll spot all these contributions throughout this edition but I can't resist thanking by name the people I worked most closely with; it's really the very least I can do in return for the hundreds of questions I asked and the challenges I posed, for their huge toleration, support and commitment, and for explaining their research and development findings to me. Long live the daily 10 am 'Creative Meetings' at Beyond Distance! So thanks, and here's to the future of learning, to: Ola Aiyegbayo, Alejandro Armellini, Kelly Barklamb, Terese Bird, Rob Cane, Sheetal Chudasama, Emma Davies, Roger Dence, Palitha Edirisingha, Sylvia Jones, Simon Kear, Suzanne Lavelle, Louise Lubkowski, Matt Mobbs, Richard Mobbs, Jaideep Mukherjee, Ming Nie, Samuel Nikoi, Rakesh Patel, Madelaine Peene, Sandra Romenska-Aggarwal, Tania Rowlett, Paul Rudman, Lee Taylor, Matthew Wheeler, Helen Whitehead and Gabi Witthaus. Our visiting professor since 2005 has been David Hawkridge: I thank him for his advice and editing, which have been invaluable yet again for this edition, as for the previous two.

Thank you to Phil Candy, Michael Sankey and Shirley Reushle for enabling me to get fast into the swing of things at the University of Southern Queensland, and for their suggestions and contributions to this book.

And of course my thanks to Rod, Glenn, Emily and Paula, and many other friends and family for always saying 'Yes . . . and we will help you!'

Part 1:

CONCEPTS AND CASES

Throughout this book, I use real online messages from courses that I design or run as illustrations. I indicate a screen message by shading, like this paragraph. Messages have had to be pruned to reduce the amount of space they take up in the book, but I have not attempted to correct their grammar or informal language. By the way, looking at selected messages in print after the interactive event makes them seem more organized than they really were. Live e-moderating is likely to be messier!

Chapter 1

E-moderating – the journey

This book is set in the context of the rapid development of technologies of all kinds, addressing communication, business, life processes and entertainment. A few have been developed specifically for learning and or knowledge dissemination purposes (these are usually called 'learning technologies') but many others have been 'harnessed' by educators and adapted and exploited for learning use – often called 'technology enhanced learning'. This book's key focus and emphasis are on the advantages to learning made possible by technology and the best ways of achieving this aim, but I look at these changes through the eyes of online teachers, for whom I have used the term 'electronic moderators' – 'e-moderators'.

This chapter introduces e-moderating to you and starts to explore the contexts and environments in which it thrives.

The term 'online' came from the days of the telegraph, when messages could be tapped directly onto the line rather than prepared 'offline' on perforated tape, for sending when the machine was later connected to the telephone line. Today, 'online networking' covers a range of technologies. In education and training, technologies that concentrate on computer-mediated communication are commonest. They fall into three broad categories as originally defined by Santoro (1995):

1. Informatics, particularly involving electronic access via telecommunications to catalogues, library resources, interactive remote databases and archives, including those on the World Wide Web.

2. Computer-assisted instruction, also known as computer-assisted learning and computer-based training, which may or may not require tele-communications.
3. Computer-mediated conferencing is based on computers and tele-communications.

From 2002, there was a new view of the generations of online learning environments (Dirckinck-Holmfeld, 2002). These are:

1. First generation: computer conferencing, asynchronous and text based.
2. Second generation: web based, still asynchronous but now including more linked (hyper) texts and multimedia resources.
3. Third generation: includes more synchronous communication.
4. Fourth generation: virtual reality and mobility. And more as yet un-imagined.

E-moderators undertake most of their work at present with first and second generation technologies. However, I now include a much wider range of learning technologies and those that have been produced for business, social networking, entertainment and harnessed in the service of knowledge sharing and construction. The Horizon reports, which started in 2002 and continue annually, are a great way of viewing the rapid changes and deployment of technologies in the service of learning, teaching and creative expression (Horizon, 2010). Many defy highly structured categorizing, at least at this early stage in their development.

Another way of considering ideal 'types' is the level of interactivity between the learner, the learning resources and the learning group. The research and stories in this book could be considered as Ellis and Goodyear's (2010) Type 2 – that is, using largely web-based resources and software but with significant human intervention. In practice, the cry that is heard so frequently 'it's not really about the technology' has been proven through research, through practice, through the learners' and teachers' voices – whilst learning design creates the pedagogy, the human intervention by an empathetic teacher enables the learning. I make no apologies for stating and restating this absolute truism for me. I am indebted to the fresh and valuable experience of my fantastic colleagues at the University of Leicester, where we have had the opportunity to research many ways of creating humanness in technology through the Media Zoo (www.le.ac.uk/mediazoo). I am also learning from my new colleagues at the University of Southern Queensland, from their wisdom and experience (see for example Reushle and Mitchell, 2009; Candy, 2010).

A moderator is a person who presides over a meeting. An e-moderator presides over an electronic online meeting or conference, though not in quite the same ways as a moderator does. Computer-mediated conferencing, often shortened to (CMC) actually requires e-moderators to have a rather wider range of expertise, as I shall explain and demonstrate.

There are many different definitions and applications of e- or online learning. One main difference is between those who see online as based on instruction and transmission, and those who see the learner's experience as central to knowledge construction. In this book I focus mainly on the second definition. This is the world where the role and skills of the e-moderator are critically important.

I hope you will come to see the word 'e-moderating' as an active verb – like learning and teaching. The essential role of the e-moderator is promoting human interaction and communication through the modelling, conveying and building of knowledge and skills.

An e-moderator undertakes this feat through using the mediation of online environments designed for interaction and collaboration. To learn to undertake an e-moderating role, whether coming to it fresh or as a change to previous teaching, coaching or facilitating practice, takes a mixture of new insights and some technical skill, but mostly understanding the management of online learning and group working.

In our highly complex world, of course I acknowledge that the place of human intervention is highly complex. The tutor, teacher, trainer – whatever you wish to call, him, her or them (I call them e-moderators when they work online) – operate in the boundary between the educational establishment (represented by the curriculum and the provided learning technologies) and the learning experience – they adopt a wide variety of roles.

Jane's diary

Here are a few pages from Jane's diary. She's an e-moderator, and it will give you the flavour of what this job can be like. Jane is a university teacher, like me, and she's an enthusiast too.

Day 1, Thursday, 10 pm

Just back from swimming. I check my course list: 16 students this time, from four continents. I hope they've all received the first mailing in the post, including their log-on instructions and my first requests. I try not to plead too hard for them to get started really early on the conferencing!

How many will have logged in by Day 1? I click on the Cross-cultural Management Conference icon. Then into the 'Arrivals' thread. And there it is on my screen! The 'new message' flag. The conferencing begins! It's great getting to know new students. Abraham is confident:

> Hi there.
>
> ABRAHAM HAS LIFT OFF! OR IS IT LANDING?
> I'VE ARRIVED IN THIS INTERESTING NEW PLACE AND I'M
> READY TO BEGIN.
> Who can tell me what's what around here?

This one's perhaps timid:

> I hope I'm posting this message in the right place. Can someone tell me?
> Marianne from Manchester

Out of my 16, eight have got there so far and have announced their arrival, as I asked them to. Another two have e-mailed me. Paula in Moscow says she's having connection problems. Ben can't find the Cross-cultural Management Conference discussion board on his screen. I e-mailed both back with ways of contacting technical support and diaried myself to follow up in a few days.

So, I e-mail the arrivals to thank and encourage them for their first conference messages. I mention to Abraham that capital letters are equivalent to shouting online. I check the message history for the arrivals conference – two more have been reading the messages but haven't contributed yet. I'm sure they will soon. I make that 12 on the runway.

I check the conference for their second task: to use the 'resume' facility to tell the group a little about themselves. Time online: 45 minutes.

Day 3, Saturday, 10.45 am

Super! Two more in arrivals, one from Beijing, one from London. Fourteen on the runway now. Some interchanges occurring in 'arrivals' between those already there. I need to archive to avoid too many unread messages (especially as six were from Abraham). For the final arrival I post a message asking people to move across to the café conference and I put a couple of chatty messages in there myself. Time online: 15 minutes.

Day 5, Monday, 10 pm

Out for sushi then log on. Fifteen chatty messages in café conference and one more new arrival – Sylvia from Vienna. Set first conference for carrying out course activities. As a 'warm-up' activity, I post this message:

Task 1 Over the next few days, visit a local store that sells soft drinks. Try and find the cheapest of the kind on offer of:

Coca–Cola,

Local cola brand.

Check out how each type of cola is priced, the place where you found it and the type of promotion it was being given. Please give price per can or bottle.

Then convert your currency into sterling through a currency converter website. Post your results in this conference by next Sunday 7 pm GMT. Abraham and Marianne have agreed to collate and post comparative results.

As an example, I went to my local supermarket in Loughton in North East London in the United Kingdom. Here are my results:

Price for Coca-Cola: £0.38, ie 38p (but sold only in packs of 6 for £2.25)

Price for local cola: Safeways 'Select' Cola £0.28 (but sold only in packs of 6 cans for £1.69)

Promotion for Coca-Cola: displayed at eye level on soft drinks shelf (Pepsi Cola was below eye level)

Promotion for local cola: displayed at eye level along with options, e.g. caffeine-free. The packaging and colour very similar to Coca-Cola.

Time online: 10 minutes.

Day 10, Saturday, 6.45 am

Going out for the day so I log on early.

The facilitators for the cola activity, Abraham and Marianne, report by e-mail that they have 13 results in. They are chasing the other two.

Check message histories throughout the conference. I'm still one participant completely missing online. Check participants' list, this is a Philip Brown from Dublin. Time online: 10 minutes.

Phone technical helpline. They've had no requests for help from P. Brown. Fax him to ask what problems?

Day 13, Tuesday, 7.15 am

Log on before leaving for work.

Marianne has posted a spreadsheet giving 15 results (14 from students plus mine) for the 'cola' exercise. I set up a sub-conference with starter questions:

> What do the results tell you about the way soft drinks are marketed in your home location, compared to the others? What do they tell you about:
>
> 1. The economy of your location?
> 2. The habits of cola drinking throughout the world? Are there any indications of cultural differences?
> 3. Your views on the nature of global brands?

Time online: 5 minutes.

Day 18, Sunday, 7.30 pm

Log on quickly while the family are clearing up the garden after a barbecue.

E-mail from the course administrator that P. Brown from Dublin has dropped out of the course due to connection problems. Very annoying, wonder if it's recoverable? I will compose a snail-mail letter to him.

The cola exchange sub-conference has really taken off. There are 36 messages in it. I do a quick analysis:

> Four people had posted one message each;
> Three people had posted five messages;
> Four people had posted two messages;
> Three people had posted three messages;
> One reading everything but not contributing.

I summarize the relevant contributions into one 'key points' message and archive the originals so participants can access them if they like. Two people – Anton and Jeremy – had started a conversation in the cola conference about alcohol and their local driving laws. I archive these messages with the rest but e-mail A. and J. to suggest they continue this conversation by e-mail. Time online: 35 minutes.

Day 20, Tuesday, 12.30 pm

Log on from the office in my lunch break to set up the first assignment.

I divide the 'class' into two groups for this exercise – one group of eight and one of seven. I mix up activists and reflectors in the groups, based on my experience of them so far. Post URL with notes on forming virtual teams and online collaboration. Appoint facilitators for each team, and e-mail them basic e-moderating points to help them.

Make as clear as I can the requirements for assessment and deadlines for submission. Time online: 35 minutes.

Day 30, Friday, 4 pm

Log on from office and look in on Assignment 1 discussions.

Team A have built themselves a clear objectives and a triple conference structure for their team. They've spent the first few days in dividing up tasks and responsibilities. In Conference 1 'Data', the student facilitator has asked each participant to post a set of data about themselves. In Conference 2 'Concepts', Peter's summarized the data in Conference 1, and put his views on how this relates to Hofstede and there is the start of a discussion. Conference 3 'Meanings?' is currently empty except for its introduction message, saying this is the place for developing the written assignment!

Team B has started with just one conference, where they introduced themselves, explained their backgrounds, education, families, interests and the places they had lived in the world. People seem to be enjoying explaining about themselves and only two messages have gone over the suggested 'one screenful' in length. There are several interesting threads, where participants are finding their similarities and differences. No leader has emerged yet but two participants appear to be taking responsibility for progressing the discussions, while another is complaining about the two who are reading but not posting messages – saying this is not 'fair'. I'll wait for a few more days to see if they start putting some structure into this before intervening.

I post a message in our 'information' conference to say I'll be away for three days and offline. Time online: 20 minutes.

E-moderating, a new way of orchestrating learning

E-moderating along the lines of Jane's conference has become an accepted way of teaching, particularly in higher and professional education.

The early adopters of teaching with computers were considered mavericks. They found it necessary substantially to change their teaching practice, to welcome computers with open arms; they took online courses for themselves, incessantly asked questions of experts, acquired the earliest computers for teaching or for home use. Some worked out how to use computers to enhance their usual ways of facilitating, others saw computers as a way of transforming their agenda for student-centred learning. Since then there has been a worldwide increase in the adoption of networked computers for teaching and learning, and whereas the staff involved used to be considered innovators or early adopters, now learners and teachers of all kinds expect to be online.

Many colleges, universities and training organizations have moved online, with the associated issues of student satisfaction and quality. In higher education the move to online in a wide variety of forms continues unabated. There is less uncertainty about the value of e-learning. But, time and time again, studies have shown that the role of the online teacher or tutor – in whatever disciplinary context, level or type of technology in use – has a major influence on learners' flexibility and achievements (Ruey, 2010; Dawson, 2010; Loureiro-Koechlin and Allan, 2010).

What we now know for sure is that concepts of time, motivation and teacher development are the key factors in e-learning success. We need to improve our online teaching in terms of both quality and quantity, whether in a blended, online-only or technology-enhanced mode. We cannot succeed in scaling up without enabling the role and training of the e-moderator. E-moderators need new attitudes, knowledge and skills, and ways of operating successfully and happily in the online environment.

The availability, speed and usability of networked computers in homes for education and at work have rapidly increased, while costs to online participants have fallen, making online learning and interaction accessible to large numbers of participants. Online learning raises extremely challenging issues for education, however, including complex partnerships, funding and intellectual property. Most of all, online learning calls for the training and development of new kinds of online teachers – the e-moderators of this book.

As the internet and the World Wide Web have expanded, opportunities to use them for teaching and learning have expanded too and we now have a very wide range of opportunities to engage with learning, creativity and knowledge construction. Educationists all over the world are experimenting with various forms of distance, open, blended, mobile and flexible learning. Networked computing offers the chance to build a learning community: this can be in a university or college, in an industrial or commercial setting, or based on common interests or objectives rather than geographical location. I have met many academics and trainers who are very keen indeed to adopt these new ways to enliven teaching and learning in their subjects. Their institutions and organizations have invested heavily in technological systems, thus creating conditions in which networked learning can be widely available.

Monash University in Melbourne, Australia, was one of the first universities in the world to explore and exploit networked computing for learning, and to train academic staff and e-moderators. It continues to be committed to the philosophy that effective e-moderation underpins in the delivery of quality education in the online environment. Sandra Luxton, senior lecturer and director of the online Master of Marketing, reports on the role that e-moderation has played in the development and delivery of online marketing education at Monash.

E-moderating at Monash

The Marketing Department at Monash University has been involved in distance education since the late 1980s and in multimedia education from the mid-1990s, with the initial development of an online version of the undergraduate foundation subject, 'Marketing Theory and Practice'. From this experience in electronic course delivery, a second development phase was undertaken: that of an entire graduate program – the 12-subject eMaster of Marketing. In 2010 the topics continue to expand and now include environmental (green) marketing. The eMasters is based on a hybrid educational model comprising a text-based study guide, CD with multimedia enhancements and networked learning through Blackboard.

We now have significantly more students enrolled in our online programs than we have studying on campus, which reflects the increasing demands on postgraduate students' time and their desire to have flexibility and mobility in their study options.

Expansion from one online undergraduate subject to an entire post-graduate degree program was a major feat, and not without problems! The scaling up included servicing a much larger cohort of students than earlier and ensuring a consistent, high-quality experience for them as they completed each subject throughout the degree program. Furthermore, the target market shifted from young, computer savvy, full-time undergraduate students to groups of middle and senior managers, studying part-time, returning to study after many years, travelling often, time poor and with varying computer literacy. So an effective approach to maximizing time spent in the online environment became paramount.

We needed to increase the numbers of staff involved quickly, so our first leap was to take the Virtual Learning Environment (VLE) to the on-campus faculty. The reaction from staff was varied. Some staff were excited and have since become great advocates, but initially were somewhat the 'cowboys' with their own ideas about how they would manage this new environment. At the other extreme, some staff became involved reluctantly. In both instances, the need for careful management became evident. This realization encouraged us to explore online teaching models, and subsequently adopt Gilly's five-stage model for e-moderation to support staff in systematically building the confidence and competencies of the students. By the way, several units have now very successfully incorporated regular audio podcasts into their courses, with dialogue from their e-moderator. This dialogue includes an additional welcome to help set up expectations, provide advice on assessment tasks and additional information on the subject content. The students have responded very positively to the podcasts as they feel it gives them a closer connection to the program.

Monash e-moderator training took place with faculty staff who were accustomed to face-to-face classrooms in a traditional university setting. We introduced them to teaching and learning in the online medium. This involved a major change to their workplace culture and their comfort zone. We found a combination of online and offline training was most effective for them.

Approximately 60 per cent of the training was offline for local staff. We conducted this training in a computer lab so that they could participate in online activities. The online discussion forum provided staff with an opportunity to learn in a familiar environment. We found we could then assist their transition to working in the online environment whilst minimizing their anxiety. Our experience suggests that e-moderation training increases confidence and comfort with online teaching and dispels preconceived ideas about the 'unmanageable workload', as well as fears and myths of the unknown online world.

We also remotely trained lecturers working outside Australia as e-moderators. Their training took place 100 per cent online. These staff members were selected on the strength of their pre-existing familiarity with the online environment. The absence of face-to-face or offline training proved unproblematic for them.

On completion of training, each staff member was given an e-moderation CD and a mentor appointed from the pool of more experienced e-moderators. Now we have a trained and stable set of staff who are able to moderate effectively and support the learning across the programs.

Teaching and learning online

Millions of words have been written about technology and its potential, but much less about what the teachers and learners actually do online. Thousands of online discussion groups have started up among people with shared interests. Some prosper; others wither. Many change and grow with very little structure and no one person providing direction. The advent of a wide variety of enticing Web 2.0 applications have dramatically increased social networking (Hamid, Chang and Kurnia, 2009). Networked computers can provide vehicles for learning materials and interaction but students still need the 'champions' who make the learning come alive – the e-moderators.

Education and training are always undertaken for a purpose. Unlike social networking of all kinds, casual browsing or playing games on the web, a key distinction of online education and training is that they are highly purposeful and have planned goals, outcomes and directions. E-moderators, whether working remotely or in blended mode, have to think through the design of structured learning experiences for their students. To exploit online for teaching, they must understand its potential.

Systems and platforms

If you have already used online teaching and learning software, you may want to skip this section, in which I want to say just enough to introduce the software to those who are unfamiliar with it.

Nearly all educational institutions now deploy web-based Virtual Learning Environments (VLEs). VLEs include asynchronous ways of interacting in groups. We used to call these Computer-Mediated Conferencing (CMC), now they are usually called discussion groups, forums or occasionally online conferences. Participants may post messages for other participants to read anytime; participants do not need to be logged in simultaneously. 'Synchronous' – at the same time – sessions use similar technology, and are also often used as part of web-based virtual classrooms.

To take part, participants need access to a computer or mobile device, a network connection and fixed or mobile broadband. They will usually need a password to access the VLE.

Three types of technology are involved in computer-mediated conferencing:

1. *A server (special computer) and software system*: the server can be anywhere, though often it is maintained and housed by the institution or organization that sets up the service. It is a special computer, with its own software, that can store and organize well the messages, of which there may be tens, even hundreds, of thousands in a year. Fast, powerful hardware and reliable, sophisticated software enable many thousands of participants to access the platform through a single server.
2. *A 'terminal' for each user*: these can be fixed 'tethered' computers, or mobile laptops or devices with wireless access. Students can access conferences from a work or campus computer, a computer at a study centre or student residence. Access to the discussion forums are usually provided through standard web browsers and interfaces. Access to online networking through web browsers needs no special installation and free browsers are now factory-installed on computers. On mobile devices such as iPhones, an application programme is typically downloaded to the device to make them easier to use on a smaller screen.
3. *A communications system to connect the computers to the server*: connections can be connected by always-on broadband connections that can carry much more traffic at much higher speeds than were previously feasible. Networks are linked, so that a message may cross several networks before it arrives in the relevant conference in the server. Connection through wireless networks, with broadband, is now possible in most places, and on-the-move discussion boards only require low band width and can also be accessed through modems and dial-up telephone access.

There are two main types of VLEs owned and operated securely by educational institutions, which enable and support collaboration for learning. VLEs are also called MLE or LMS in some countries. Some educational providers choose a commercially available system because they want the benefits of support and development, year in, year out, Blackboard is the commonest in use in the UK but there are many others. Each has its own underlying software, with a slightly different 'look and feel' for the participants, and a variety of facilities and functions for learning. Most offer technical support facilities but not much specially for e-moderators. Others choose open source platforms of which the most popular is Moodle, which offers a community of developers and contributors. The code to run the platform is freely available. The university or other provider needs more people in-house to support the development and running of an open-source platform, so costs are shifted to different places and purposes, compared to commercially provided VLEs.

In addition, there are many Web 2.0 applications, usually called 'social networking' sites, which can be deployed. They are not provided specifically for teaching purposes but they can be deployed with suitable design and e-moderating. Examples include Facebook, Twitter and Second Life – there are hundreds of others and they come and go. These cannot currently be owned and hosted by the educational institution. Chapter 3 describes the application of the five-stage model and e-moderating principles to some of the newer technological applications

Students frequently set up web-based applications, which are freely available to them to share and work together outside the institutionally provided platforms.

A postgraduate management student reports:

> We had our own say too, over and above what the institution provided. My study group of seven students on our course set up a carefully designed set of folders and files on an iDisk [a free web-based file store, accessible and editable from anywhere and by anyone], which we edited remotely and individually, adding our latest versions of our work to this shared drive for the benefit of all. This was very useful for revising for our exam. We could have achieved the same via GoogleDocs or another system, but the iDisk was simple and neat. AA

The examples throughout this book, originally published in 2000 and again in 2004, are drawn from e-moderating experiences using many different systems. Some of these platforms have merged, disappeared or become highly marketed commercial systems. Others, especially those based on open source systems such as Moodle, continue to develop. In my view, if the e-moderators are keen and competent, the precise nature of the platform and its functionalities are less important.

Online networking for education and training

Working together, perhaps informally, in groups, for learning purposes is a tradition in many parts of the world. For example, a group of Scandinavian educators write about the concept of *'folkbildning'* (Axelsson, Bodin, Norberg and Person, 2001). They say the term is not really transferable to English (although their book about it has been translated). Nordic *folkbildning* traditions of over 100 years are based on meetings intended as learning and opportunity-generating groups, stimulating curiosity and critical thinking. The democratic nature of the meetings promotes tolerance towards differing opinions and respect for developed arguments. Courses are also structured in this way, and participants are involved in the shaping of their learning processes with others. When we move such concepts online, and restrictions of travel and location are no longer significant, then we open much new potential.

Online participant interaction is used in three main modes of learning. First, in distance learning – where e-moderators and participants never meet. Second to supplement campus-based learning – where students can easily meet face-to-face but also frequently benefit from the use of a VLE and e-tivities can be provided. Third is a different form of 'blend', where activities can take place in seminars, in classrooms or online, and often mixtures of all.

Compared with face-to-face group teaching, online is readily available, and does not require participants to travel to a certain place. Many participants find that the time lags involved between logging on and taking part encourage them to consider and think about the messages they are receiving before replying, rather more than they would in a class situation. Participants can ask questions without waiting in turn. Because of these characteristics, rather different relationships – usually based on shared interests or support – can develop compared to those between learners or teachers who meet face-to-face. Although many people find the lack of visual clues strange, messages are 'neutral' since you cannot see whether the sender is young or old, nor do you need to consider their appearance or race. This characteristic tends to favour minorities of every kind and encourages everyone to 'be themselves'. Online it's now easy to include pictures and videos of all kinds. However, it's often a good idea not to rush in too much with the visual images until after the learning community is established. Meanwhile with text-based conferencing it is possible to 'rewind' a conversation, to pick out threads and make very direct links. Therefore online discussions have a more permanent feel and are subject to reworking in a way more transient verbal conversation cannot be. This means that the medium is good for giving praise and constructive critiques.

Working online should be viewed as a new context or environment for learning, not just as a tool. It enables individuals and groups of people to carry on conversations and discussion over the computer networks. Networking works like a series of notice boards, each with a title and purpose. For example, an individual may set up a conference and post a message on it to begin a conference. This message could be, 'This area is for our discussion on your next assignment'. Each participant then logs on through his or her personal computer, reads the message and can post one of his or her own. When the originator of the first message logs on to the conference a few days later, 20 others may have made their contribution to the discussion and perhaps responded to each other's questions. Participants continue to log on, read the contributions of others and the discussion proceeds. Online networking's ability to engage its users is remarkable.

The asynchronous nature of bulletin boards and forums relates to many of their special characteristics. The benefits include the convenience of choice over when to participate. Participants can have 24-hour access to the system and can log on when they wish, for as long or short a time as they want or need to. Many participants can be logged on at the same time although each message appears in a list. Online networking is less intrusive than face-to-face conversations or telephone tutorials because participants can choose when to read messages and when to contribute.

Online networking involves a hybrid of familiar forms of communication. It has some of the elements of writing and its associated thinking, and some of the permanence of publishing, but it also resembles fleeting verbal discussion. The typical participant's discursive style lies somewhere between the formality of the written word and the informality of the spoken. From the earliest days, experienced e-moderators explained to their students, 'Consider this medium as like talking with your fingers – a sort of half-way house between spoken conversation and written discourse' (Hawkridge, Morgan and Jelfs, 1997). Now, for many people, being online is a normal part of their everyday interactions.

Being able to reflect on messages and on the topic under discussion, in between log on times, has always seemed important to researchers into computer-mediated conferencing, and to some at least of the e-moderators I have known. It does seem that quite a few participants reflect on issues raised online and then mould their own ideas through composing replies. It's interesting to revisit some of the first feelings about asynchronous networking – long, long before anyone had ever heard of Facebook and the like. For example, a very experienced Open University teacher described his first participation in an online conference:

> I was struck by how I'm still in touch with the conference even when away from my computer and busy with other activities. Somewhere in my unconscious I continue to debate and new lines of argument keep occurring to mind unbidden. And it is always so tempting to take just one more peep at the screen to see if another participant has come up with something new or built upon the last message one posted oneself.
>
> (Rowntree, 1995: 209)

Online networking can offer the opportunity for a whole series of ideas to be pulled together, too, and we now know that the role of the e-moderator is critical in enabling contribution to become learning opportunities. Many forum discussions promote openness and participants typically expect some freedom to express their views and to share their experiences and thoughts.

The online environment mediates the communication but also shapes it. Participants do not need permission to contribute and individuals can receive attention from those willing and able to offer it. Face-to-face identities become less important and the usual discriminators such as race, age and gender are less apparent. Successful participation online does not depend on previous computer literacy and it often appeals to inexperienced computer users, including those unlikely to use open social networking sites.

The lack of traditional hierarchies in online networking and its ability to support synthesis of knowledge lead to somewhat different styles of communication and knowledge sharing, compared to synchronous meetings. Programmes of study aiming at a spirit of wide access and openness, crossing industry, professional and international boundaries and applying research to practice are therefore well served.

Here a lecturer describes her experience of designing and delivering in an online programme aimed at 'transformational pedagogy':

> The text-based nature of dialogue enabled learner-learner, learner-facilitator and learner-content interaction to be visible and accessible to all students. The layers of interaction stimulated peer conversations, collaboration and a collegial atmosphere that allowed me . . . to operate socially and affectively in a virtual learning space. The online environment also provided opportunities for . . . access, sharing, digesting and critiquing information quickly and easily.
>
> (Reushle and Mitchell, 2009: 16)

The online environment is such that mistakes are recorded for all participants in the group to see. Tardiness, rudeness or inconsistency in response to others tend to be forgiven less easily than in a more transient face-to-face setting. Minor complaints can escalate when several individuals in a conference agree with each other and create a visible 'marching about with banners' online.

A graduate student expresses her views on unintentionally upsetting a peer online:

I was asked to write about a 'critical incident' for my learning. One occurred when I least expected it. As I was reading through other people's critical incidents, I came across a report by one of my fellow students that caused me so much emotional upheaval that it became a critical incident in itself, and became the subject of my report. My classmate described a situation in which she had posted a message to the discussion forum as a 'helping hand', and had been rebuffed in a response that included an 'onomatopoeic exclamation', and that she had been severely hurt by this incident. While reading this, I had no idea what she was referring to, but having had several interactions with her, I anxiously checked the discussion threads to see if I might have been to blame. To my great embarrassment, I came across a message I had posted in which I had spontaneously expressed my frustration at not being able to grasp what two other people were saying, and had graphically embellished my message with an 'aaargh!' and a plea for help. It did not occur to me at the time that anyone would take this as a personal attack, and came as a resounding shock to me when I realized how insensitive I had been.

Even though my classmate noted in her report that in retrospect she felt she might have overreacted, I felt extremely distressed at how easily and unwittingly I had caused offence – ironically, in the midst of an exercise on online communication norms and netiquette.

I think this incident highlights quite a dramatic difference between face-to-face and online learning, which is that physical presence in a group setting enables a far easier, more relaxed communication style than online communication, where contextual clues such as body language, eye contact, laughter, etc. are absent. I doubt that this misunderstanding would have occurred in a face-to-face setting, where both of us could have sought instant clarification. I think it highlights the concept of 'social presence', as defined by Gunawardena and Zittle (1995) in McDonald and Postle (1999) – 'the degree of salience of the person in the interaction and the consequent salience of the interpersonal relationships . . . the degree to which a person is perceived as a real person in mediated communication'.

How could I recover my sense of dignity and self-confidence to continue contributing to class discussions without being paralyzed by the fear that anything I said could be misunderstood. I resisted the urge to e-mail everyone in the class and beg forgiveness for anything I might have said which could have caused them offence, but I did post an apologetic reply on the discussion board to my classmate, who responded very graciously and in good humour.

My longer term significant question concerns issues of emotional intelligence (Goleman, 1995) in the world of online interaction. Is a greater degree of emotional intelligence needed for online communication than for face-to-face communication, or is the difference one of quality/kind? Are there ways for learners to develop the emotional skills and strategies needed to survive the jungle of ambiguity that is online communication?

I now see the value of the 'netiquette' activity as being something far more significant than just an ice-breaker or an introduction to the concept of online communication, which was how I originally viewed it. I think the very fact that our class had focused so much on developing ground rules for effective communication meant that the person I had offended and I were able to confront the issue and overcome any obstacles to our learning and our relationship that might otherwise have ensued. I will be sure to include some form of discussion/negotiation on netiquette in the early stages of the online courses that I help to develop in future.

Gabi

Working online has attracted the attention of leaders of graduate-level courses, those involved in professional development of people such as managers and teachers, and those attempting to build online learning communities. In addition, many campus-based universities and colleges are seeing the benefits of enhancing classroom-based work with technology, some of them very successfully. The term 'blended learning' has come into common use – recognizing that currently few learning experiences are entirely online or completely offline (Jaques and Salmon, 2007). Blend can mean many things but typically refers to a blend of media and/or activities for learning (Littlejohn and Pegler, 2007).

Dr Carol Russell tells us about running project work in large classes using a blend of distance-only learning for some participants and blended with face-to-face classes for others.

Engineering design for large numbers

The University of New South Wales Faculty of Engineering runs a faculty-wide first-year project-based design course with over 1,000 students. Although all the main interactions are in class, the course relies heavily on online tools to facilitate students' selection of projects and formation of project teams and to support peer feedback on individual and team tasks.

The course has run on several online learning management systems – now Moodle. The current version uses Moodle's default functions of groups and groupings used along with selective release criteria. Students first view project briefs for around 12 projects and select which option they want to join. The selective release criteria allows them to see further information for that project stream – such as timetables and teaching contacts – along with project-specific resources and discussion forums. They also form small teams of four or five to undertake the project work.

There is a need to form teams including a range of experiences – for example, mixing language backgrounds and experience with hand tools. To do that, we ask the students to complete a short quiz/questionnaire on their experience and use the results to create teams. We have customized the online systems to minimize the administrative workload in creating groups and setting up large numbers of project and team discussion forums. Student data, including group membership and quiz scores can be imported and exported in spreadsheet format, allowing for semi-automated team allocation.

The five-stage model provides a scaffold and structure:

Stage 1 – support for access and welcoming. The Environmental Health students are introduced to the e-platform but in a face-to-face workshop, followed by online familiarization activities and tasks. Mining Engineering are entirely distance students and welcomed directly online.

Stage 2 – introductions online and (in the mining course) support for decisions about whether to do a work-based project or take part in the online role play.

Stage 3 – each role is played by a group who have their own group discussion area. They access all the background material, discuss and flesh out the role and prepare a case to present at the planning focus.

Stage 4 – switch into role-play environment, log on in role, with facilitator also in role to promote experiential learning through the interaction.

Stage 5 – once the interaction is concluded students come out of role and are debriefed online in each course, to draw out the lessons from the experience. Their individual reflections on the roles and scenario in terms of professional issues in mine environmental impact or on public health impact analyses form the final assessments.

The e-moderating effort is mixed with classroom support and is mostly aimed at Stages 1–3 of the five-stage model.

Students log in to access information and organize who they will be working with. E-moderators check that they are able to do this, and allocate students to teams, using the online tools.

Students use the online spaces to contact their team members. Students use the online discussion forums and other communication tools to share documents, submit assignments and access information for their project work.

While there is some shared knowledge construction going on in the course – as students work on their team design projects – the online course environment is primarily for recording the outcomes and is not the prime medium of interaction. Nevertheless, some teams have chosen to set up their own online groups outside of the Moodle platform – using Facebook groups as well as meeting face-to-face. So the students are perhaps showing some aspects of Stages 4 and 5, in that they are taking control of their own use of the online environment.

Another way in which the online tools support teamwork is through using plug-in software (WebPA) to give each other anonymous feedback on team contribution. The teams do this exercise twice, once formatively and the second time with scores being used to moderate allocation of team marks to individuals. Students' individual reflections on the team processes are included as part of the course assessment. The students also use an online-calibrated peer-assessment service to mark other students' individual work. The aim of this exercise is to improve students' understanding of the assessment criteria for their project reports.

Costs and resourcing e-moderation

Choosing to spend scarce funds, time and effort on something – even as enticing as promoting students' online learning – is challenging. It's reasonable to try to judge the benefits, and expect others to do so! Most of this book is about the benefits and how to realize them in a low-cost, sustainable and high-value way, but as yet I've not come across any widely agreed method for working out online teaching costs (Meyer, 2006). Nor is there a standard way to separate and measure the educational or other benefits of using interactive online learning. What students and teachers actually do changes when online is introduced, so meaningful comparisons with other forms of delivery are difficult. The costs and measured benefits of e-moderating alone have not been studied, since e-moderating is always associated with online or blended learning.

There are some clues rather than absolutes. For example, a president of a private college in the USA suggests that careful learning design reduces costs and increases student satisfaction:

> we started searching the literature for instructional designs that require fewer resources and result in high levels of student learning. The ones we found shared certain characteristics. They were driven by clear learning goals and involved extensive assessment and feedback to students. They stressed active learning and took maximum advantage of technology. In each design, faculty spent less time lecturing and more time coaching, proactively asking and answering questions with groups of students. And faculty were assisted in their coaching role by teaching assistants or peer mentors. Finally, economies of scale helped to produce significant cost savings.
>
> (Bassis, 2010: 1)

We can perhaps look at four areas that are significant in their use of resources for e-moderation and online conferencing.

First, to learn online you need to make good provision for the technology platform – most educational establishments now have a VLE provided centrally: it could be considered a 'sunk' cost. All VLEs have asynchronous bulletin boards and some have synchronous chat. Most have wikis and blogs and ways of providing podcasts. Almost all VLEs are underused, especially from the perspective of interaction between staff and students. Most institutions are very happy for the investment, which has been made to provide a secure accessible platform for learning, to be used more extensively and productively for learning purposes. In the event that an institutionally owned VLE is not available, there are many good conferencing systems that can be hired for seminars, and even more Web 2.0 applications are available for free (Salmon, 2005). My preference is to build capacity throughout the staff of the organization. In this way low-cost high-value technologies for learning can be deployed rather than building up expensive unsustainable centralized technology units (Salmon, 2005).

Second, there are two kinds of staff associated with the provision of suitable technology platforms. Technicians are the first kind – these are usually in place already. Learning technologists are the second – people who bridge the gap between pedagogy, design and delivery. In big pedagogical change programmes, learning technologists may need to be employed, but in most cases academic and teaching staff can, with some help, acquire the necessary skills themselves.

Third, providing course materials online has always been seen as a major cost – the design and delivery of multi-media quality materials can be a big challenge and gobble up resources. Academics spend many hours designing and developing the materials and require support from a range of technical staff (Rumble, 2009; Rumble, 2010). However, if this is appropriately managed, they can 'design once – deliver many times' (Salmon, Jones and Armellini, 2008), so creating a beneficial Return on Investment (ROI) of materials development. No matter how good the materials are, students crave feedback and support. The costs of providing this part can be low if done well, and highly successful.

Currently the Open Educational Resources (OERs) movement is gathering strength (Hawkridge, Armellini, Nikoi, Rowlett and Witthaus, 2010); so over time some costs may reduce to those associated with finding and repurposing, rather than with constant fresh development. Some commentators suggest that OERs could make a major contribution to reducing costs in the future (Kanwar, Kodhandaraman and Umar, 2010). Similarly, students are increasingly seeking resources and developing their learning more independently and more constructively (Daniel, West and Monaghan, 2008).

OERs include freely downloadable, reusable e-tivities and sequences of e-tivities designed to meet a specific objective, such as writing a literature review or dissertation proposal (Hawkridge et al., 2010). These help e-moderators design for interaction. Savings are generated at the *design stage* by re-versioning successful e-tivities, rather than creating them from scratch, and at the delivery stage by adapting and incorporating time-efficient e-moderating practices.

Fourth, the biggest over time costs and benefits come from what staff actually do. Designing for participation is important. Structured, paced and carefully constructed e-tivities reduce the amount of e-moderator time, and impact directly on satisfactory learning outcomes, adding value to the investment in learning technologies (Salmon, 2002a). E-tivities can be very rapidly developed and students are quickly engaged.

If well-constructed programmes are used, skilled and trained e-moderators can often handle large numbers of students online. Using lower-cost assistance, such as from (trained) graduate students, to support participants often helps. From the perspective of costs, an optimum is around 30 or more participants to one e-moderator (Rumble, 2001). Good pedagogical design suggests a lower ratio of 15:1. Most well-designed e-tivities run successfully with a ratio of up to 20:1, so perhaps it is best to have one (well-trained) e-moderator running two separate groups for optimum cost-benefit.

Costing each activity related to online staff development is difficult, but not impossible. Much depends on the assumptions behind the figures. For example, I compared the estimated costs of training Open University Business School e-moderators face-to-face with the actual costs of training them online. My estimates were based on costs in 1996 of a face-to-face weekend for 180 e-moderators, drawn from all over the United Kingdom and Western Europe, including travel and subsistence, attendance fees and set up costs, but excluding staffing costs and overheads. These came to £35,000 in 1996. The actual direct costs of the online training for 147 e-moderators were £8,984. The two sets of figures do hide quite a few assumptions, but the cost advantage of using online was apparently considerable. Online staff development costs only about a quarter of the cost of face-to-face training – so it's worth considering! You can also read about the huge cost and carbon savings for running an academic conference entirely online on page 118. Chapters 5 and 6 describe how to undertake online e-moderation training and development.

Summary: High value, low costs – sustainability for e-moderation

● Design for interaction, participation and feedback (rather than 'content delivery').
● Avoid expensive materials – for example, spending a lot of money on development and copyright; instead use Open Educational Resources.
● Use low-cost technologies or those already provided.
● Employ trained and developed e-moderators and train graduate students and others to help.
● Require students to do more themselves, with each other, focusing on what staff must rather than can do.
● Build capacity and capability in your academic and teaching staff rather than outsourcing materials development or building up an expensive internal technology support unit.

Online and flexibility

In the OU Business School, I chaired a large open entry course leading to a Professional Certificate in Management. The programme developed as a response to customers' requests for flexibility in learning provision for the twenty-first century. We deployed the well-rehearsed OU-supported open learning method, including high-quality materials together with on and offline tutor support for individuals and groups. We used custom-built websites and FirstClass online conferencing for interaction. The programme was highly modular and customizable, with a wide range of choices for participants, including four start and finish dates each year, special versions for some employment sectors, study breaks and online options.

The management students defined 'flexibility' in 73 different ways! Their top requirements could be met by online provision. They wanted fully searchable, portable, course materials and extensive help with pacing of their study. They expected 'anytime, anywhere' assessment, and feedback on their exams of the same quality as the feedback provided on assignments (personalized and individually crafted by their tutors).

The management students' greatest wish was for increased access, not to technology, but to human support. Their expectations were demanding: an 'always-on, broadband tutor'! The issue of access to tutors and to others was a key aspect of making the course not only more flexible but also more friendly, more motivating, achievable and satisfying. How could we do this successfully?

One student wrote:

> In my experience, my tutor was very good, knowledgeable of his topic and willing to help, but he was tied to email and phone as his technological repertoire, with a bit of FirstClass here and there. He could have had more impact with less effort, I think, if he had used the OU's VLE more effectively or indeed a Facebook group for his tutorial group. BC

Ultimately, the kind of flexible provision students expect needs loving adoption by experienced e-moderators, and rather more than promise and the hand of fate from technology provision. The rest of this book will show you some pathways towards flexibility and success. Chapter 2 introduces my early research in this area.

Chapter 2

A model for collaborative online learning

About the OU

My original research into online networking for education and training was carried out in the Open University (OU) of the United Kingdom, therefore you should know its context.

The OU is an excellent 'test bed' for new ways of teaching because it:

- is 'open as to people, places, methods and ideas' – and to new media;
- is one of the largest distance teaching universities with around 250,000 students;
- provides a very wide range of supported degree-level distance courses;
- awards its own internationally recognized degrees and other qualifications;
- is known for the quality of its teaching and research – and the success of its students.

Course design, production and distribution are located centrally at the OU's headquarters in Milton Keynes, England, together with personnel, finance and administrative systems. As the OU website shows (www.open.ac.uk), on the Milton Keynes campus are the academic schools, faculties and institutes, as well as the administrative and operational departments. I worked in the OU's Business School for some 15 years to 2004.

Services to OU students, such as registration, advice and arrangements for short residential schools and examinations, are devolved to 13 regional centres in cities of the United Kingdom and worldwide, through local offices. These are manned by administrative staff and faculty representatives with responsibilities for students and tutors. They look after hundreds of study centres, in which face-to-face tutorials take place, and they organize the residential schools, essential for students taking certain courses. They also recruit, appoint, induct, develop and supervise tutors, who are employed part time by the OU as Associate Lecturers.

Tutors or Associate Lecturers (or mentors, instructors or teaching assistants as they are called elsewhere in the world) have always had important roles in the OU system. Many people believe that the OU's success can be attributed to the support it gives to its students, through the tutors. Until the advent of online, each one tutored up to 25 students, mainly through the postal system but also through face-to-face group tutorials in the study centres. They marked and commented on students' assignments, and students could phone them for support, direction and counselling. Now, most communication is electronic and assignments are submitted through a complex e-system. Critically, for OU courses online group working computer mediated conferencing vastly changed some of the roles and functions for tutors (Hawkridge, 2003) and course and programmes are now using a Virtual Learning Environment (VLE).

Building a model of online teaching and learning

Although e-mail was available to some OU students and tutors much earlier, computer-mediated conferencing (CMC) was first introduced in 1988, in a new course made by a team from the Social Science and Technology Faculties (*DT200 Introduction to Information Technology*). As you can see from the title, CMC was peculiarly well suited to such a course. The course team, the tutors and the students were very keen to try it, if a little apprehensive about how successful it would be. The software available was CoSy; today, it looks very primitive, and it of course did cause some problems.

The Information Technology course served about a thousand students each year for four years. The experiment was sufficiently successful for other course teams to want to include online conferencing as part of their media mix. By 2000, online conferencing was used in 160 courses, studied by about 100,000 students; by 2003, 150,000 students were taking courses in which CMC was used. For the first time, one very large-scale foundation level course (*T171 You, Your Computer and The Net*) was taught entirely online (Weller and Robinson, 2001). You can get a flavour of the quality of materials from the OpenLearn site (http://openlearn.open.ac.uk/). In 2010, all OU students work online in some way and attendance at residential and face-to-face schools and tutorials are reducing.

In 1991, the Open University Business School (OUBS) started experimenting with computer-mediated groups in its Master of Business Administration (MBA) courses. During the early 1990s general interest conferences were provided covering topics of the students' choosing. They were available to those MBA students and tutors who wanted to use them and could – typically 20–30 per cent of students or 100–200 individuals per course. These first online discussions were seldom e-moderated except to start and stop conferences and to ensure that nothing inappropriate occurred (this was extremely rare).

I used these early voluntary conferences in the MBA to build simple working models of CMC use in the Business School. I developed a framework for action research, which allowed for pathways, ideas and feedback to be explored. My action research was aimed at solving problems rather than establishing theory. However, the models I created and developed provided a set of constructs that could be tested as well as a basis for later online induction and training programmes. I thank James Slevin for his exploration *and* critique of the impact of grounded work such as mine in the growing importance of learning online for the twenty-first century (Slevin, 2008).

Methodology

My model as described below in some detail is therefore grounded in my research. Here is a very brief summary of my content analysis and focus group work, for those interested in exploring action research in online environments.

First, I analysed the content of messages. I concentrated on understanding the naturally occurring online behaviour. I was the observer. Online, every piece of information entered into the system, including all the messages, is stored and can be accessed. These messages are suitable units for content analysis (Holsti, 1968). There are many possible methodologies for studying communication patterns, but apart from content analysis they are too complex for non-specialists and not suitable for analysing a huge volume of messages (Henri, 1992). Online messages are in textual form but they have little in common with printed texts, the usual medium for content analysis, since they have been produced in collaborative and asynchronous ways. Each person's contribution has its own meaning and can be considered individually, although patterns of interaction and discourse also can be ascertained. Messages online have several advantages over printed texts when it comes to content analysis: the exactness of expression and the direct, brief and informative styles, sometimes limited by software; the messages also form a distinct body, usually united by a joint purpose (Mason, 1993).

For my research, I printed around 3,000 messages over two years from the voluntary MBA CMCs. I used 'idea units' for analysis (Potter and Wetherell, 1989). An idea unit is a single idea or piece of information, with its context attached. It forms a 'unit of meaning'. Like Halliday and Hasan (1989) I divided the idea units into univocal (received and understood) and dialogical (the text ceases to be a passive link in conveying information, and becomes a thinking provocation device).

Later, I did a content analysis of the responses to feedback from Open University Business School (OUBS) tutors undertaking online tutor training (described in Chapter 4). I created special conferences called 'reflections' where tutors could place feedback messages. I drew on Kelly's construct theory (Kelly, 1955). I used a computer programme, COPE, based on cognitive mapping for data entry and analysis of the tutors' statements (Eden and Ackermann, 2004): COPE is now called Decision Explorer (/www.banxia. com/dexplore/). It provided a powerful way of capturing the natural language used by the individuals in the conferences. I copied each statement from the reflections conferences in its entirety into the COPE software. I entered words and phrases exactly as the respondents gave them in their messages. COPE then acted as a database and enabled manipulation of the data to determine the most important ideas in a quantitative way, without loss of the original text.

After I had entered all the phrases and statements from the reflections conference, I searched for relevant text using the word search facilities and by listing concepts. The COPE database then provided a vehicle by which tentative classifications were made, changed, or extended. It provided basic retrieval and presentation commands and a variety of text-based and graphic displays and printouts of data (Pidd, 2003). This enabled me to build a more complete picture of the statements. At any point in the analysis, I could ascertain the source of any statement. I colour-coded the statements according to whether they appeared to refer to technical aspects of the software, learning aspects, or e-moderating and teaching. This analysis led me to revise the categorizations of some messages, and to a greater sense of the sequence of activities pursued by the online participants. In this way I was able to discern patterns of behaviour without resorting to intervention or questioning.

Second, I used focus groups (a rich source of qualitative data) to improve my understanding of participants' experiences (Morgan, 1988). I ran focus groups of 35 online participants who produced lists and mind maps. They employed brainstorming techniques and nominal group techniques (Stewart, Shamdasani and Rook, 2007: 153–54). I also asked them to draw causal maps of their experience. The focus groups provided a large amount of data in a short time, answering specific questions I had formulated from the content analysis.

From the lists and causal maps, I created diagrams of what the participants considered were key activities for learners online, the significant technical skills needed, and the kind of support and help required. I built a simple model first, then obtained feedback and comment by showing the diagrams to further groups, to add to my focus group results.

From 1996 onwards, with my Open University Business School colleagues, I built and ran an e-moderators' training programme based on the first model. I was able to extend and test the grounded ideas in the model. At the end of the first training programme in February 1997, accessed by 187 trainee e-moderators, I developed an extended model based on participants' experiences and opinions. I collected my data through online evaluation and reflection conferences during the training. Online training of a further 200 e-moderators in the OUBS during 1997–99 provided even more data, through 'reflection' conferences and exit questionnaires.

From 1999 to 2003, my research was through analysis of interactions, online messages and exit questionnaires from 600 participants on 40 courses, using ten different online platforms.

My ongoing research continues in the tradition of the action research that I started in the mid-1990s (Salmon, 2002a, 2002b, 2002c, 2002d, 2005, 2006; Salmon and Edirisingha, 2008). For an interesting worked example see Reushle (2008).

> Action research is highly appropriate to the development of e-learning, where experience suggests that significant modifications are required to the traditional paradigm . . . changes imply not only alterations to course models but also development of new attitudes.
>
> (Baptista Nunes and McPherson, 2002: 17)

Action research is widely used in studies of web-based education (Mann, 2006; Reushle, 2008). Researchers in this field have been criticized for failing to employ robust research designs and/or for relying too much on survey data (Lowenthal and Leech, 2010). Content analysis is the primary method for analysing online discourse (Lowenthal and Leech, 2010); Friesen (2009) suggests it is effective for studying learners' experience. Conole (2005), however, claims it is too rigid in coding and fails to capture the complexity and context of the online events. She suggests that new methods are needed in e-learning research. Some online researchers argue in favour of using 'mixed research' methods to improve rigour and quality (Johnson and Onwuegbuzie, 2004; Ross, Morrison and Lowther, 2010). Creswell and Clark (2007) and Jones (2010) suggest that mixed research involves stating the philosophical assumptions behind collection and analysis of data and using both qualitative and quantitative approaches. Another fairly new methodology is design-based research. Its proponents (Design-based Research Collective, 2003; Kelly, 2004; Wang and Hannafin, 2005) argue that it can strengthen studies of online learning because it fits into the world of technology-based learning more readily than traditional experimental or even quasi-experimental approaches (Van den Akker, Gravemeijer, McKenney and Nieveen, 2007). Hence my most recent research uses a variety of methods, with a strong systems thinking focus (Flood, 2010) but still includes cognitive mapping based on Decision Explorer (Curşeu, Schalk and Schruijer, 2010; van Kouwen, Dieperink, Schot and Wassen, 2009; Harris and Woolley, 2009).

Five-stage model

The consolidated model that I built from my action research is shown in Figure 2.1. I hope you will explore it and use it in your own context wherever you can.

I will now summarize the model before going into detail. The underlying assumption to the model is that learning involves very much more than undertaking activity on a computer. Indeed, online 'Learning . . . includes an intricate and complex interaction between neural, cognitive, motivational, affective and social processes' (Azevedo, 2002: 31). Second, learning is a transformation where energy flows and impetus grows, not smoothly, but in leaps and bounds. Learners online move from the known to the unknown (Dirckinck-Holmfeld, 2002). A further assumption I make is that participants learn about working online *along with* learning about the topic, and with and through other people. Much literature until now has distinguished between learning *about* technologies and learning *with or through* technologies, whereas in practice, success comes from the integration of both. You will see that the stages I describe illustrate the complex interplay between communicating through computer mediation, communicating with others, growing personal confidence and the dynamics of the online group as well as learning about the topic (Macdonald, 2004).

When I discuss online interaction, I acknowledge that when working online there are three types: interaction with 'content' (course materials or references), interaction between the tutor and the student (Berge, 2007) and, third, the much wider interaction between groups of peers usually with the e-moderator as the mediator and supporter. It is this third kind that the model focuses on whilst seeking to integrate the other two.

Individual access and the ability of participants to use online learning are essential prerequisites for group learning to develop later (Stage 1, at the base of the flight of steps in my model). Stage 2 involves individual participants establishing their online identities and then finding others with whom to interact. At Stage 3, participants give to each other information relevant to the course. Up to and including Stage 3, co-operation occurs in the form of support for each person's goals. At Stage 4, course-related group discussions occur and the interaction becomes more collaborative. At Stage 5, participants look for more benefits from the system to help them achieve personal goals, explore how to integrate online into other forms of learning and reflect on the learning processes.

Each stage requires participants to master certain technical skills (shown in the bottom left of each step). Each stage calls for different e-moderating skills (shown on the right top of each step). The 'interactivity bar' running along the right of the flight of steps suggests the intensity of interactivity that you can expect between the participants at each stage. At first, at Stage 1, they interact only with one or two others. After Stage 2, the numbers of others with whom they interact, and the frequency, gradually increase, although Stage 5 often results in a return to more individual pursuits. The nature of the interaction and the

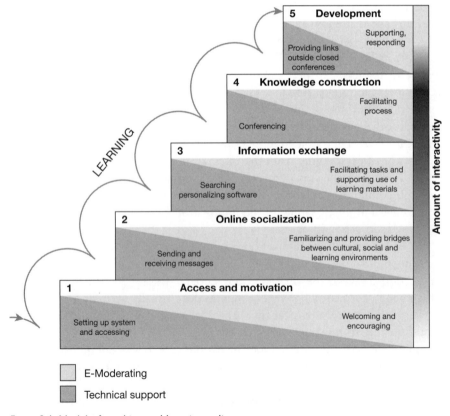

Figure 2.1 Model of teaching and learning online

kind of information and messages that participants exchange also change through the steps and stages of the model.

Given appropriate technical support, e-moderation and a purpose for taking part online, nearly all participants will progress through these stages of use. There will, however, be very different responses to how much time they need at each stage before progressing. The model applies to all online software, but if experienced participants are introduced to new-to-them software, they will tend to linger for a short while at Stage 1 or 2, but then move on quite rapidly up the steps.

The chief benefit of using the model to design a course with online networking and group work is that you know how participants are likely to exploit the system at each stage, and you can avoid common pitfalls. The results should be higher participation rates and increased student satisfaction. E-moderators who understand the model and apply it should enjoy working online, and find that their work runs smoothly. Participants, in turn, are more likely to be in control of their own learning, focused both on tasks and processes, and able to pursue more obscure and hypothetical solutions to problems (Hopson, Simms and Knezek, 2001–02: 117).

The five-stage model can be used not only to give insight into what happens with online discussions groups, but also to scaffold individual development. The more successful and scaled networked learning courses use scaffolding approaches (Reiser, 2004; Cummings and Bonk, 2002; Nussbaum, Alvarez, McFarlane, Florencia, Claro and Radovic, 2009; Sharma and Hannafin, 2007). Scaffolding is also a way of gradually moving from what we might call directed instruction to a constructivist approach, from short-term needs to the longer term, and from immediate to more holistic learning (McNaught, 2003; Roblyer and Edwards, 2000).

By using the model, you can structure tasks and processes for students to shape and support their learning and you can e-moderate to help them succeed. This task is complex enough in familiar circumstances, but you also need appreciation of the impact of the mediation of technology. Essentially, you are looking for synergy in multiple forms of pedagogical support: between design and delivery of learning, between the software platform and the human intervention and the increasing contributions of the participants in online and group learning (Tabak, 2004).

But now, I will go into more detail about the stages of the model.

Stage 1: access and motivation

For e-moderators and students alike, being able to gain access quickly and easily to the system is a key issue at Stage 1. Participants' attitudes towards learning online and their ability to get effective help are the two key variables at this stage (Tsui, 2002). Another important issue is their becoming motivated to spend time and effort, and to return to participation regularly.

In short, participants need to know what they will get out of the system when they are involved in logging on. The purpose at this stage is to expose participants to the platform (not train them) and to enable them to become successful in using technology as well as to see the benefits.

I kicked off my own e-learning unit this week. Really interesting timing now that the Uni is shut down for 3 days! So I have been thinking a lot about 'sparks' to get the students going. I set up a group discussion forum for them and invited them to post their feelings about launching into e-Learning – I told them it was perfectly fine to say they were uncomfortable or nervous. There was zero response! They all had their laptops yesterday so I got them to go into the online discussion board and I (jokingly) said no-one goes to lunch until I get a posting from everyone – then there was an explosion of responses! There were some great posts and they had a lot of fun. What was happening, of course, was that no-one wanted to be first to post (even though I had posted my own feelings to give them some idea of what to do). It is interesting how a little hesitation can lead to a big block. BM

I associate this online discussion with a new swimming pool. Everyone's perhaps waiting along the sides for the other person to jump in first. Test out the water. How do we get them in?
Be in the water and do the coaxing or
Get behind them and do the shoving.
KP

If, like me, you are an organizer of online provision for education and training, you want to be sure that the student, trainee, delegate (I'll use the term 'the participant' for short):

- gets to know about the availability and benefits of the system;
- sets up his or her own system of hardware and software;
- obtains a password, dials up or accesses the system through a network;
- arrives in the VLE at the point where the conferences are available on the computer screen.

The participant needs information and technical support to get online, and strong motivation and encouragement to put in the necessary time and effort.

Like learning about any new piece of software, mastering the system may seem fairly daunting to start with, though many participants sail through quickly. Some participants need some form of individual technical help at this stage, as well as general encouragement. Problems are often specific to a particular configuration of hardware, software and network access, or else related to loss of a password. Access to technical support needs to be available, when the participant is struggling to get online on his or her own.

Stage 1 is when e-moderators can look out for any sign of life online from new students. This is the time to welcome participants and offer them support.

Motivation to take part, and continue to take part, occurs when there is a balance between regular and frequent opportunities to contribute, and the capacity of learners to respond to the invitations. The best participant experiences occur when both the challenges and the skills to respond are high. There is a key challenge at this stage as participants want to feel competent in their learning and to have just enough difficulty but not too much. It is a mistake to assume that at this stage participants will be motivated by very challenging tasks, but of course they can also be put-off by those that are too easy (Berge, 2007). The teacher or course owner of the course material will be the best to judge this – conferencing design should be in their hands rather than in an instructional designers alone.

The difficulty is that what is challenging to one person may be a barrier to someone else, so it is always necessary to expect to offer some individual support and to appeal to personal interests (Skinner, 2009). However, try to avoid dependency on this mechanism being set up. The need for individual support is higher at Stage 1 than later in the model, before the establishment of personal online identity, trust and group dynamics kick in (Salmon, 2002d).

It is also motivating at the start to make it very clear to participants the value of online, its links to and integration with the rest of the course, its role in assessed components (tests and assignments) and the amount of time they should allocate to its use. It is a great mistake to assume that any participant will want to divert hours and hours to online conferences without good reason. Clarity of purpose from conference designers and e-moderators is critical from the very beginning. My book *E-tivities* gives more information about learning design for interaction (Salmon, 2002a)

Even at this early point, the e-moderator should encourage constructive critique and confidence in what constitutes a valuable contribution to the conference, by acknowledging and giving feedback. Participants should start to get the idea that they can look for meaning and value from the contribution of other participants (not just the e-moderator).

Stage 1 is over when participants have posted their first messages, and responded to at least one other.

Stage 2: online socialization

John Seely Brown and Paul Duguid's influential book (2000) argued that technologies that do not have a strong social 'scaffold' are inadequate and may even be harmful. An underlying assumption to the five-stage model is that learning involves very much more than a simple shift in cognition or the experience of using a computer. Online learning offers the affordance of online socializing and networking. Affordance means that the technology enables or creates the opportunity, that is, it has an inherent social component. However, online group working will not in itself create the social interaction (Preece, 2000; Berge, 2007). Sensitive and appropriate learning design and the e-moderator's intervention enable the socialization for learning to occur.

In Stage 2, participants get used to being in the new online environment. There are two motives for groups of people to work together. Many of the benefits of online networking in education and training flow from building an online community of people who feel they are working together at common tasks. However, such power is not inevitable but depends on the participants' early experiences with access to the system and integration into the virtual community. One is self-interest, and the other, common interest. The first can be promoted through extrinsic factors, such as incentives, but the second needs trust and mutual respect. So from the start of Stage 2, e-moderators should seek to create a climate that will strongly enhance the well-being of the online group, based on respect and support for each other, rather than corner-cutting in the service of instrumental personal goals. In this way, intrinsic motivators will gradually emerge, and learning will be promoted.

Online, people have the ability to convey feelings and build relationships. This is not a demanding concept to understand – but in the rush to 'get on with the learning' is frequently missed. Study after study (Aubert and Kelsey, 2003; Rovai, 2002; Rossi, 2010) has shown that an online team or small community must be built up for engagement between participants to occur, and relevant authentic and purposeful e-learning activities must also be simultaneously introduced to sustain the community. To reinforce, Downing, Lam, Kwong, Downing and Chan's (2007: 212) research clearly found that, 'early engagement with an asynchronous discussion board can be greatly facilitated by the design of a simple yet appropriate socially formative assignment'.

Virtual working has taken on much more importance with the growth of the deployment of the internet and fabulous tools of all kinds but throughout the ages, trade and the sharing of knowledge has relied on dispersed collaborators (Aubert and Kelsey, 2003) and most researchers determine that trust is a key factor in the effectiveness of any complex system requiring co-ordination, sharing and action (Skinner, 2009). Hence, at Stage 2 e-moderators are attempting to create what we might call a psychologically 'safe' climate that enables every participant to express themselves but with respect and appreciation for the unique qualities of others, their experiences, and the avoidance of stereotyping or labelling (Swann, Polzer, Seyle and Ko, 2004).

More than a century ago, Émile Durkheim, the French sociologist, explored the issues and consequences of socialization and the implications of shared customs, beliefs and heritage for human behaviour and welfare. He is perhaps best known for his concept of 'collective representations', the social power of ideas stemming from their development through the interaction of many minds. He was of course writing long before anyone thought of the internet, or talked about the 'Wisdom of Crowds' (Surowiecki, 2005) but perhaps we could learn from the basic ideas as we start to build online societies? Durkheim showed that a sense of security and progress depends on broad agreement both on the ends to be pursued and on the accepted means for attaining them. Every grouping of people develops its own culture with formal and informal rules, norms of behaviour, ways of operating and sanctions against those who fail to understand or conform. An individual cannot easily replace a familiar culture or values with those of a new community – he or she is more likely to selectively adapt or modify features of a new group that seem attractive or useful. In this way a newcomer to an environment is assimilated but also changes the nature of the environment and the interpersonal interactions within it.

If e-learners become alienated from their online group and their e-moderator, they may distance themselves also from the topic they are studying (Mann, 2001), losing interest in learning more about it. Therefore, at Stage 2, e-moderators should create opportunities for socialization, not only into the online group but also to understand how online contributes to learning for *their* topic, *this* course, *this* discipline.

If there is hope that a community of learning and/or practice will develop, then the e-moderator needs to give very explicit attention to enabling and promoting all aspects of online socialization. To succeed in fully engaging the participants and promoting their active involvement, imaginative and creative approaches will be needed. Energies can be harnessed towards the shared enterprise and purposefulness of the learning community. In a sense, e-moderators create a special little cultural experience belonging to this group at this time and through discussion and negotiation. This is called a virtual 'third culture' (Goodfellow, Lea, Gonzalez and Mason, 2001). Although these socialization components can gradually develop throughout the five stages of online provision, success comes with a strong foundation at Stage 2.

Collaborating for *learning* online is a new and potentially alien world for some participants, even if many already use web networking for information, entertainment or communicating with friends and family. An influential discovery from early research on computer-mediated conferencing was the impact of the lack of non-verbal and visual clues in online interaction. Some participants regard this as an inadequacy that can result in a sense of depersonalization and hence negative feelings, and rapidly seek to post videos and images. Others consider the lack of face-to-face interaction to be a freedom and prefer that participants are undistracted by pictures of or the accents of participants, or by social games. Participants can disagree without arousing excessive emotion by creating a positive emotional atmosphere (Tsui and Ki, 2002), they can debate without clashes apparently based on conflicting personalities and without shyer individuals having to 'fight their way in'. Some participants find it easier to ask for help online than face-to-face.

Joining in with a new educational experience (or any novel situation) inevitably creates some confusion and especially so for participants coming from different cultural and language backgrounds from that of either the majority of the group or the provider of the learning experience. Such uncertainty and puzzlement may provide a barrier for interaction. However, if plenty of 'space' and encouragement is given at Stage 2 for dialogue of all kinds with the group, there is a greater likelihood that productive communities will build up.

The virtues of a sense of time and place are those of finding 'roots' – provided by continuity, connectedness with place and others who share it and our own internalized set of instructions for how to behave, how to make judgements, feeling comfortable and 'at home in one's world' and the reassurance of the familiar. Working online fragments and expands this sense of time and place and the usual pillars of well-being may be less available. There is evidence at Stage 2 that individuals struggle to find their sense of time and place in the online environment. Hence the importance of e-moderators enabling induction into online learning to take place with support and in an explicitly targeted way. When opportunities for induction into the online world are taken, participants report benefits to their later online learning.

I am now coming to regard the adjustment to working online as if to one to a different culture. My first language and cultures are British English, my second are Japanese and my third North American (most of my social interaction is with people from that part of the world). Therefore I am something of a hybrid, which has advantages and disadvantages and affects my interaction with indigenous members of all cultures.

For example, British people find me excessively courteous to the point of thinking me uptight, sarcastic or humorous (my Japanese influence).

They also find me too enthusiastic, friendly or gung-ho (the North American influence).

When entering any other culture there are initially acclimatization problems. With Japanese, it took me a long time due to not only great cultural differences but also learning the language. In North America the process was thankfully a lot quicker. With both, the acclimatization was fraught with emotional peaks and troughs of elation ('Wow! Japanese trains are so punctual', or 'Great! Americans are so enthusiastic') and depression ('Why are the Japanese people so uptight when I am 2 minutes late?', or 'Why are some Americans so warm at first and then go cold?'). Gradually the amplitude and frequency of these extreme emotions decreased as I acclimatized, defined my identity and started to function to my full potential in the new culture.

I currently feel I have been through the maximum and minimum amplitude of troughs and peaks of acclimatization last week during the first stage of our online course. There were messages I sent, and have since unsent, that I now look at and cringe. There were also moments when I thought I had been kicked off the course because I had posted something extreme and by chance the server had gone down a few hours after: effectively denying me access. I know the amplitude and frequency (feelings of insecurity exacerbated by distance) will continue to decrease from here on in. I apologize to those of you who happened upon some of my more extreme postings. There are some interesting ideas behind them, which I intend to explore in due course.

I thank everyone on the course for treating us newbies with support and compassion, and I hope that, one day when I am an old hand, I too will have the wisdom to read through the emotional rantings of newbie postings, like my own, to the heart of what they are trying to say. Thank you for your time.

Nick

In my own experience, online participants display all these behaviours, needs and feelings, immediately following their gaining access to the system, when they reach Stage 2. This is regardless how familiar they are with the web or even with each other! They recognize the need to identify with others for knowledge exchange, to develop a sense of direction online and they need some guide to judgement and behaviour. A wide range of responses occurs. Some are initially reluctant to commit themselves fully to participation in online groups, and should be encouraged to read and enjoy others' contributions to the conferences for a short while, before taking the plunge and posting their own messages. This behaviour is sometimes known as 'lurking', although the term can cause offence (Bax, 2010). 'Browsing' is perhaps a safer word. Some e-moderators become annoyed with lurkers but it appears to be a natural and normal part of online socialization and should therefore be encouraged for a while as a first step.

When participants feel at home with the online culture, and reasonably comfortable with the technology, they move on to contributing. When we interact with other people through face-to-face communication, we use much more than words. We use gestures, breaks, intonation and 'body language', all of which we are skilled in 'reading'. Online, this kind of communication must be made more explicit through the medium itself. For example, you might shrug your shoulders in answer to a question from someone who is standing in front of you (Mathiasen and Rattleff, 2002). Online you would need to type 'don't know' or 'I don't care!' If you failed to reply at all, the questioner would not know whether you had left the computer or were outraged at the question. However, the benefits of writing are huge for the development of thinking skills, especially if written messages are exposed to the responses of others and to feedback (Tsui, 2002). (You can read more about the early stage of the renaissance for the human voice in Chapter 3.)

E-moderators really do have to use their skills to ensure that participants develop a sense of community in the medium. Group discussions on the web frequently demonstrate how quickly and easily group thinking and shared understanding can develop, often around the simplest of identity-bonding issues such as PC versus Mac, Canon versus Nikon. All of us who teach through groups know the tricks to get small face-to-face groups working quickly together – handing out a badge or a flag, allocating a space to sit, or working with a flip chart. We wouldn't dream of facilitating a learning or collaborating group without applying such basic principles!

The empathy developed through this stage of online interaction provides an essential prerequisite ingredient for later course- and knowledge-related discussions. At this stage e-moderators should take the lead in promoting mutual respect between participants, defusing problems and counselling any apparently alienated or offended individuals. They should also try to help those participants with similar interests and needs to find each other.

It is essential to create an atmosphere where the participants feel respected and able to gain respect for their views. E-moderators should deal with strong differences of opinion or objections to procedures. The best way is in private through e-mail rather than allowing participants to 'flame' and cause discomfort in conferences. This is quite different from encouraging productive and constructive exchanges of views, which occurs at Stage 4.

Some e-moderators assume that varying cultural backgrounds and experiences from participants result in very different approaches to learning, and try to adapt their e-moderating accordingly. It is extremely difficult to get to know and understand someone else's culture, and attempts to do this can result in unhelpful stereotypical views. Instead we find it's best to promote interest and respect for the backgrounds of all participants. The nature and support of the learning environment are just as important as participants' cultural backgrounds. We find that online students are very adaptable and able to respond to challenges and new opportunities, and we avoid simplistic views of cultural influence on online learning. Building a 'third culture' which values different perspectives and strokes seems the best way (Goodfellow et al., 2001).

Research supports exploring feelings along with reflection (Taylor, 2001). Transformations happen through reflection, but also through experience and feelings, thoughts and actions. In other words e-moderators should try to promote emotional literacy as much as information technology literacy (Eshet-Alkalai, 2004).

Stage 2 is over when participants start to share a little of themselves online. E-moderators should ensure that the social side of conferencing continues to be available for those who want it. Usually this is done by provision of a 'bar' or 'café' area and through special interest conferences. Skilled e-moderation will always be needed to ensure that conferences can be scaled up beyond small groups. The balance between delegating the e-moderating responsibility and avoiding creating many, many small, unproductive conferences is a delicate one. E-moderating these can be time-consuming, and some large online programmes allocate e-moderators specifically for the social host role, perhaps recruited from experienced participants or alumni.

A trainee e-moderator reflected:

> For me, the key learning point from taking part online is the realization that I am not alone in the problems I encounter. This is where this medium of communication scores over all others. Through reading the other messages you quickly find that whatever is concerning you, others have faced the same problem and that gives you confidence to carry on. CR

Stage 3: information exchange

If Stage 2 has been successful, your participants will have gone beyond seeing your system as a 'fast food' IT tool and into viewing it as an active and lively human network. A key characteristic of working online is that the system provides all participants with access to information in the same way. At Stage 3, they start to appreciate the broad range of information available online. Information exchanges flow very freely in messages since the 'cost' of responding to a request for information is quite low. In my experience, participants become excited, even joyful, about the immediate access and fast information exchange. E-moderators can help them all to become independent, confident and enthusiastic about working online at this stage.

Critically, by this stage, you need to ensure that every participant has a role to play and is actively participating. I'm not suggesting you should treat browsers, lurkers or vicarious learners as criminals, but instead you should continue to design and e-moderate both for active participation and for workable online relationships (Bax and Pegrum, 2009).

For participants, their learning requires two kinds of interaction: interaction with the course content and interaction with people, namely the e-moderator(s) and other participants. 'Content' or learning resources are now typically provided on the web-based Virtual Learning Environment – it is particularly important to ensure that they do not dominate and prevent group learning. Participants often find that references to course content, including links to online resources such as websites, provide welcome stimuli during, and sparks for, group interaction (Salmon, 2002a). The growth in the availability of high-quality, freely available open educational resources on the web adds considerably to the range of resources that can be deployed (OECD, 2009).

E-moderators and participants alike soon find that the 'messiness' of conferencing is in stark contrast to well-crafted text or multimedia materials. Networked learning makes demands on the participants: they have to find what they really want. As two e-moderators in management education put it:

> It is very easy to see forums as a fun medium. This is possibly a valid use but my advice to participants would be to focus very clearly on what they want to get from group discussions and to pursue this objective as in any other management activity. RA
>
> What a lot of files/conferences/folders – call them what you will. If I imagine a shelf of files for the various topics covered by our various conferences then it doesn't look too large and unwieldy but I must confess to a slight degree of cross-eyedness when scanning through all this. Having said the above, it is a super facility and great fun – as long as it stays manageable! CT

At Stage 3, e-moderators should ensure that discussions and e-tivities concentrate on discovering or exploring easily accessible answers, or aspects of problems or issues. Presenting and linking of data, analysis and ideas in interesting ways online will stimulate productive and constructive information sharing. E-moderating at this stage calls for preparation and planning, as in any good teaching. At this stage there will be evidence of participants able to take strategic approaches with particular interest in assessment (Mann, 2001). It is critically important to convey clear instructions and expectations to your participants (Berge, 2007). *E-tivities* (Salmon, 2002a) gives detailed instructions on ensuring success.

Participants develop a variety of strategies to deal with the potential information overload at this stage. Some do not try to read all messages. Some remove themselves from conferences of little or no interest to them, and save or download others. Others try to read everything and spend considerable time happily online, responding where appropriate. Yet others try to read everything but rarely respond. These participants sometimes become irritated and frustrated. They may even disappear offline. E-moderators need to watch out for each of these strategies and offer appropriate support and direction to the participants. Information overload and time management are much less a problem for those participants who are already well organized, or who rapidly learn to share the workload in teams.

At this stage, participants look to the e-moderators to provide direction through the mass of messages and encouragement to start using the most relevant content material. Demands for help can be considerable because the participants' seeking, searching and selection skills may still be low. There can be many queries about where to find one thing or another online. E-moderators should be introducing some discipline online through providing guidelines and protocols. For participants, learning how to exchange information in conferences is essential before they move on to full-scale interaction in Stage 4. If participation starts to flag at this point, e-moderators have an important role to play in empathizing and encouraging. Participants can be encouraged and developed to take on some e-moderating tasks from this point.

The temptation at this stage may be to provide some kind of 'automatic' answering of frequently asked questions (usually called FAQs). Ng'ambi and Brown (2009) and Ng'ambi and Goodman (2009) report interesting researched examples. It is common for overstretched e-moderators to insist that participants check electronic FAQs before asking online. This may work for technical issues or rules and regulations about the course if a good search programme is provided. However, it is unlikely to inspire appropriate communication around course material and best practice or lay the basis for more in-depth interaction at Stage 4. At this stage, the motivation and enjoyment come from personal and experiential communication. Supportive, formative feedback is motivational and will contribute to modification of participants' thinking.

A key skill for e-moderators at this stage is to look beyond the obvious in participants' questions (Castelfranchi, 2002). E-moderators should celebrate, give value to and acknowledge contributions to discussion processes and knowledge sharing by participants, and give credibility, authenticity and verification of information offered. Summative feedback and assessment can be introduced at Stage 3, especially if aligned with the online processes and achievements. You may also want to try some voice-based feedbacks – we have found that these can be welcome and effective (Nie, Armellini, Harrington, Barklamb and Randall, 2010).

Stage 4: knowledge construction

You may feel tempted to skip to Stage 4 from the start of your online programme! However, the previous stages provide an important scaffold for success. Most studies show that you can get students to exchange information (Downing et al., 2007) but a learning and interaction scaffold and skilled e-moderation intervention are essential for high-level constructivist collaboration. At this stage, participants begin to interact with each other in more exposed and participative ways. They formulate and write down their ideas or understanding of a topic. They read such messages from other participants and respond to them frequently and often successfully. As conferences unfold and expand, you will discover that participants engage in some very active learning, especially through widening their own viewpoints and appreciating differing perspectives. Participants' grasp of concepts and theories is enhanced through the debate and by examples advanced by other participants. Once this process begins, it has its own momentum and power. Rowntree put it this way:

> Participants are liable to learn as much from one another as from course material or from the interjections of a tutor. What they learn, of course, is not so much product (e.g. information) as process – in particular the creative cognitive process of offering up ideas, having them criticised or expanded on, and getting the chance to reshape them (or abandon them) in the light of peer discussion. The learning becomes not merely active . . . but also *interactive*. The learners have someone available from whom they can get an individual response to their queries or new idea and from whom they can get a challenging alternative perspective. In return, they can contribute likewise to other colleagues' learning (and themselves learn in the process of doing so).
>
> (Rowntree, 1995: 207)

Communal constructivism puts emphasis on the building of knowledge in groups, and drawing on real situations and experiences (Wenger, McDermott and Snyder, 2002; Fulantelli, 2010; Redmond and Lock, 2009; Redmond and Mander, 2009). The use of networked technologies enables access to the communication and sharing of such knowledge, the opportunity to present and publish individual and collective views, and easy ways of building on the ideas of others. At Stage 4 these are the aims. At best, highly productive collaborative learning may develop. As one e-moderator says:

> Conferencing is a medium that can add an extra dimension to developing ideas and increasing understanding of the course material. It gives the opportunity to stop and think and refine ideas without immediately losing one's place in a debate, and holds on to those ideas for future reference. It is important to accept that it has to be structured and focused in order to do that. IN

The issues that can be dealt with best by online participants at this stage are those that have no one right or obvious answer, or ones they need to make sense of, or a series of ideas or challenges. These issues are likely to be strategic, problem or practice based. However, avoid the temptation to load masses of questions and challenges into one message – better to keep them separate and be able to e-moderate the threads (Salmon, 2002a). The e-moderator needs to be aware of how the students are thinking, and remain open minded to new ways of considering many topics (Cheung and Hew, 2010).

By this stage it's important that participants appreciate that knowledge is not something that is fully 'fixed' or that can easily be codified and transferred from one person to another. However, some participants may feel uncomfortable at expressing potentially controversial views (Tsui, 2002). It takes skill in online activity design and interventions by the e-moderator to overcome such reluctance. E-moderators may need to ask more questions, seek more discussion, motivate, challenge, compliment and encourage all participants.

Attempts can be made to reduce gradually the virtual group's dependency on the e-moderator. E-moderators should design for group interaction, create a feeling of 'presence', but also make it clear they are not always available, perhaps 'handing on the baton' to leaders of small groups.

However, e-moderators have important roles to play at this stage. The best demonstrate online the highest levels of tutoring skills related to building and sustaining groups. Feenberg (1989) coined the term 'weaving' to describe the flow of discussion and how it can be pulled together. Online forums make weaving easier to promote than in face-to-face groups, since everything that has been 'said' is available in the conference text. The best e-moderators undertake the 'weaving': they pull together the participants' contributions by, for example, collecting statements and relating them to concepts and theories from the course. They enable development of ideas through discussion and collaboration. Weaving is an active and somewhat time-limited activity that enables full and beneficial participation during active conferencing.

Another important e-moderating role is summarizing. Summarizing tends to occur regularly but after the main discussion has occurred. A skilled e-moderator needs to know when to weave and when to summarize. E-moderators summarize from time to time, span wide-ranging views and provide new topics when discussions go off track. They stimulate fresh strands of thought, introduce new themes and suggest alternative approaches. In doing all this work, their techniques for sharing good practice and for facilitating the processes become critical.

While it is important to allow interest and engagement to flourish, it is also critical to allow discussions and e-tivities to die away naturally. The value of an online discussion can be very high while interest and focus last. There is no need to extend these artificially.

Here is an example of a woven message.

Week 2 started with a shock e-tivity. We were asked to simulate affordances of the online environment but in the physical one, with small groups of colleagues or family. Simulating the online environment offline was quite an eye opener! On her review, Gilly suggested 'real learning here!' and asked 'whether anyone might choose to do a summary of it?' I volunteered . . .

Here is my woven summary.

This activity aroused in some the feeling of 'virtual frustration' as Patty put it. 'The pace of conversation and contact needs to be steady or students will be deluged by, possibly, conflicting instructions.' The typical chat-room scenario? Patty suggested also 'instructions need to anticipate likely problems . . . If ignored the student may well . . . disappear.'

But Frankie was quick to point out that 'for online to work well, it has to be useful or interesting enough to move individuals beyond negative feelings'.

Wanda bravely started the exercise 'moments after Ricky arrived home from 2 days in Berlin'. She experienced similar irritation: 'Frustrating that the object of our messages didn't always read them immediately, odd to not be acknowledged and understood immediately' and of course 'lacking in that extra dimension that accompanies a f2f message – so information was flat if not read in detail and with concentration'.

Communication problems – communication out of sync – were highlighted by Tony: 'The exercise was a real eye-opener for me', as for many, concluding a 'need for simple structure and language, for empathy, for reformulation to check meaning', and 'for awareness of time and constraints on communication'.

Participants chose to solve real-life problems using this exercise. Dylan 'tried this exercise with my wife on discussing where to go on holiday this year' and found progress slow!

I found my own experience of the virtual offline activity to be 'a good demonstration of the online messaging environment . . . to highlight what we are missing when we communicate online'.

Anton observed that 'When somebody doesn't answer a message . . . I feel . . . more affected than I would be if fellow students in a class were not to pick up on an observation or an interjection I've made.'

The discussion now became more interesting and reached new depths. The focus shifted to the dynamics of online communication.

Rupert noticed how 'the core group were communicating far more often than the others, including myself, but I was reading all the messages'.

. . . and communication breakdown: Jonathan said, 'My subject area is TQM.' Anton said, 'Whatever is TQM, Johnnie? I've no idea!'

. . . and the issues facing on-line communication – as Myrna says 'on one side pushes you on revealing more of yourself but on the other hand you can hide more easily' while Anton finds the medium 'all so strange isn't it'.

The focus then shifted again to the importance of the words themselves in this environment.

Bertie became 'much more aware of the starkness of the online environment – all the missing cues of voice, tone, nuance, body language, and getting the messages in the wrong sequence! Yet we find ways to compensate – online or otherwise – perhaps through better use of words?'

To which Frankie added that 'seeing *through* the words to the person behind them . . . someone's personality still comes through strongly online despite (because of?) the focus on just one medium'.

Prompting Bertie to respond that 'we sometimes reveal more of ourselves this way than in face-to-face verbal communication' but Myrna was '. . . not so sure . . . It seems to me that you can either create very deep relationships or completely false.'

Anton agreed – 'This thought is often at the forefront of my mind as I read people's messages and as I post my own.'

The importance of language came to the fore, as illustrated by Myrna 'It is really important to pay careful attention to the language you are using . . . think of how many times you got angry for a misunderstood e-mail.' Barry continued 'the written words themselves become more important and more subject to scrutiny than in a hasty verbal utterance', and Patty graphically illustrated the point 'I can't remember the last time I spent so long deliberating over a sentence . . . but . . . as time goes by and the correspondents become more familiar, then you slip into easier patterns of speech. Just like making new friends.'

Wanda observed that online communication 'does feel odd at times . . . but . . . the opportunity to plan your contribution carefully seems to make up in part for not being able to read body language'.

So, to summarize we explored:

- the importance of careful use of language and words
- the absence of non-verbal cues and ways of compensating and benefiting
- and the permanence of the written word and its impact on group dynamics and our communication.

For me I found this a really educational e-tivity that helped us discover the advantages, how the careful use of language and extra time available in this environment can lead to greater depth and expressiveness. BM

The locus of power in more formal or traditional learning relationships is very much with the tutor, teacher or academic expert. At Stage 4, however, there is much less of a hierarchy and some would say, well into the Web 2.0 era, very little. Betty Collis and Jef Moonen were among the pioneers of technology-enabled learning in Europe and have extensive long-term experience. They are now Emeriti Professors of the University of Twente in The Netherlands. They emphasize that technology can bring new forms of learning activities, especially those where participants contribute to each others' learning through what they share and build together (Collis and Moonen, 2005).

You could say there is a 'flattening' of the communication structure between e-moderators and participants. E-moderating is not the same as facilitating a face-to-face group. In Stage 4, it may be necessary to explain this to the participants, especially if they still expect the e-moderator to provide 'the answers', although in the contributory world of Web 2.0, this is increasingly less of a problem. At Stage 4, we see participants start to become online authors rather than transmitters of information.

Online networked technologies have the potential for knowledge construction (not just information dissemination) at Stage 4 – this potential has been recognized since the early days of computer-mediated conferencing. It is perhaps only now that we understand the importance of building up to achieve it most successfully. Jonassen, Davidson, Collins, Campbell and Haag (1995) assert that:

> Dyads and groups can work together to solve problems, argue about interpretations, negotiate meaning, or engage in other educational activities including coaching, modelling, and scaffolding of performance. While conferencing, the learner is electronically engaged in discussion and inter-action with peers and experts in a process of social negotiation. Knowledge construction occurs when participants explore issues, take positions, discuss their positions in an argumentative format and reflect on and reevaluate their positions.
>
> (Jonassen et al., 1995: 16)

At this stage, e-moderators need to appreciate the differences between cognitive methods of teaching and learning (where new information is assumed to be assimilated directly by participants) and constructivist approaches (where learners create their own meanings) (Fibiger, 2002). Stimuli for this construction process can happen through interaction with other participants' messages, by the introduction of 'sparks' of information (deliberately placed at the start of discussions and online activities to stimulate dialogue), or through the interventions of the e-moderator. Keep the sparks light however – at this stage, there is a tendency to engage in 'feature creep' and introduce more text, more visuals and links (Salmon, 2002a). These should be used cautiously if group collaboration is required.

During my research I undertook a study of groups of participants who had already reached Stage 4 in their use of online conferencing. I examined three conferences in an OUBS MBA course (*B820 Strategy*). The participants were charged with discussing the strategy of their chosen industry, with a view to deploying this new knowledge in their assignment.

In each of the three conferences different approaches developed. One group discussed the voluntary and not-for-profit industry. This sequence of messages started with a participant posing a series of questions. The e-moderator behaved like a participant and was unafraid to express a personal opinion. Message three, from a participant, suggested a structured way of capturing opinion – based on an audit. Several participants responded to this message and the audit reports became interwoven with a debate on stakeholders as customers. The participants were very aware of the need to be supportive and build on each other's contributions and of the communication protocols of conferencing, such as optimum length of messages, avoidance of mere lurking, and so on.

The second group discussed strategy in the brewing industry. This group had an interesting mix of participants, widely scattered geographically, who had never met. They appeared to be confident communicators and were operating in only the information sharing and knowledge construction modes – there was no 'socializing' or technical discussion. The e-moderator was the managing director of a successful local brewery. Of the participants, around half were working in brewing and the rest were 'users', accustomed to drinking beer. The conference began with a participant drawing attention to a report on the brewing industry. He suggested that what he saw was the impact of the data and he asked for views. He also used a little self-disclosure about himself and his own job. Message two suggested that although the statistics were interesting, a wider view of the industry should be taken. Message three knitted together the first two messages and resulted in a very productive sequence of messages that attempted to weave understanding of quantitative ideas with notions of wider strategy. Many participants stated a view or gave information and then finished their messages with a question. Several messages from participants and e-moderators summarized and modelled ideas as well as supporting the contributions of others. The designated e-moderator had to do very little. About halfway through the sequence he too threw in a short message based on a question. The sequence closed after a participant commented on how useful the discussion was for the assignment.

The third conference was about strategy in the information technology industry. This conference also included a mix of participants, all managers working in the IT industry and customers. It had 30 active participants plus some lurkers. Although it had an e-moderator, this is an example of a conference where the participants effectively adopted and shared the e-moderating role, with one participant taking the lead. The participants spent considerable time and effort in defining their task and sharing ideas on how to collaborate. One participant adopted the e-moderating role by posting a starter suggestion and then continued to weave together other contributions. He then posted a plan which he later said 'has now been read by 31 members of the conference, i.e., a majority, without any objection'. He continued to facilitate the discussion throughout and his fellow participants much appreciated his role. This probably contributed later to their negative reactions to the official e-moderator's well-intentioned but directive interventions.

The conference continued by others posing questions, suggesting an online brainstorm and adding links to relevant websites. At the right moment, specific questions proved helpful in summarizing and focusing. While some participants interacted regularly, others came in only occasionally but nevertheless contributed effectively to the collaboration. Other participants acted as cheerleaders and timekeepers and reminded their colleagues of the need for focus. They were extremely supportive and encouraging of each other's contributions, which led to continuous development of the information sharing and knowledge construction. One participant managed a little humour – which is not easy online due to the lack of non-verbal expression. One 'lurker' apologized for his absence. There was good demonstration of search and share skills and of summarizing by participants.

The appointed e-moderator eventually felt he had to assert the requirements of the assignment in a very structured way, thereby establishing his authority rather than participating in the discussion. He thus gave the impression he was the teacher/assessor rather than adopting an e-moderating role. He asked for contributions from lurkers but this seemed to have no effect. He also asked participants to reduce the amount of 'techie' debate and for them to focus on the strategic issues. This resulted, some four days later, in one participant suggesting that they should join another conference. The e-moderator gained access for them and signed off with a 'good luck'. I conclude that the participants felt that the e-moderator was not helping them in the way they expected and that he was less skilled and understanding of online working than they were. Because of his inappropriate e-moderating approach, they sadly failed to succeed in tapping into any expert knowledge he had to offer.

All three of these e-moderators had been through the training programme using the model. Two had become very effective and successful e-moderators, one somewhat less successful. The latter continued to assert some authority, to the detriment of knowledge construction online, although he was known as a valued and effective face-to-face facilitator. I conclude that face-to-face facilitation skills, while having many of the same attributes as online e-moderation, are insufficient in themselves to ensure successful interactive conferences. If some participants are also trained and/or experienced in conferencing skills, they may be able to take on successfully some at least of the e-moderating roles.

As I write at the start of the second decade of the twenty-first century, there is strong interest in learners as authors and as authentic contributors, and in their ability to effectively self-direct and to lead. Indeed many e-moderators dream of enabling, advocating, promoting and encouraging the increased ownership, choice and contribution amongst their students (Redmond and Lock, 2009). The idea is that whilst educational institutions take the responsibility for provision of the technology and the direction, equity, access, participation and standards (see for example the impact and power of mobile devices, Traxler, 2010), the students take much more responsibility for the learning.

As Traxler says:

> Students are acquiring their own personal technologies for learning and institutions are challenged to keep pace. These allow students to produce,

store, transmit and consume information, images and ideas; this . . . realises the educators' dream but for institutions is potentially a nightmare, one of loss of control . . . quality, consistency, uniformity and stability that delivered the dreams of equity, access and participation.

(2010: 149)

Ensuring the deployment of a scaffold to the point of much freer engagement with learners (whether access through the web or a mobile device) provides a structured 'half-way house' to student contributions. At Stage 4 authentic examples for discussion on the conference are of great value and the linking of web-based conferencing with the deployment of the capture of critical incidents in teaching is an increasingly easily accessible way of participants making such contributions. For example, Aubusson and colleague's study at the University of Hull in the UK (2009) tell us that:

> mobile technologies have the capacity to add new dimensions to teacher professional learning. Mobile learning provides an unrealised opportunity for the facilitation of observation, critique and sharing of activities in the classroom. There is an important knowledge production and knowledge sharing capacity afforded by mobile learning as the audience to a critical incident is able to be much broader than the teachers in the staffroom or the local region. The ability to share events and deconstruct them with a large number of critical friends suggests that feedback will be more extensive . . . asking students to be co-researchers, both capturing moments and using them to indicate what learning they felt was occurring in that moment, has tremendous power for teacher learning . . . The strength of this kind of learning lies in its spontaneity, immediacy, honesty and agility.
>
> (p. 245)

The authors conclude that their participants were liberated by the combination of mobile 'capturing' combined with peer discussion and feedback.

Stage 5: development

I hope by now you have been convinced that technology itself does not lead to independent learning, and that there is much that e-moderators can do to promote and build increasingly productive use of the system. There are powerful reasons to scaffold online learning, not only for gradual knowledge construction but also to promote individual cognitive skills and reflection (Salmon, 2002c). Cuevas and colleagues' studies (2002, 2004) show us the importance for learning of supporting metacognitive processes. Metacognition promotes integration and application of learning experiences (Brown and

Reushle, 2009; Pettenati and Cigognini, 2009). Therefore Stage 5 is just as important as the other four!

At Stage 5, participants become responsible for their own learning through computer-mediated opportunities and need little support beyond that already available. Rather different skills come into play at this stage – those of critical thinking and the ability to challenge the 'givens'. At this stage, participants may demand better access, faster responses or more software. They become extremely resistant to changes to or downtime on the system. However, participants also find ways of producing and dealing with humour and the more emotional aspects of writing and interacting. Experienced participants often become most helpful as guides to newcomers to the system.

Some may resent 'interference' and wish to start conferences of their own, in Web 2.0 applications of their own choosing, perhaps asking the designated e-moderators to withdraw. The participants are sometimes confident enough in the medium to confront an e-moderator when his or her interventions seem unhelpful or out of place. Some e-moderators are naturally concerned or upset about this since their roles are then difficult to negotiate.

A critical activity at this point is to ensure the participants are independent online and can personalize and appreciate the incredible experiences that are on offer and evaluate the personal learning benefits – they should be able to articulate what has really made a difference to them, helping them to achieve that extra value from taking part.

At Stage 5, e-moderators and participants are essentially using a constructivist approach to learning. Constructivism calls for participants to explore their own thinking and knowledge-building processes: social dialogue is important to trigger knowledge construction (De Wever, Van Keer, Schellens and Valcke, 2010). This personal knowledge includes not only ideas about the topic area under study, but also the teachers' and participants' responses to the experiences of teaching and learning (Hendry, 1996). A key principle of constructivism is that the meanings or interpretations that people give to incoming information depend on their previous mental models and maps of the topic area or issue, drawn from experience (Seel, 2001). Challenge and argument at this stage will foster deeper thinking and reflection (Warren, 2008; Carrington and Gitta, 2010).

When participants are learning through a new-to-them medium such as online networking, their understanding of the processes of using the software and of the experience of learning in new ways is being constructed too. It is therefore common at Stage 5 for participants to reflect on and discuss how they are networking and to evaluate the technology and its impact on their learning processes. These higher-level skills require the ability to reflect upon, articulate and evaluate one's own thinking. Participants' thoughts are articulated and put on view online in a way that is rarely demonstrated through other media. In that sense, the role of reflection contributes in a unique and powerful way to each individual's learning journey (Hunt, 2001).

When conferences are set up to discuss the role of online conferencing in learning, they are always well populated with messages and ideas. The discussion probably includes uncertainties and problems with the content and design of conferences and an awareness of the social, ethical and technical dimensions of the experience of conferencing. E-moderators need to be prepared for this and should welcome it as evidence of real cognitive progress in their participants. E-moderators should set up exercises and online events, for Stage 5, that promote critical thinking in conference participants, such as commenting on each other's writing.

If suitable technical and e-moderating help is given to participants at each stage of the model, they are more likely to move up through the stages, and to arrive comfortably and happily at Stages 3–5. These stages are the most productive and constructive for learning and teaching purposes.

Blumer (1969) wrote of action learning (before networked computers). He described people involved in directing their actions, individually and collectively, around shared understandings of their world. Each persona carries cultural, philosophical, physical and psychological luggage, and shapes his or her learning experiences to meet ends associated with these.

At university level, lecturers are extremely keen to develop critical faculties in their students, which are considered essential for high-order thinking (Fisher, 2003). At Stage 5, this kind of experience becomes very obvious. In the conferences, participants comment time and time again on meeting online with colleagues, sharing views and receiving support, especially in terms of actions.

I'm an enthusiast for getting in touch with someone (with more experience, or generous-spirited, or patient, or in an appropriate formal position, or stimulating to talk to. . .) and asking for help. All of you are here with me! RB

I do like having the opportunity to computer conference. It breaks the isolation, it enables self-help, it networks, it allows for all kinds of learning styles. I wish I'd had this when I was studying my MBA. CB

This experience has forced me to rethink, review and refocus! JB

Anita Monty, an e-learning consultant at the IT Learning Centre in the Faculty of Life Sciences (LIFE), at the University of Copenhagen, helps academics to design and deliver online courses.

Climate Change: a course using the five-stage model

In 2005, we decided to deploy Gilly's five-stage model, to get our students involved in discussions. Very soon we noticed a difference!

LIFE's first online courses were not that successful. Though our academics worked very hard to design online courses in the VLE, the students didn't really engage with them. The courses included questionnaires and online discussions, all based on literature that the students were supposed to study carefully. Each VLE forum had a question from the academics for students to discuss; they expected the students to raise questions and discuss the literature, but nothing happened. Students dropped out from the courses.

We had to change the course design. We used the five-stage model, with e-tivities and e-moderating, in some pilot courses to see if we could help students to start writing together in the forum and to complete their programmes. The results were promising: students were active, their achievements were very good and they were satisfied with the courses. This success inspired us to develop Climate Change, an interdisciplinary 15 ECTS (European Credit Transfer and Accumulation System) online distance learning MSc course about climate change and humans' response to it. The 17 online modules and a final exam were delivered by the University of Copenhagen, the University of California (Berkeley), the Australian National University and the Danish Meteorological Institute. From these institutions, 22 academics were e-moderators and we divided them into small same-discipline teams for each module. They were supported by four student assistants.

We delivered the course in 2009 and 2010, starting with 60 students each time: 92 per cent completed in 2009 and 91 per cent in 2010. We think the low dropout was due to the scaffolding provided by the five-stage model and the assessment, which gave credit to students for their activity during the course.

The students worked in four groups of 15, with a student assistant in each group to help the e-moderators by monitoring students' participation, suggesting additional sources and summarizing discussions. Each module contained an introduction, the purpose and learning objectives, a short study guide, exercises called E-lessons and suggested learning resources (text, audio and/or video files managed by the library and provided online).

For many of the academics it was their first attempt to teach online. I introduced them to the five-stage model, e-tivities and being an e-moderator. They learnt how to encourage their students to continue writing and collaborating throughout the course. We had a weekly webcam meeting with the current module's teachers, the next module's teachers, the assistants, course coordinator and me as pedagogical consultant.

We started the course with a two-day workshop for students who could attend, with others joining by webcam. The e-moderators welcomed and encouraged them. In groups, they engaged in e-tivities at Stage 1, 2 and 3 to socialize online and to learn to start writing messages for the discussion forum. At Stage 1 they were expected to answer briefly a message from the e-moderator; at Stage 2 they answered a message from the e-moderator and responded to other students' messages; at Stage 3 they co-operated. After the workshop students went home, all students continued to take part online in e-tivities at Stage 4 and Stage 5. The e-tivities all had the same structure but with different tasks. The task might be a question for students to discuss together with fellow students and the e-moderator. Students were expected to post at least two different messages to the discussion during the weekly module. We required this since we were afraid that they wouldn't respond to other students' messages, posting only one statement before leaving the discussion for the rest of the week. We wanted them to be responsive to other students so there would be a real dialogue between students and e-moderators in the weekly module. This requirement about posting at least two messages ensured that students spent time on reading postings from fellow students and that they responded to other contributions. We were pleased by the healthy dialogue throughout the course, with some students posting much more than twice because they really got involved in the discussion. The e-moderator's job was to comment on students' e-lessons, correct mistakes and ask more questions during the week to encourage students to engage actively. We asked the e-moderators to spend at least two hours online each week in these discussions because students wanted their teachers to reply, comment and/or to ask new questions.

Here is an example of a Stage 4 e-tivity designed in LIFE by C.B. Henriksen:

E-lesson 1.4: Estimate your e-learning emission reductions

Spark: *Humans need to fly – or do we?*

Objective: Estimate and reflect on the CO_2 saved by taking this course as an e-learning course

Task: In this E-lesson you should work together with your fellow group members to estimate how much CO_2 your group will save by taking this course as an e-learning course. Use the carbon calculator in the suggested resources to calculate the saved CO_2 emissions for each group member and for the group as a whole, and post your calculations in the E-lesson 1.4 discussion forum.

Suggested resources: http://www.carbonfootprint.com/calculator. aspx

Start: Thursday 4 February at 14:00 CET

Deadline: Friday 5 February at 17.00 CET

For this e-tivity, the e-moderators answered questions, commented, clarified, weaved, summarized and joined students in the forum, but students posted 90 per cent of the messages. The VLE's discussion tool enables open and flexible exchanges, but using the five-stage model provided a good atmosphere, which made it easy to start writing together and comment on each other's messages.

All e-tivities in the course have a similar structure, designed to ensure that students know what to do and when, and how to make an active contribution. Students receive 3–50 per cent of the final grade for their contributions, with 50 per cent from the final exam. Each week the e-tivities consisted of one or two tasks and three or four discussions; there were also two team assignments for students to collaborate on. These were compulsory for students wishing to take the 24-hour written exam: after we released the exam questions, the students had 24 hours to submit the answers, individually.

Many students said the course was the best they had ever had; I think because they were actively involved in learning. They found it more demanding, interesting and fruitful. I'm very happy to say that we are already planning new online courses. We can't wait to find another hot topic for a new course!

Simon Rofe, who lecturers in International Relations at the UK's University of Leicester, explains how he made the concept of the five-stage model, and e-moderating, his own to very good effect on his students' achievements.

International Relations and e-moderating with the five-stage model

The Salmon Five-Stage Model is at the heart of the 'International Relations IR Model' which has supported the successful development of a suite of Masters' programmes in International Relations. It has provided the pedagogic framework onto which subject specific knowledge has been mapped in an online programme that has seen student attainment at all levels outstrip campus based counterparts by 5–10 per cent. This means students, and staff, have been able to address the challenging issues facing scholars of International Relations in the twenty-first century.

The successes we have enjoyed demonstrated clearly the manner in which the Five-Stage Model builds skills and knowledge alongside each other. These two elements of the academic endeavour are married to great effect so that they build curiosity and confidence in a varied student body ensuring student engagement and improved performance. With the foundation provided by the Five-Stage Model, student learning is operationalized through a series of e-tivities which require an increasing level of analytical skills and knowledge of our students. In line with the Model they begin by offering access and socialization as students become familiar with their online learning environment and then progress through collaborative learning e-tivities towards completion of a 5000-word end of module essay displaying independent analytical understanding in the field of International Relations. The model's robust pedagogic underpinnings, coupled with inbuilt flexibility to reflect subject-specific knowledge, has allowed for comprehensive and coherent programmes to be designed, developed and delivered.

While the immediate focus of academic endeavours has been the student experience, the programme's successes would not be possible without the role played by an Associate Tutor who plays the role of 'e-moderator'. These individuals play a crucial role as the intermediaries between our students, the subject-matter academic convenors and the Distance Learning Administrator. They provide an invaluable service to students in addressing queries on any manner of subjects. Many initial queries are of a simple straightforward nature with respect to the mechanics of the course, and a prompt response is important to illustrate to the students that they are supported in their learning. The queries develop throughout the course, in line with the Five-Stage Model, to reflect increased levels of student engagement with the course material and therefore call upon different skills and areas of knowledge for the e-moderator. As such they are a conduit to knowledge about the programmes, the department and the university as a whole, and need to know where to direct students if they are not able to answer a query themselves.

In our Master's programme, informed debate is an integral part of the learning experience for our students and this is done in dedicated discussion boards, known as forums within the programme. The e-moderator plays a vital role in facilitating discussion to ensure it is focused on the desired learning outcome and at the same time encourages the involvement of all students. Given many issues within the field of International Relations are keenly contested, particular care – in tone and content – must be given to allow dissenting voices to be heard, which in itself can encourage greater all-round understanding. Knowing when to intervene and when such an intervention might stifle the debate is a critical attribute to successful moderation of our discussion boards. The skills to be able to address student queries in an honest and friendly manner and to facilitate student discussion are learnt via an online e-moderating programme which all our Associate Tutors undertake prior to working with our students. The development programme provides ideal training for the role of e-moderator by placing the Associate Tutor in the role that their students occupy once registered on the course.

As first point of contact our e-moderators provide a mission critical role and are, in short, the face of our Distance Learning programmes to our students.

Their contribution is acknowledged by our students – for example:

> Excellent degree of support! I always feel that someone is there to answer any question.

Such sentiment is testament to the framework provided by the Five-Stage Model and the skills provided to e-moderators, without which our programmes would not be the success they are.

For more see Rofe (2011).

Chapter 3

More technologies – and the five-stage model

In addition to safe institutionally owned VLEs, there are many new technologies that can be deployed to enhance learning, most of them currently outside of the control of the educational organization. Many are those that might be termed 'Web 2.0' – these are hosted in a wide variety of places by different groupings and organizations – some intending to try to establish money-making ventures, others have more public and altruistic motives.

Some innovative academics are experimenting with Web 2.0 for group learning. The keys in using Web 2.0 for learning are threefold: identifying a pedagogical or learning challenge that introducing the Web 2.0 innovation might solve, then purposeful design and e-moderating. I have chosen six examples to demonstrate these principles together with a detailed case study of the power and impact of innovation and a case study of the impact of blend.

Facebook

Some Web 2.0 applications are very popular for social networking purposes, as I write, notably Facebook. It's early days as yet but interesting to try to harness (for pedagogical purposes) those platforms that are very popular with students.

Dick Ng'ambi from the University of Cape Town explains the benefits of using Facebook for his undergraduates.

Facebook is already in use by most students – but mostly not with and for their classes. At the University of Cape Town, we offer three first-year undergraduate courses in Information Systems (IS). In addition to using the university's Learning Management System (LMS) students are also invited to join a Facebook group created by the course convenor. Our pedagogical motivation is to mediate active academic engagement; to serve a catalytic role for student collaboration; to empower students who could otherwise not talk in face-to-face sessions as an incentive to engage. They communicate with each other and the lecturer via the Facebook group 'wall', the Facebook forum discussion and Facebook messages. The intention of the Facebook group is to create a knowledge-sharing space where learners informally consult one another on course-related issues. Students are encouraged to join the Facebook experience by both an allocation of 2 per cent of the term marks and the opportunity to expand their social networking friends.

The Facebook 'wall' (a shared writing space) assists in familiarizing and introducing the students to each other (Stage 2), offers administrative help in answer to questions and encourages mutual support on course-related issues (Stage 3). Through deploying and working together on Facebook as an information sharing space, we notice that the students progress through increasing levels of interactivity between themselves. We also feel that Facebook presents few barriers – people of a similar race normally tend to group together in the classroom – whereas through Facebook they socialize more with others from different groups.

Blogs

The use of blogs as an educational tool is increasing in education (Hookway, 2008). Weblogs, or blogs as they are more commonly known, have proved to be valuable tools for learning. A blog can be set up on an institution's VLE within seconds, or you can choose a free one to try. Blogs require only a low level of technical ability by authors, contributors and responders. Blogs are asynchronous, which lends a greater level of flexibility for mature students who often work full time as well as having a range of domestic responsibilities. The entries appear chronologically, which makes tracking the progress of a blog simple.

Jackie Musgrave, who is co-ordinator of the Early Years Foundation Degree at Solihull College in the UK, tells us about her success in using blogs to work with educational professionals on an undergraduate degree programme.

I have used blogs as part of our partner university's blended learning approach with mature undergraduate students on an 'Early Years' foundation degree programme. There are 24 students in the group and they are in college on just one day a week. The blog helps the group to form relationships with each other and stay in touch. It also allows me as a tutor to keep the students focused on their studies in a variety of ways.

The blog is set up on Moodle, the college's Virtual Learning Environment. The focus of the blog is a series of curriculum-related issues posed by me, in the role of e-moderator. One of our first issues is the students' thoughts about becoming undergraduates as part of the government's 'widening participation' policy and initiatives. Many of the students are regarded as 'non-traditional', having left school with few public exams. They are returning to College, sometimes many years after they left school. Understandably, there are many concerns about the academic requirements of higher education. Because the blog requires low technical ability to access, many students were surprised and thrilled about this aspect of the use of IT. The blog helped the students to express their concerns, share ideas and they evaluated its effectiveness as a helpful way of getting through the first term when they were exploring new territory in the murky waters of formal education!

My role is to act as e-moderator in the blogging process. This involves a range of responsibilities. First and foremost, it is important that some rules of netiquette are agreed with the students to avoid embarrassment and ensure that the blog maintains its role of helping with academic progress and providing a framework for mutual support.

As e-moderator, it is important to respond to students' comments, sometimes to all, sometimes one to one. Occasionally, it is necessary to make corrections. On the other hand, if a student makes a particularly notable contribution, this needs to be fed back with specific explanation as to why their contribution is so valuable. Sometimes, contributions to the subject of the blog can flounder and it is up to me to pull the threads together by summarizing, adding value to their contributions, making suggestions or extending the questions for them to consider.

If I notice that a student has not contributed, I give them a little nudge. I may remind them that their contribution to their blog will be reflected in a summative essay that analyses their higher education journey at the end of the semester.

Still in e-moderator role, it is important to have a firm beginning and end to a blog. The students are given a warning that the blog is about to close and this generally produces a late flurry from them. Finally it is important to thank them and acknowledge whatever qualities have been demonstrated by the students in their contributions, for example, honesty, thoughtfulness, depth of reflection or whatever is evident in the blog.

Students make contributions at unexpected times. I noticed one blogging after midnight on New Year's Eve! I like to think that this was an example of how the flexibility of an online environment can accommodate the students' busy lives.

The blog runs for the first semester and the students are able to identify how far they had progressed by reading their entries at the start and the finish. The final question I pose in the study skills blog asks the students to self-assess their first submitted assignment after they had submitted it and before receiving the marked scripts back. They are given clear guidance about how to identify their emerging strengths and areas for improvement from their first summative assignment. Their contributions were insightful and many students correctly predicted their awarded grades.

One student wrote in her blog entry:

> I have just had a go at grading my essay, it is difficult. Overall I think I have a grade D which I would be happy with. But what I think and what I get are 2 different things. I did find it interesting as when reading my work. I could see that it didn't flow as well as it could, and also there were some sentences that I repeated. It's scary reading it back as you can't remember what you wrote so you see your work differently.
>
> On a positive note I did see some strengths with my referencing and using a variety of evidence!
>
> There is still a lot for me to learn and in the future for the next assignments I shall be rechecking my work more to make sure it flows and makes sense, and also try to follow the criteria sheet more so that I have an understanding of what they are looking for.

This is powerful reflection and progress in a student who had struggled at first making the step up to the academic requirements for higher education. She continued to make excellent improvements, as well as producing a beautiful baby during the week handing in her second summative assignment.

So I conclude that blogs have great value for self-assessment, expressing thoughts and feelings and a framework for support. The students identified their blogs as valuable tools and in keeping the connection between college attendance days and with each other during the times that they were not physically together. More importantly it became a place for them to share reflections on their practice and academic ability in what was made to be a safe and encouraging environment for them. An added bonus for me was how humorous some of their comments were.

Microblogging for learning is also becoming more popular using applications such as Twitter (see for example Cann, Badge, Johnson and Moseley, 2009).

Podcasting

Podcasts offer a unique opportunity for the e-moderators to improve the use of the five-stage model for collaborative learning online.

Podcasts are digital media files that play audio, or audio with still and/or moving images that are made available from a website, that can be opened and/or downloaded and played on a computer, or downloaded from a website to be played on a small portable digital device (music player, mobile phone or an e-reader) designed to play the sound and/or vision. Podcasting is the action of both creating podcasts and distributing them (Salmon, Edirisingha, Mobbs, Mobbs and Dennett, 2008).

The voice of the e-moderator or tutor and the participants coming through short well-worded podcasts but with an informal style and tone can add a new dimension to the text-based communication in discussion boards. At first, tutors may worry about their voices sounding professional but we find that very quickly, they stop worrying about making their podcasts sound perfect, and the students give positive feedback about the more informal, natural styles of speaking.

Table 3.1 How podcasts can support the five-stage model

	Functions and benefits of pedagogical podcasts
Stages	
Access and motivation	Short, portable, easily accessible audio files provide reassurance, spark learners' interest and offer guidance and workable alternatives if things go wrong.
Socialization	Human voice and personalization, encouragement to initiate engagement, share basic personal interest and information and respond constructively to others.
Information exchange	Low-cost, high-value intervention to illustrate the type of resources that participants are invited to exchange and why, and demonstrate how they can be shared effectively to benefit the group.
Knowledge construction	Capturing key issues in e-tivities via appropriate, accessible and highly reusable audio interventions at key points, including weaves and summaries. Encouragement of participants to generate and upload their own podcasts.
Development	Consolidation and confident application of acquired knowledge and lessons learned in context demonstrated through participant-generated podcasts. Evidence of increased self-regulation and autonomy.
Techniques	
Weaving	As in text-based discussions, an audio weave looks forward by capturing key aspects of an earlier task that have not been discussed in sufficient depth and encourages additional exchanges.
Summarizing	A podcast summary acknowledges participants' input and brings the discussion to an end, highlighting its key contributions. It may be produced by participants

Here, in Table 3.1, I suggest how podcasts can be used to support each stage of the five-stage model.

Wikis

Discussion boards have served online teaching and learning well for many years. Wikis (editable web pages) offer features that enable e-moderators and participants to achieve certain objectives that can be more cumbersome using a discussion board (Kovacic, Bubas and Zlatovic, 2008). Wikis can make the e-moderator's work easier and the learning process more efficient and rewarding. Table 3.2 compares and contrasts traditional text-based discussion boards with wikis on the basis of the five-stage model and key moderating activities.

Using social bookmarking and wikis can also lead to more independent student contributions. One project found:

> Initial student feedback has been very positive, indicating that this method of learning is seen as interesting, challenging and effective, and that it is very fair in ensuring that non-contributing group members are not carried; a matter which is of significant concern to many hard-working students.
> (Behan and Boylan, 2009: 1)

See Table 3.2.

Virtual worlds[1]

Three-D Multi-User Virtual Environments (3D MUVEs) provide virtual three-dimensional spaces, tailored by their designers, which can accommodate more than one participant at a time. Many virtual games are played out in such spaces, but our interest was in Second Life, a 3D social software application. Its developers, Linden Lab in California, say, 'It is a free online virtual world imagined and created by its residents' (http://secondlife.com/whatis).

Second Life was the third most popular social software application in the UK in 2009, after Facebook and YouTube. As I write, Second Life is by far the most widely used 3D MUVE for teaching and learning (Warburton, 2009) and although it is starting to decline in general popularity, hundreds of universities have a presence in virtual worlds (Hew and Cheung, 2010). Warburton (2009: 415) notes 'a virtual world provides an experience set within a technological environment that gives the user a strong sense of being there'.

---

1   This section was first published in 2010 as 'Developing a five-stage model of learning in Second Life', *Educational Research*, Special issue: Virtual worlds and education, 52 (2), June 2010, pp. 169–82. Many thanks to the publishers, Taylor & Francis, for agreeing to reproduce it here, lightly edited and adapted, and to my co-authors Drs Ming Nie and Palitha Edirisingha for their permission.

Table 3.2 Comparing and contrasting discussion boards and wikis using the five-stage model and key moderating activities

	Discussion board	Wiki
Stages of the five-stage model		
Access and motivation	Easy access via a link within the VLE or to a fixed URL in the 'cloud', ideally with no additional sign-on. A suitable spark to start a dialogue or activity, a clear purpose and a well-worded seed contribution by the e-moderator will ensure participant engagement and willingness to get started.	
Socialization	Safe, known environment to contribute ice-breaking and socialization messages. The e-moderator and the participants feel in control of their posts. Each contribution takes the form of a message. The e-moderator provides suitable activities and hosting.	Less familiar, vulnerable and more exposed environment. Contributions can be directly edited by others, hence less control. The e-moderator initially populates the wiki with examples to encourage participation and to illustrate the type and length of the expected contributions.
Information exchange	Participants and their individual contributions are clearly identified. Messages need opening one at a time. The relevant contribution for weaving or summarizing may be buried several clicks away, and under several messages in a thread.	Contributions are not immediately attributable to individual participants. There is a holistic view of the shared information and resources. Relevant parts of the content are easy to identify, extract, edit and repurpose. Participants' self-regulation is encouraged and anarchy can be avoided through tight design and the provision of relevant examples, which ultimately reduce the workload of the e-moderator. The e-moderation becomes embedded in the same page and forms part of the new, emerging shared resource.
Knowledge construction	The representation of new knowledge takes the form of separate messages by different contributors.	The emerging wiki page is a representation of new group knowledge, which needs personalizing if it is to be useful and relevant to each individual group member.

Development	The links between messages are not always easy to make. A skilled e-moderator brings together lessons learned by individuals in formats that others can benefit from – by weaving them into a new message.	A personalized version of the wiki, showing each person's learning, may take different forms. A skilled e-moderator will intervene to encourage participants to distil the group outcome. Participants shift from inter-dependence to independence. They extract relevant lessons learned from the prior stages, adapt them as appropriate and apply them confidently in their contexts. They convey their new knowledge to others and generate additional benefit. The e-moderator facilitates this process but his or her participation diminishes as participants' autonomy and self-regulation increases.
E-moderating skills		
Weaving	Can be time-consuming for the e-moderator though beneficial to the participants. The components of the weave can be spread across dozens of messages and even threads. The resulting message is crafted and posted by one individual – usually the e-moderator.	The weave draws on information readily available on one page and can be edited by all contributors over time.
Summarizing	The resulting summary is unique, as contributed by the summarizer (often the e-moderator), who owns the text. Discussion board summarizing is an important way to acknowledge and encourage further individual contributions.	Key information is available on a single page and structured for quick and easy access by all participants. The summary is the result of all contributors collaborating on the same text, with shared ownership.
Evaluating the effect of contributions	The impact of the e-moderator's contributions is easy to visualize and measure in terms of participant engagement and breadth and depth of traffic, and creates value and presence. It is easy for the e-moderator to identify appropriate places and time points when additional contributions will generate further exchanges and enhance the learning process.	
Enabling effective group work	Groups of participants are easily allocated to different areas of a discussion board to carry out specific tasks.	Groups of participants are easily allocated to different pages of a wiki to collaborate on specific tasks.

Virtual worlds are social environments, not games; their participants each have at least one avatar (a virtual representation of themselves), able to move around in the 3D environment and interact with other avatars. Avatars do more or less whatever they like, including teaching and learning (Salmon and Hawkridge, 2009). Potentially, virtual worlds provide very powerful new cultural experiences for learning and for groups to work together in innovative and engaging ways (Salmon, 2009; Salmon, Nie and Edirisingha, 2010).

However, reflecting on the experience of developing the Schome Park Programme, Twining suggested that 'open virtual worlds are unclaimed spaces as far as education is concerned – educators have not yet established norms of how to support learning within them' (Twining, 2010; Salmon, 2009: 503). I agree that a key challenge is to design educational activities in virtual worlds, while exploiting the social nature of the visual environment, and of course to train e-moderators to exploit the new ways of learning.

Testing the five-stage model

Instead of designing for learning in the virtual world from 'scratch', my colleagues and I chose to test the five-stage model that had proved so useful in text-based 2D environments. Interestingly, Zane Berge in the US has also examined the impact of moving e-moderators from text to 3D (Berge, 2008). Within MOOSE (MOdelling Of Second life Environment, www.le.ac.uk/ beyonddistance/moose), a JISC-funded research project, our three case studies investigated the model's usefulness for teaching and learning in 3D envirion-ments. They involved students and tutors from three courses at two higher education institutions: the University of Leicester – a postgraduate distance learning course in Archaeology and a postgraduate campus-based course in Media and Communications; and the London South Bank University – a campus-based undergraduate course in Digital Photography.

Development of artefacts and activities in Second Life

We supported the Second Life (SL) tutors in their design of activities in SL (SL-tivities) based on the model's stages, including interesting collaborative tasks, thus scaffolding students' learning and group work. We ensured that artefacts were built in SL to provide 'a stimulus or a start (the "spark") to the interaction' (Salmon, 2002a).

Research methodology

As this was an early study, students were recruited on a voluntary basis. Their engagement with SL-tivities and learning experiences at each stage of the model was studied using qualitative methods. We captured data from the students in two ways. We conducted semi-structured interviews, lasting 40–60 minutes,

Case study 1

At Leicester, the Department of Archaeology developed two artefacts to support learning about the concept of using space and landscape. One simulated an aspect of the lives of ancient Saami people in Northern Scandinavia. The other simulated a village of the Kalasha, an ethnic group from the Hindu Kush Mountains in the northwest of Pakistan. In both Saami and Kalasha cultures, access to social spaces depends on the individual's gender and social status.

Students were inducted into SL through creating their avatars and given opportunities to navigate around the Saami tent and Kalasha village, see the layout and division of the space, and explore where they could and could not go according to the gender assigned to their avatars. They were encouraged to interact with each other (avatar–avatar) about what they found, experienced, thought and felt.

A version of the Saami tent is available as an open educational resource (http://slurl.com/secondlife/Media%20Zoo/177/222/24/) under the OTTER (Open, Transferable, Technology-enabled Educational Resource http://www.le.ac.uk/otter) project.

Case study 2

At London South Bank, the Department of Digital Photography deployed 'virtual story cubes' for teaching. Students as avatars practised taking snapshots in SL, using camera control commands and changing SL 'environmental' settings to take high-quality digital photographs. They 'set off' to visit different islands in SL and captured a variety of digital images representing different subcultures. They learned how to create a cube with their pictures and manipulate it by changing the size, the texture and moving it. Student avatars then demonstrated their individual cubes to others and shared experience about places they had visited and why they had taken the photos. Finally, they put all the individual cubes together and created illustrated stories from them, negotiating on the shape of the combined cubes, the order of them and which sides to show.

Case study 3

At Leicester, the Media and Communications Department designed two SL-tivities to enable students to investigate digital identity issues. Avatars were teleported to different places in SL where they met and interacted with others. They were teleported back to the university's Media Zoo Island to share together news of what and whom they had encountered and how their experiences had enhanced their understanding of digital identity.

focusing on their personal experiences of learning and using SL and on contributions to their learning at each stage of the five-stage model. We recorded the chat logs of students' discussion in each teaching session. The chat logs enabled mapping of student dialogue against each stage of the model, going back to my original research.

Cognitive mapping was the method used to develop the original five-stage model. We analysed the interview data by using cognitive mapping (Bryson, Ackermann, Eden and Fin, 2004), to create unique visual causal representations of individuals and groups and their changing views, feelings and experiences. The methodology is grounded in theories of personal constructs (Kelly, 1955), and supported by Decision Explorer software (www.banxia.com/demain.html).

When conducting SL-related research, there are ethical considerations in collecting and using data from chat logs, observations and the use of images of avatars. We ensured that participants knew how data would be used and that we had their informed consent.

Findings: the 5-stage model in Second Life

Stage 1: access and motivation

Gaining access is an essential precondition for learning in any online environment. By comparison with simpler text-based 2D environments such as computer conferencing, SL presents additional challenges but also advantages. Participants must create their avatars and learn to manipulate them in SL. MOOSE showed the importance of preparing learners in SL itself, helping them to acquire the basic skills of moving, navigating and communicating effectively. Acquiring these avatar-driving skills is a more complex process than being inducted into text-based learning environments which feel familiar to e-mail users. However, for a small greater investment, SL skills lead to exciting, motivating and fun experiences for participants.

Stage 1 applies equally to students and their tutors (SL-moderators). We found that it was best to split the stage into two steps.

Step 1: learning individually. The first step focuses on helping individuals to gain access to SL, creating an avatar and choosing its avatar name, logging on, teleporting, movements and group communication tools. We developed a MOOSE guide for participants to work through at their own pace (Wheeler and Salmon, 2008). The guide incorporates YouTube videos that demonstrate the basic skills. Students told us that they found this guide useful and the videos easy to follow.

Step 2: learning in a group in-world. Competence in more sophisticated in-world skills such as movement including flying, gestures, navigation, camera control, private chat, searching and use of simple development tools need to be developed. Mastering such skills in SL is a prerequisite for students to appreciate the whole environment, to feel comfortable and confident in exploring its resources independently, and to engage later in SL-tivities.

We provided a one-hour training session for students and staff, delivered in-world, avatar to avatar. Participants were shown and practised skills useful for taking part in SL-tivities. Students appreciated the opportunity to have an in-world training session, especially to avoid 'getting lost' and for building confidence in the environment. We consider this gaining of personal control and confidence a key prerequisite for motivating them to return and take part.

Students also appreciated the opportunity to learn in an avatar group and interact with others at the same level of understanding, through their avatars. The nature of engagement in SL is somewhat different from that of text-based asynchronous discussion forums, where socialization with others occurs via postings, reading and replying to each other, possibly over days or weeks. However, the 3D and immediacy of SL, the realistic feel to the artefacts and the co-presence immersion result in the personal experience of socialization in SL 'feeling' similar to that of RL. This co-presence in SL means that opportunities for socialization are available from the moment the participants meet each other in-world. They demonstrated high motivation to engage with each other.

We conclude that it is beneficial to build in-world skills development for small groups of learners together from Stage 1, and ensure that participants meet each other's avatars in the first group training session, rather than attempt individual training for everyone. The Stage 1 experience contributes to continuing access and motivation, and provides the basis for more complex avatar–avatar interactions at Stage 2.

Stage 2: online socialization

Stage two of the original five-stage model involves participants establishing their online identities, finding others with whom to interact online, understanding the nature of the online environment and how it is used for learning, and developing trust and mutual respect to work together at common tasks. All these are necessary for Stage 2 in SL but perhaps especially the establishment of online identity through avatars which is a more complex experience. SL presents opportunities as well as challenges for establishing online identity.

Our study found that for some participants the visual appearance of their avatar on the screen and their learning to 'drive' it are powerful enough for them to feel that the avatar is part of themselves. One participant said that she immediately 'felt attached to her [the avatar]'. Another said, 'I feel like I am an avatar' and a third, 'my avatar is a fantasy extension of me'. A significant milestone is reached when participants begin to feel that they are establishing a new and coherent identity through their avatars. This critical moment took longer for some than others.

Meeting other avatars helps develop personal avatar identity. We ensured that, by the end of Stage 1, participants had each constructed their first avatar. When they ventured around SL and met other avatars, they began to realize the social nature of the immersive world; the interactions with other avatars in SL 'felt' real. For example, one participant felt threatened when an avatar that she met offered to teleport her to another place in SL. Another participant wanted to change the look of her avatar when she met an avatar with similar looks and outfit!

We will be planning more SL-tivities to enable personal and group development through participants focusing on their avatars and developing a sense of 'inhabitation' for future projects. We recommend that sessions should include activities such as changing the appearance and making modifications to avatars, animating avatars by learning how to make gestures and movements, taking avatars shopping and field trips to different places in-world, by interacting with other avatars living in SL, and sharing, exchanging and reflecting on the in-world experiences.

In the original five-stage model, online socialization stands for more than merely 'socializing'. It includes understanding how being online contributes to learning for *their* topic, *this* course, *this* learning group. Our study concludes that SL sessions offer two more ways for socialization than in text-based environments. The first is enabled by artefacts available in SL which encourage avatars' interest and dialogue. The second is through the meeting, greeting and seeing the avatars of others, that is, impactful co-presence. As Meadows observed, identity is a vital aspect to consider in developing learning activities in SL (Meadows, 2008).

SL offers opportunities for socializing around artefacts that cannot be provided in text-based environments. For example, Box 3.1 is a conversation in text between avatars (students) gathered around the Saami tent.

Box 3.1 Students commenting on the artefacts around the Saami tent

[6:55] *Avatar 1: I like the crackling fire :)
[6:55] Avatar trainer: my pot over the fire is new! It cost me $L155.
[6:55] Avatar 1: Oh, how nice! What are you cooking? :)
[6:56] Avatar trainer: some special broth!
[6:56] Avatar 1: The rugs look so real.
[6:57] Avatar trainer: I knitted them the weekend that's why!

[6:57] Avatar 1: You're You're very talented.
[6.57] Avatar 2: :-)
[6:57] Avatar trainer: Well, some people have the skills! :-)
[6:57] Avatar 1: Do you have to knit in the middle of the tent or in the men's section?

Note: * The names of all avatars have been replaced by numbers to respect their anonymity.

Our analysis showed that there was laughter in the early SL sessions. In text-based environments, humour can be difficult to achieve until the group is well established. In Box 3.2, students are joking when they can't get into the Saami tent.

Box 3.2 Humour and laughter in SL

[7:09] Avatar facilitator 1: Well I can't move at all – I think I'm a lost reindeer.
[7:10] Avatar 1: No luck getting in?
[7:11] Avatar facilitator 1: Let's try again – we're all blocked from somewhere. It shows how strong these cultural conventions are!
[7:11] Avatar 1: I think we need to make our own tent :)
[7:12] Avatar 2: No problem :-)

Observation and interviews with participants showed that they were aware of SL as a *social* environment from the very start of their participation. They reported that SL allowed them to get to know each other better and faster than in text-based environments. As one student put it, 'due to the interaction, you quickly sort of get to know somebody, like E, she is very polite, very nice, so I got this first image of her'. A view of others' characteristics occurred earlier and more easily than in text-based environments where there is often some discomfort and much more effort needs to be put into establishing presence and trust (Salmon and Lawless, 2006). The characteristic recognition by new avatars of the high social presence encourages self-disclosure; they express feelings and emotions and they contribute further to online socialization and group building.

Box 3.3 shows an example of self-disclosure in SL. This happened in the in-world training session where the avatars of a group of distance learners met in SL for the first time. They quickly started sharing some aspects of their personal life with each other without prompting by the SL-moderator.

Box 3.3 Self-disclosure in SL

[7:00] Avatar 3: Are all of you taking the theory module?

[7:00] Avatar 2: Yes.

[7:00] Avatar 1: I was but deferred it because I was in the hospital . . . so I'll be starting again in July.

[7:00] Avatar 2: Are you well again?

[7:01] Avatar 1: Yes, thank you!

[7:01] Avatar Trainer: I need to pop away and set something up please keep chatting

[7:01] Avatar 1: Are you both from the UK?

[7:01] Avatar 5: No, I'm from Germany. And you?

[7:01] Avatar 2: I'm from the US.

[7:02] Avatar 3: I'm from Germany as well, but living in France.

[7:02] Avatar 1: Wow :)

[7:02] Avatar 2: Where from?

[7:02] Avatar 1: New Jersey

[7:02] Avatar 3: Born in Freiburg, but grew up in Kempten, in Bavaria. How about you?

[7:02] Avatar 2: I've been to Virginia once, I really liked it.

[7:03] Avatar 1: Yes, Virginia's pretty, I like it too.

[7:03] Avatar trainer: OK I'm back – I do not want to stop you but I'll have to!

[7:03] Avatar 1: I've been to Munich and really liked it.

[7:03] Avatar 2: I live in Sindelfingen near Stuttgart, but I was born in Munich.

Box 3.4 is an example in which avatars of a group of distance students, in their first teaching session in SL, shared their feelings.

Box 3.4 Sharing personal feelings in SL

[6:51] Avatar trainer: I'm very excited and nervous!

[6:51] Avatar 1: I'm very nervous :)

[6:51] Avatar trainer: This is the first time I have helped someone else teach in here so please be patient with us!

[6:52] Avatar 1: Of course!

[6:52] Avatar 2: And I'm nervous, too!

Being in an immersive virtual environment, with interaction through avatars, as well as making timely and seamless conversation, are all approximations of real life, and enable humour to bubble up easily. Box 3.5 is an example of humour that came through naturally during a teaching session.

Box 3.5 Humour during a teaching session in SL

[7:41] Avatar 1: I feel like I am in your company
[7:42] Avatar 1: Like a real class
[7:42] Avatar 2: Yes, a part of a group
[7:42] Avatar facilitator 1: Well, I feel like a prune standing up here
[7:42] Avatar 3: It's less anonymous
[7:42] Avatar 1: ha ha
[7:42] Avatar 3: Sit down!
[7:42] Avatar 2: :)
[7:42] Avatar facilitator 1: I'm not sure I know how to sit down yet! It might be embarrassing!
[7:43] Avatar 1: We won't laugh. :)
[7:43] Avatar 3: Right-click on sit
[7:43] Avatar facilitator 1: Thanks – that's helpful. But I might fly instead
    . . .

The Media and Communications students' avatars had no prior contact before meeting in SL. They were not informed which avatar was driven by a tutor and which by a student, nor did they try to determine RL (Real Life) roles during their SL sessions. We conclude that the avatars did not find it necessary either before or during the SL sessions to investigate each other's RL roles. However, it became apparent through behaviours!

Cognitive mapping revealed that tutors' avatars interacting with students' avatars within the immersive SL environment created an equal relationship, breaking down the old tutor–student hierarchical relationship. Again, although this is a known phenomenon in text-based environments, it was most marked and happened quickly in SL. One tutor explained that SL enabled the students and tutors to move away from traditional structures (buildings, classrooms), timetables, rules and regulations and modes of teaching and learning so typical of the higher education environment, to a new approach. The development of equal relationships, where preconceptions about who is who change, contribute to the start of a 'virtual third culture' at the online socialization stage (Salmon, 2002d).

Stage 3: information exchange

The experience of information exchange in SL is rather different from that in the original five-stage model although the key features remain. In SL it is characterized by questions and responses occurring in rapid successions similar to that occurring in instant messaging forums, but with much more context from avatars' gestures and movements and reference to artefacts in the SL space. The conversation pattern is similar to that which occurs in face-to-face meetings rather than on asynchronous bulletin boards. Conversely, in bulletin boards participants have the option and time to reflect and compose their responses, but in SL they need to compose their responses and ask questions based on what they already know about the subject under discussion. They need to do this quickly or they will get 'left behind'.

In our study, we identified two types of information exchange, both of which are features of Stage 3 of the five-stage model: sharing and recommending information to others and helping others to achieve their goals. Box 3.6 is part of a student discussion that begins with a question: 'Can you recommend any good places in SL that others can visit?' This is a direct request for information exchange. The students started talking about their encounters with artefacts in SL. They were easily able to ignore the SL moderators' attempts to get them back on track!

Box 3.6 Offering information to others

[7:47] Avatar trainer: did anyone find any good places they would like to recommend others to visit before next week?
[7:47] Avatar facilitator 3: and photo galleries as well
[7:47] Avatar 5: Alice in wonderland, or the little circus. . .
[7:48] Avatar 5: there's a lion to sit on!
[7:48] Avatar 8: okay, that's fairly amazing
[7:48] Avatar 7: did you take a picture?
[7:48] Avatar 5: no I was too busy sitting on it
[7:48] Avatar 8: I've seen a dragon!
[7:49] Avatar 5: can you sit on it?
[7:49] Avatar trainer: OK . . . BACK TO THE CLASSROOM!
[7:49] Avatar 6: I saw a whale. . .
[7:49] Avatar 8: not so sure

In the example in Box 3.7, the tutor is helping the students, and the students are helping each other to navigate around the Kalasha village.

Box 3.7 Helping others find their way around the Kalasha village

[7:46] Avatar 3: I can go up to the mountain top, isn't this limited to men only?

[7:48] Avatar facilitator 2: in theory you shouldn't be able to go up the mountain top – mountains are pure, so for men only
[7:48] Avatar 3: Can you enter the hut, V?
[7:48] Avatar facilitator 2: but try and see what your permission lets you do
[7:48] Avatar 4: I'll try
[7:49] Avatar 3: Can I open the door?
[7:50] Avatar facilitator 1: Yep just click on it

Stage 4: knowledge construction

In our study, we identified two types of avatar behaviours likely to promote knowledge construction: collaborations and sharing, that is, exchanging views and learning from each other to achieve a common goal. Unlike text-based environments, SL offers opportunities to build, create and develop objects collaboratively. Participants found the activity of building and developing virtual story cubes very interesting and engaging. They very much enjoyed the group support, discussion and negotiation mediated through developing and putting together their story cubes. The characteristics of the SL environment led to easy and productive processes and group work – qualities that are difficult to reproduce and require more effort to generate in text-based asynchronous environments. In Box 3.8, a group of students discuss and negotiate on what shape they should put their story cubes together.

Box 3.8 Interacting and contributing towards a common goal

[6:31] Avatar 8: how should we put them together? What shape?
[6:31] Avatar 5: circle, so we can walk round it easily
[6:31] Avatar 7: yep
[6:31] Avatar 8: the viewer stands in the middle? Or outside?
[6:31] Avatar 5: or a semi circle?
[6:31] Avatar 9: good idea
[6:31] Avatar 10: yeah a circle
[6:31] Avatar 5: clever
[6:31] Avatar 7: in the middle
[6:31] Avatar 8: I'd go for middle
[6:31] Avatar 8: let's do it
[6:32] Avatar 5: and won't it be FUN to see the story on the outside!!

[6:32] Avatar 8: I'm gonna start with a wonky circle
[6:32] Avatar trainer: should we all stand in the middle as you build it around us?
[6:33] Avatar 10: yes good idea ... H ... I think I am in the middle now
[6:33] Avatar 6: looks very professional Avatar 4!
[6:35] Avatar 8: now you think about the order

Boxes 3.9 and 3.10 demonstrate the need to create appropriate conditions for the smooth and regular flow of engagement and interchange. In Box 3.9, the SL-moderator facilitated knowledge construction through asking questions, promoting new topics, seeking more discussion and encouraging controversial views.

Box 3.9 E-moderating skills for facilitating knowledge construction in SL

[7:09] Avatar facilitator 1: Who wants to start – A? (being alphabetical)
[7:09] Avatar 3: All three of them, I guess.
[7:09] Avatar facilitator 1: D – do you agree?
[7:09] Avatar 2: All three, I suppose.
[7:10] Avatar facilitator 1: E? Someone start arguing!
[7:10] Avatar 1: I think it's socially structured, but maybe all three? It's neutral as far as gender goes I think.
[7:10] Avatar 1: It's virtual so it's a little confusing
[7:10] Avatar facilitator 1: Gender is an interesting one, as it is very easy to be transgender or opposite gender to real life, as we shall see next week
[7:11] Avatar facilitator 1: Can we think about how far SL conforms to these kinds of approaches in turn?
[7:11] Avatar facilitator 1: As far as I can experience it, SL uses Cartesian coordinates, so in that sense it tries to mimic the real world rather than do anything more creative
[7:12] Avatar 3: But the same time it's three-dimensional, measurable and quantifiable.

In Box 3.10, the students achieved knowledge construction through following up each other's questions, keeping the discussion growing, and sharing and exchanging views.

Box 3.10 Knowledge construction through sharing and exchanging views in SL

[7:40] Avatar facilitator 2: ok, end of that PowerPoint – any questions about burial?

[7:41] Avatar 3: Any differences between men and women?

[7:41] Avatar facilitator 2: good question – no difference between men and women for actual burial, but the ancestor statues tend to be of men

[7:42] Avatar trainer: Do they use different woods/components depending on prestige/status of the person buried? The pictures I saw (you showed me) . . . all look the same?

[7:42] Avatar 3: Or colours on the statues?

[7:43] Avatar facilitator 2: yes, interesting point – wood today in the Kalasha valleys is in short supply – deforestation by the Kalasha

[7:43] Avatar 4: is the depth of burial very little as in European Muslim cemeteries

[7:43] Avatar facilitator 2: this means that any wood that can be found is used, and also means that the production of ancestor statues is dying out

[7:43] Avatar 1: Is that why they don't use coffins? The small supply of wood?

[7:43] Avatar 3: Have they started using different material for the statues?

[7:44] Avatar facilitator 2: and because wood rots away quite quickly when exposed, we don't really know so much about what happened some year ago, only very recent burials

[7:44] Avatar facilitator 2: V first – the traditional burials and 'buried' – the coffins are placed above ground, and you'll see this in the photos next week

[7:44] Avatar 4: understood

[7:45] Avatar facilitator 2: E – the bodies are placed in wooden 'coffins' and this is the traditional practice, the coffins are then just left above ground to rot away

[7:45] Avatar 1: I see, thanks.

[7:45] Avatar facilitator 2: however, recently Muslim practices are starting to prevail and bodies are having to be buried according to Muslim traditions

[7:46] Avatar facilitator 2: A – interesting idea, but I haven't seen any trend at all to make statues out of different material. I will look out for this if I go there again soon though

[7:46] Avatar 3: OK, then

Stage 5: development

The example in Box 3.11 shows that students and tutors reflected on their experience of SL (towards the end of a learning session) and the similarities and differences towards the end of a teaching session. They were able to take a meta cognitive view of their learning through the 3D world.

Box 3.11 Reflecting on personal experience in SL

[4:26] Avatar facilitator 4: what do you think you have learnt about virtual identity from your experience in SL?

[4:26] Avatar facilitator 5: I hope we all go on adventuring in SL

[4:26] Avatar facilitator 4: So do I

[4:27] Avatar facilitator 5: It has changed a lot for me. A whole new world has opened up for new teaching and research

[4:27] Avatar 11: I think it's just like real life, but the difference is you can make it different

[4:27] Avatar facilitator 4: why not change in real life? Maybe you will now

[4:28] Avatar facilitator 5: I'm working in New York and having fun in SL with all of you. I'm here but I'm there too. Multiple spatiality

[4:29] Avatar 12: I think I've got more chance to do something that I can't do or no chance to do in real life

---

In the final stage of the model participants aim to achieve personal goals and attempt to integrate their learning experience from the online environment into other forms of learning. There is potential for sophisticated individual learning at this stage.

Summary and recommendations

Our initial study shows that using a structured model for scaffolding learning in groups has value in 3D MUVEs such as SL as well as in text-based asynchronous environments to ensure that for learners, and teachers, *confidence in the environment and in each other builds up in a productive way*. The basic structure appears to hold good (see Figure 3.1), but the potential at each stage is slightly different.

There is no need to separate the activities that support learning to benefit from using the technological platform from those needed to undertake course-related tasks and establishing a constructive learning group. Of course, at present SL is more alien to some participants than bulletin boards are, and they need support and practice. This is an echo for many of us of how it was in the early days of bulletin boards! The key aim for SL-moderators should be

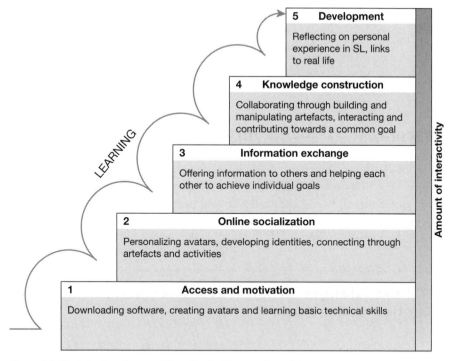

Figure 3.1 Model of teaching and learning in 3D virtual worlds

to enable each student to become comfortable in his or her avatar's identity and 'at home' in the SL environment. Then the participants will learn to relate well and early with each other through their avatars. We noted that this is somewhat easier in SL and occurs more naturally through experience of interaction, once basic skills are acquired, than through asynchronous bulletin boards. However, learning designers should avoid missing out on the critical 'online socialization' stage – it provides the building blocks in the scaffold for much more group learning later on.

Next steps

We are continuing to research into both SL activities (SL-tivities) and the social scaffolding of learning in SL, with on-campus and distance learners, through further studies focused on the students' learning experience and the use of SL in established programmes of study, as in our projects DUCKLING (Delivering University Curricula: Knowledge, Learning and INnovation Gains, http://www.le.ac.uk/duckling) and SWIFT (Second World Immersive Future Teaching, http://www.le.ac.uk/swift). We plan to continue to illuminate the benefits of the five-stages for SL and other Web 2.0 environments, and invite other teachers and researchers to explore these ideas and send us feedback on their findings.

There are many other ways of using these low-cost high-value virtual worlds – see Salmon and Hawkridge (2009) and Salmon (2009) for lots more ideas. Another example is given in the next section.

Learning in virtual laboratories

Dr Paul Rudman, researcher/developer for the Second World Immersive Future Teaching project (SWIFT) at the University of Leicester, tells us about deploying a virtual world application to support laboratory-based learning.

You can read more about SWIFT in Rudman, Lavelle, Salmon and Cashmore (2010).

The challenges of laboratory learning in higher education

At the University of Leicester, undergraduates' genetics laboratory classes involve a combination of classical and molecular genetics experiments related to a range of organisms including bacteria, fungi, fruit flies and humans. A typical laboratory holds 120 students and lecturers and contains standard tools and equipment.

In laboratory-based classes there are constraints of time, resources and space, and limited opportunities for interaction between students and staff. In particular, it is neither cost- nor time-efficient to use a real laboratory session solely to cover health and safety and equipment use issues. Instead, students are given a printed sheet with relevant health and safety procedures, while instructions on equipment use are given as and when required for each experiment.

A virtual lab

SWIFT (Second World Immersive Future Teaching) is a research and development project investigating the effectiveness of a virtual laboratory to supplement students' real-life laboratory time and expand their learning experiences.

One of the qualities of Virtual Worlds (VWs) is that they allow the low-cost simulation of real-world spaces. The SWIFT project created a VW-based simulated genetics laboratory, on the Beyond Distance Research Alliance's Media Zoo Island in Second Life.

In the virtual laboratory students, as avatars, can experiment and evaluate situations in risk-free interactive ways. For the first part of SWIFT, we

---

designed activities in the virtual world that allowed students to explore the laboratory and its health and safety issues.

The five-stage model and VW acclimatization

SWIFT comprised two one-hour VW sessions for groups of three to six Biological Sciences first-year undergraduates. The first session covered avatar skills including text chat, walking, sitting, change clothes and moving the camera (viewpoint on-screen) (Stage 1 of the five stage model – access and motivation). We were impressed at how quickly and easily participants gained the skills needed to engage successfully with the VW.

We noticed differences in participants' adaptation to learning in a VW compared to distance learners, such as with MOOSE (see page 68). For SWIFT, the equipment was set up in advance close to the main campus, addressing many practical access issues associated with Stage 1 of the five-stage model. All the SWIFT participants were attending in person a campus-based course at the University of Leicester, and several were friends with each other before the SWIFT VW experiments began.

This meant that participants tended to arrive in twos or threes for the first session, while for the second session most arrived in one group. Participants logged onto the VW from laptops while in the same physical room as each other. This made them well placed to interact with each other across both the real world and the virtual world, supporting a strong 'online socialization' (Stage 2 – in-world socialization).

The five-stage model in the virtual lab

In the second session, avatars worked together to practise and consolidate their skills (Stage 2), with the help of the VW-moderator (in real life, a Genetics VW-moderator). In the VW, avatars first congregated in a social area comprising chairs and drinks machines. The VW-moderator, as an avatar, then gave participants' avatars a guided tour of the virtual laboratory, describing the main items of equipment, and discussing health and safety issues in general and such issues for each item of equipment.

There was some integration between real-world and virtual-world socialization. Participants were sitting together in the real-world computer room whilst their avatars were interacting, allowing VW interactions to move into the real world – often as short comments or non-verbal communication (looks, smiles, sounds). Everyone knew whose avatar represented whom, and would refer to real or avatar names interchangeably, with questions about the task being asked in both the virtual- and the real-worlds. Stage 2 clearly benefited from this integration.

> [5:23] Avatar A: can I get a drink from the water fountain?

> [Voice in VW] VW-moderator: I don't know, have a go and see if
>   you can get a drink from the water fountain
> [Voice in VW] VW-moderator: Oh, do you mean the real one
>   outside?
> [5:23] Avatar A: in real life I mean sorry
> [5:23] Avatar A: yes
> [Voice in VW] VW-moderator: yes, you can
> [5:23] Avatar A: thanks
> [5:23] Avatar A: brb [be right back]

SWIFT participants were highly motivated to participate in a serious learning exercise. They were happy to treat their avatar as an extension of themselves and learn through the avatar's experience, such as seeing ethanol catch fire when placed beside a Bunsen burner.

In practice, the avatars create the impact of the social experience, regardless of the 'built' environment in which an event takes place. Early on, the avatar's behaviour is not always under the person's control. Relative beginners find their avatar inadvertently walks into walls, stands on benches, flies or loses its hair, to name just a few unexpected behaviours. Thus, VW sessions with beginners are best treated as informal settings – it is hard to maintain a formal environment when one cannot be sure of walking in a straight line!

The SWIFT VW-moderator adapted to this by switching between the formal task (explaining about the lab) and informal assistance and patience with VW difficulties. Thus, while SWIFT participants were often briefly sidetracked by difficulties in controlling their avatar, the VW-moderator was able to complete her tour of the virtual lab, and participants complete their group tasks. Most participants agreed that they learnt valuable health and safety information and recommended the VW lab as a helpful induction prior to entering sessions on the real-world lab.

Occasionally, a participant would blame themselves for their avatar's misbehaviour – seeing themselves as 'stupid' or suchlike. The VW-moderator acted quickly to help and reassure them that such difficulties with avatars are usual in the VW environment.

The sequence below shows an example of how the group collaboratively dealt with one avatar's mistake, using humour to cover possible embarrassment. Note the VW-moderator offers practical advice on solving the problem and allows time for the mistake to be rectified.

> [Voice in VW] VW-moderator: . . . the laminar flow hood. Last
>   piece of kit that you may have used to set up some of your
>   experiments
> [5:09] Avatar B: [Avatar C] still has something in her right hand

[Voice in VW] VW-moderator: [Avatar C] has something in her right hand
[5:09] Avatar B: souvenir?
[Voice in VW] VW-moderator: Oh!
[5:09] Avatar C: oops what?
[Everyone laughs in real-life]
[Voice in VW] VW-moderator: That's fantastic [ironic]
[5:09] Avatar C: what is that
[Voice in VW] VW-moderator: Whoever's that is, it looks like a planet, Pluto
[Several laugh in real-life]
[5:10] Avatar B: it's Saturn without rings ;)
[Voice in VW] VW-moderator: Could maybe take it back, put it back in their inventory, that would be nice
[Spoken in real-life] Participant with avatar D: What is it?
[5:10] Avatar D: Pluto isn't a planet
[5:10] Avatar E: halo over my head
[5:10] Avatar F: it's reminding me of Maltesers
[5:10] Avatar D: a planetoid
[5:10] Avatar C: an asteroid
[5:10] Avatar F: a planet?
[5:10] Avatar D: uh huh
[5:10] Avatar B: an astero-planetoid so no one will be upset

After the lab tour, participants, as avatars, worked together in pairs or groups of three. Again, the exercise took place simultaneously through avatars in the virtual world, and in the real world. Participants were given the task details on paper in the real world but accomplished the tasks as avatars in the VW. Communication was by group text chat in the VW, whereby participants only saw messages typed by the other group member(s). Thus Stage 3 (information exchange) also spanned both the real and the virtual worlds.

The next sequence shows an example of information exchange (Stage 3). Groups have the task of taking three photos of (virtual) lab equipment and placing the photos in a public display area in the VW.

[3:20] Avatar G: [Avatar H], which one do you want to take a photo of?
[3:21] Avatar H: um, I'll take a pic of the gel tank
[3:23] Avatar G: OK, I will do the Bunsen and whoever finishes first will do the next one :)
[3:25] Avatar H: I've done the gel tank
[3:26] Avatar G: oh, I just can't take myself out of the way :(

[3:26] Avatar G: would you mind if you do the 3rd one?
[3:26] Avatar H: yes ok I'll do it
[3:26] Avatar G: thanks :)
[3:26] Avatar H: try pressing alt and the arrows to focus on an object . . . that's what I did
[3:26] Avatar G: OK, good idea :)
[3:26] Avatar G: will do
[3:28] Avatar H: I've taken them both,
[3:28] Avatar G: OOOH
[3:28] Avatar G: I am almost done
[3:29] Avatar G: done
[3:29] Avatar G: where are the cards?
[3:29] Avatar G: do you know?
[3:29] Avatar H: click on the name card
[3:29] Avatar H: and it'll come up . . . u have to keep them
[3:30] Avatar H: I've got the answer for the gel tank . . . u have to wear gloves
[3:30] Avatar G: OOOH, well done

Overall, the virtual lab classes ran successfully. The only technical difficulties participants encountered were with putting on and removing lab coats, something we have addressed with more specific training. The VW environment supported all activities well, except for detailed demonstrations of picking up and manipulating objects.

Participants were overwhelmingly positive about the virtual laboratory, finding it more realistic than they had expected and reporting a learning experience, especially of health and safety information. Participants cited new learning, such as learning about a new piece of equipment, as well as revision, such as of the safety rules, or both new learning and revision.

Being synchronous and looking somewhat like the real world, VWs are in many ways closer to real-life classes than to discussion forums. Students can be placed in a position similar to real-life classes, where contributing is expected of them by their peers. Choosing not to participate becomes obvious and may engender similar feelings of 'letting the side down' as in real-life group work. Where a group knows each other and is sitting together in real life, this effect is amplified. We saw this effect greatly benefiting progression through Stages 1 to 3 and we expect Stage 4 (knowledge construction) to benefit as well. Stage 5 (development) is more a personal journey; it is not yet clear how effective SWIFT will be in facilitating this stage.

SWIFT found that the virtual lab can provide both good preparation for the real lab and good revision afterwards. The participants' existing real-life friendships and their co-presence in real- and virtual-worlds simultaneously appeared to facilitate greatly their moving through Stages 1, 2 and 3. Subsequent phases of SWIFT will allow participants to observe and carry out experiments in the virtual lab, thus addressing Stages 3, 4 and 5 of the model.

Asynchronous voice boards

Asynchronous voice board discussions

Voice discussion boards are low-cost, high-impact tools for providing a viable alternative to text-based conferencing, and bring their own special qualities. On an asynchronous voice discussion board, all participants can post audio messages which are linked together in a discussion thread, just as in a text-based discussion forum. The difference is that the voice is used rather than text. Popular VLEs include voice discussion boards, or you can set them up separately from the VLE (though then everyone will need a separate log in and password).

Voice discussion boards in action

As part of a research and development project called DUCKLING (www.le.ac.uk/ducking) at the University of Leicester, the MA TESOL (Teaching English to Speakers of Other Languages) and Applied Linguistics course team piloted use of the Wimba voice discussion board with students taking the *Language Discourse and Society* module in 2010. Staff wanted to generate interaction between students and encourage them to discuss concepts and issues in preparing for formative assessment tasks.

The MA is aimed at graduate teachers with at least two years of English Language Teaching experience who want to further their academic and professional development. The programme attracts about 90 students each year, almost all of whom are in employment throughout their studies. Every student has a personal tutor, who gives them feedback on their assignment outlines and drafts and provides ongoing support throughout the programme. Students can also choose to engage in discussion about the course through a text-based discussion forum on the Blackboard VLE if they wish to. Each module has an e-moderator for the discussion forum; for the purposes of the pilot, two e-moderators worked together to moderate the voice-activities (v-tivities).

Voice discussions and the five stages

STAGE 1: ACCESS AND MOTIVATION

Students who signed up for the pilot were provided with a log-in, a Wimba voice discussion board user guide, a link to the voice board from the VLE and ongoing technical support. In practice, we found that throughout the study, students did not require much technical support.

The board opened up in a new window in students' browsers. The e-moderators sent out a brief text guide to using the board and students had three weeks to try out the board before starting on their tasks. Because the navigation and functionality of the voice boards are similar to the Blackboard forums, we did not offer any new training. Students had no difficulty with access. However, some of the students' expectations were not fulfilled. They were not able to attach sound files or any other attachments to their posts; nor were they able to download each other's audio posts onto their hard drives to listen to them offline. The e-moderators had access to these functions as 'super-participants'; it would have breached the university's security protocol to give students super-user status. The 'subscription' function (i.e., receiving an e-mail alert whenever another participant had posted something to the voice board) did not work and had to be disabled. These problems were unsolvable technically: students and e-moderators had to accept the platform's limitations.

STAGE 2: SOCIALIZATION – PRELIMINARY VOICE-TIVITY (V-TIVITY)

Students were invited to participate in a preliminary voice-tivity (v-tivity). They were asked to share a little information about themselves on the voice board, and to say why they had chosen to participate in the pilot. This gave everyone the chance to sort out any technology access issues and to play with the technology, while also establishing rapport with one another before beginning the assessed tasks. Many students commented on how appealing it was to hear one another's voices at this stage, and that they felt more connected than on the text-based discussion boards.

STAGES 3 AND 4: INFORMATION EXCHANGE AND KNOWLEDGE CONSTRUCTION

Four voice-based online v-tivities were prepared, following the five-stage model. The v-tivities were based on an e-tivity template from the Beyond Distance Research Alliance's 'Carpe Diem' workshops (Armellini and Jones, 2008; Armellini, Salmon and Hawkridge, 2009). Each v-tivity had a 'spark' to start the dialogue, an explanation of the purpose, a mini-research task for students to conduct and share via the voice board, and the requirement to respond, using voice, to two other postings. Students were also asked to reflect on their experience of using the voice board.

As an example, V-tivity 1 focused on the concept of World Englishes, and asked students to elicit a voice recording from someone else (a friend, colleague or student). The respondent was required to speak about their experience of learning and using English. Students then gave an audio commentary on the recording, analysing both the speech style and the content of the recording in terms of sociolinguistic criteria discussed in the module materials and the literature. Each student was then required to respond to the commentaries of at least two of their peers, adding any further insights they could think of.

The requirement to respond to peers' contributions proved critically important in enabling a positive learning experience. The students' responses to one another's posts fostered further dialogue. They constructively built upon what other students had said in the thread, or in other threads. These responses were the key to enabling positive interaction between the peers.

STAGE 5: DEVELOPMENT

The v-tivities were designed to provide students with food for thought for their longer assignments, which they wrote as individuals, and which encouraged them to pursue their own specific professional and developmental interests.

The voice board e-moderating role

The first v-tivity took place over three weeks, and the second, third and fourth v-tivities took two weeks each to complete. The e-moderators explained the task at the beginning of each v-tivity and at the end of each provided feedback: they did not want to direct or inhibit the students' conversations during the v-tivity.

In setting up the threads for the v-tivities, the e-moderators paid attention to the structuring of the voice board. According to e-moderator Gabi:

> Unlike in written discussion boards, you can't just skim through all the contributions at a glance. You actually have to take the time to listen, and if a message isn't relevant to you, that can be quite frustrating. So it is important to set up the voice threads with clear headings, and make sure students post their contributions in the right, relevant place. It is also a good idea to ask students to write a very clear and descriptive subject line (rather than just re-using the existing heading for the thread, which appears in the subject line by default). For example, if your post contains a detailed explanation to help one person solve a specific technical problem they are experiencing with the voice board, this is unlikely to be of use to everyone, so a clear heading will help to avoid frustration.

The e-moderators supported individual students via e-mail; for example, by reminding those who had not yet posted their contributions when the deadline was approaching and by answering specific questions.

The e-moderators gave audio and text feedback at the end of each v-tivity. Both moderators chose to give the more academic feedback in written form and the more emotional feedback (praise and encouragement) in audio form. Studies of using voice podcasts for guiding students taking a Master's in Psychology at Leicester indicated that the best results occurred when e-moderators gave audio as well as written feedback to students on their dissertation drafts. The e-moderators tended to focus more explicitly on giving positive feedback when using audio. Clearly this is an area for more research studies.

The value of voice boards for learning

Asynchronous use of voice boards for learning is still in its early days, but studies at Leicester have shown some distinct advantages.

INCREASING THE USE OF HUMAN VOICES FOR REMOTE LEARNING

On many distance learning programmes, students still express feelings of aloneness or isolation. The students who participated in the voice board pilot at Leicester valued the opportunity to have direct communication with their e-moderators and peers through the voice board. The voice board helped to add an interesting humanizing dimension and 'breathed additional life' into the learning programme. Other studies have noted similar impact with the use of the human voice and podcasting (Nie, Armellini, Harrington, Barklamb and Randall, 2010).

Student feedback:

> I thought it was just an excellent way to bring the course to life really. The interactive nature, the voice, even though it wasn't in real time [was] very useful. It takes you one step closer to be in a seminar kind of environment.
>
> I think the main thing is the principle of using something to kind of re-create the seminar environment over the Internet.

Students felt that the use of voice added an element of personalization that helped to bring them closer together.

> It's so nice to hear from classmates around the globe . . . But for me it's been particularly good this time, just to be able to hear your tutor's voice and imagine what you sound like . . . This is a good course. This is a good programme. But it does seem very distant at times. When you're dealing with people's emails, you don't really get a chance of knowing what people look like or what people sound like.
>
> One of the drawbacks about a distance learning course can be the feeling [of being isolated] . . . When I was an undergraduate, you could

really see where your money is going. I would have lectures and seminars. But with a distance learning course, I felt just like (I was) reading and doing all the work by myself and getting a few points (via e-mail) from my tutor every couple of months. It (the voice board) is really a good way to personalize the delivery of the degree.

It's so interesting, . . . the world does seem much smaller.

It makes it generally a lot more real, it feels a lot more personal.

The two e-moderators also felt that being able to hear students' voices added a personal touch and helped to bridge the remoteness of distance learning. One reflected:

I found this very stimulating. I really enjoyed hearing the voices of the students. Often this distance course feels quite remote because we are just in communication by writing. [But with the voice board] it sort of would come to life. We could often measure the degree of emotional involvement of some of the students.

I like it very much. It brings a personal motivating element to the learning process.

ADVANTAGES OF VOICE- OVER TEXT-BASED COMMUNICATION

Students identified some advantages of voice-compared to text-based communication for interacting with e-moderators and peers. Some felt that voice was better at conveying emotions than text:

The expression in the voice and emotions and things like that . . . rather than having to kind of type emotions . . . The emotions [and] tone are better expressed in the voice [through the use of intonation] than in text.

The use of voice also provided more clarity:

Messages are a lot clearer in voice communication, whereas they can be misinterpreted when you use text only.

Some students said that voice was better than text at capturing people's personal views:

Of course with voice, you get a better idea about people's attitudes and opinions on things as well.

Using voice in real time also challenged students to develop their arguments in ways that would be easily understood by their peers:

> It challenges me to articulate my points. Points that are quite easy to make on paper can be quite difficult to do in real time by voice.

Some also found that listening to other people's voices motivated them to read and explore the topic more.

> But I think more importantly, it's just that other people have made [voice] contributions . . . they made such interesting comments, that it actually made me go away and think, 'That's quite interesting', and I'd actually like to read an article on that, or I would read a chapter of a book. So from talking and listening to other people on the same course, it's actually a lot more stimulating. Obviously when you're emailing your tutor, they will give you examples of journal articles and books . . ., but when you've got a whole host of people . . . then we'll be having a lot more input. I just think it's really good. It stimulates the discussion. It stimulates the knowledge. So I do feel that I read a lot more than I know I did for the regular structured activities in Module 1 and 2.

DIFFERENCES OF VOICE COMPARED TO TEXT-BASED COMMUNICATION

Students clearly experienced differences, but on the whole were joyful about the voice aspects and repeatability. Typically they developed new strategies, such as taking notes whilst listening.

Participants sometimes became more self-conscious when using voice to communicate than using text-based discussion boards, as one student reflected:

> When I was speaking I found it a bit difficult to know what I was going to say. So I had to keep notes and try to follow those guided notes to say what I wanted to say.

Others expressed that recording a post on the voice board was more difficult than they expected it to be, although, like the tutors, they soon got used to it and relaxed.

> I had asked Stuart (a respondent for v-tivity 1) to record his part before I had properly had a go and only realised after how difficult it was. I'm trying to record my thoughts in one go rather than doing a number of different recordings to get it 'perfect'. I feel that this is more natural.
>
> I agree with the natural as compared to prepared speech too. Though if you heard my rambling you may disagree. It made me realise the difficulty of asking my colleague to speak about her language use.

ASSESSMENT THROUGH INTERACTIVE TASKS

Through the voice board, it was possible to offer students more feedback (it is quicker by voice) and a greater variety of feedback from peers compared to text, whereas they received limited written feedback when assessed though the portfolios. We are still researching the longer-term impact.

Students enjoyed being assessed through interactive tasks via the voice board. They liked receiving constructive feedback from the tutors and peers.

> I think it's much, much better than text. The reason that I do is because for Module 1 and 2 . . . for the structured e-tivities . . . the comments we get are limited to one or two sentences, which is ok, but there could be more. Something like this [voice boards] is great because not only you get constructive feedback from the tutors, you get it from your classmates too.

Students appreciated the opportunity to exchange views, have in-depth discussions, and receive quality feedback from peers via the voice board.

> It was really cool just to listen to people's views on the things that we are all reading, and some interesting topics. We had some great discussions, and some good feedback from each other . . . It's a really useful tool for me to hear people talk about something that I'm interested in . . . It gives me a lot of interesting thoughts from other people.

The students considered that the v-tivities enabled discussion around the tasks with peers. Students appreciated the opportunity to conduct more readings recommended by peers on the voice board.

> It's great to read articles [recommended by peers] that I generally wouldn't read. I read a lot of articles online, but it's always good to read from papers that I haven't read. This really opens things up to me in many ways.
>
> I feel I'm actually doing more reading than I was actually doing for Module 1 or 2 just because there are added inputs to require more information . . . I think because you have a chance to interact with people on the course as well, it does give you a bit more added input. I mean I try to read as much as possible.

Rapid exposure to peer review is encouraging for many students.

> In Module 1 and 2 I read quite a bit. But this module, I read a lot more. Because I think partly I don't want to come across as not having read material on the voice board . . . I don't know whether it's a case of not wanting to look stupid because your voice is on the voice board.

Students appreciate the interactive element of the v-tivities and are happy about their formative assessment being done this way: 'From my point of view, the v-tivities have been a great success.'

A tip from the e-moderators for assessment on voice boards:

> The clearer the assessment criteria for v-tivities on the voice board, the better our students performed. It was necessary to stipulate maximum length of contributions (four minutes seemed about right for the v-tivities we used, although some students struggled to stay within this limit), and to state the scope of the content areas we expected students to cover in their commentaries. After the first few v-tivities, we also realised that the use of voice seemed to encourage more subjective commentaries from students than they might have given in writing, and sometimes less rigorously considered statements. We therefore took pains to remind them to justify their comments with reference to the literature or their research – as well as to prepare what they were going to say in advance, so that they did not use up too much of their talk-time in 'rambling'.

STUDENT PERFORMANCE

Comments from tutors about student performance throughout the pilot are mixed.

> I think that the students have done a very good job on the whole. They kept to the guidelines, included academic references, and have certainly kept on task, including some interesting points about the language that is being used.

Some students followed the instructions carefully and produced more satisfactory responses. The best responses included references to models relating to the topic, mentioned appropriate references, cross-referred their statements to other students' statements, and backed up assertions with careful evidence. The worst responses rambled, did none or only few of the above and asserted their beliefs/opinions without providing evidence.

LEARNING PREFERENCES

Some students express an initial reluctance in using the voice board. For example, this student's learning preference determined that he valued text- rather than voice-based communication:

> I guess my first reaction was a bit negative because I got used to writing papers, writing assignments. And I enjoyed it a lot researching and

referencing. I thought I lose that using the voice board . . . My learning style is through writing things. It's enjoyable to listen to different people. I find that I really like to see a reading copy, what people write also on the voice board . . . As for Blackboard, I like to see the written. I've gotten used to Blackboard, especially in its written form.

This student also found that using voice for communication wasn't intuitive enough for him. He had to prepare notes before he recorded his speech:

Before I record something, I take notes and try to speak freely, but upon the notes taken . . . If someone recorded something, in order to respond, I have to take notes.

However, his views changed as he used the voice board more. He still preferred to see the text conference on Blackboard discussion board or voice board; however, he enjoyed more using the voice board and viewed it as a different approach to writing:

I actually have a very positive attitude now towards the voice board because it's a different experience. It's an optimised approach . . . I would prefer to see written text as well. It's a new experience, which is good. It's a different sort of challenge, which I'm enjoying a lot.

We do not yet know whether there is a qualitative or quantitative difference between voice boards and text. More work will establish whether learners will interact better and longer with their peers through voice or text. It probably depends most, as always, on the quality of the structuring of the online tasks and the skills of the e-moderator. For now, it seems it adds variety and novel dimension and is worth continuing.

The role of the voice moderator (v-moderator)

The key role of the voice moderator, when introducing a voice board for the first time, is to encourage students to participate and to be available to quickly solve problems that might prevent individual students from contributing. The v-moderator's role then shifts towards summarizing key points and weaving feedback and appropriate challenges into the discussion, in order to scaffold students through Stages 3, 4 and 5 of the collaborative learning process.

Limitations with the technology

Students and e-moderators identified limitations with the voice technology: the interface and lack of functionalities. We recognized that we were in the early days of the use of voice boards, but if you are choosing one for learning purposes, I suggest you check:

- the interface and navigation (in our trial if you clicked on another title while listening to a post, this would stop the recording you were listening to);
- if you need to move more easily from one voice posting to another;
- if you need to open it to full screen (not available to us);
- the editing of voice postings (not available in our trial);
- the ability to download a voice message (not available in our trial);
- the ability to attach voice or other attachments (not available in our trial);
- the ability to subscribe to receive a notification of a new posting (not available in our trial);
- the ability to identify which voice posts you had listened to and which not, and those that were new (not available in our trial).

Summary of advantages

A summary of the advantages of asynchronous voice boards is provided in Table 3.3.

Table 3.3 Advantages of asynchronous voice boards

Findings	Key points
Adds a welcome human voice	Reduces isolation, remoteness
	Creates feelings of realness and personalization
	Draws people closer, builds relationship
	Brings distance learning programmes to life
	Enables a feeling of being in a seminar environment similar to face-to-face
Advantages of voice- over text-based communication	Expresses emotions, tones and intonations better than in text
	Clarifies messages to avoid misinterpretation
	Captures participants' attitudes and topical stands
	Stimulates and invites to read and participate more
	Encourages to articulate points
Assessment through interactive tasks	Enables feedback from tutors and peers
	Generates additional discussions around the tasks
	Encourages to study readings recommended by peers
	Motivates to study more and perform better (to avoid 'sounding stupid')

Summary of limitations

A summary of limitations with the voice boards for learning (in our trial in 2010) is provided in Table 3.4.

Table 3.4 Disadvantages of asynchronous voice boards

Findings	Key points
Lack of functionalities	Difficulty in navigation
	Unable to edit and delete posts
	Unable to add attachments
	Unable to subscribe
	Unable to identify new and old posts
Technical and access problems	Students in certain countries may experience long delays that cause sluggishness of the programme due to the internet connection, wireless and firewall.
Learning preference	Students who prefer learning through writing might not find using voice easy and intuitive.

A successful blending story

Professor John Fothergill, Head of the Department of Engineering at the University of Leicester, UK, tells us about his use of newer technologies, within a traditional university setting. He also offers us clear examples of blending: different technologies, students based on campus but working mainly online, and the pathway from discussion boards to assessment.

Learning in traditional university engineering departments, at least in the UK, is probably not as you would imagine. The students do not necessarily become experts with soldering irons and milling machines! Whilst they certainly should experience practical work through laboratories, engineering design sessions and project work, they still spend a lot of time in lecture courses 'learning things'. I could argue that there is too much emphasis on knowledge delivery rather than discovery. (Physical scientists and engineers tend to discover knowledge rather than construct it in the Social Science sense – although there are lots of arguments to be had on this about mathematicians!) Whilst there are initiatives to counter this, which generally involve putting into practice what is learnt, I felt that even in a more theoretical module, it must be possible for students to discover the context of their studies. This would give what I was teaching a conceptual frame-work, one in which they understood how the development of important practical systems (in my case the infrastructure of internet transmissions) relied on knowledge and understanding of fundamental concepts, in my case the materials science underpinning the components of optical fibre transmission systems.

Coincidentally, I was also no longer able to give my module in a traditional lecture theatre setting, together with its inevitable final unseen written examination, as I acquired the incessant duties, along with the respons-ibilities, of Pro-Vice-Chancellor for the University, with overall responsibility for Learning and Teaching. Making an opportunity to lead developments in e-learning out of the threat of not having the time to teach in a conventional setting, I felt that online techniques could also be a successful way to break away from the conventional relentless pushing out of knowledge. It would enable engineers to develop their online group skills, which surely must count as an important, if somewhat overlooked, engineering competency (aka transferable skill).

It might seem surprising then, that in considering how to organize my module, I decided to present the main material that I felt it necessary for the students to know in mini online lectures, which have been referred to as e-lectures (Edirisingha and Fothergill, 2009). However, I felt that engineering students would naturally relate to this format, rather than, for example, giving them a large amount of reading material to study. These e-lectures were not video recordings of lectures but PowerPoint presentations with narrative and some interactivity converted into a low bandwidth format using products such as Impatica and Adobe Presenter. The lectures can be watched whenever students want as many times as they like. They can be stopped, paused and rewound and they have a rolling transcript, which was particularly popular. The 'talking head' was felt by the students to be the least important part of the presentation; an interesting comment as many recorded lectures are only talking heads.

A set of these e-lectures, together with video clips, website links, animations, background reading, a list of desired learning outcomes and formative quizzes, were compiled into *learning units*, the building blocks of sections of the course. In this context, a learning unit may be considered as the 'smallest self-contained learning lesson, providing at least one learning outcome' (Han, 2006). The learning units were organized into the four sections of the module and each section was concluded with a summative assignment – usually an online computer-marked test taken under examination conditions in a computer suite.

In the first couple of years of presentation of this course, whilst the students did well, there was little interaction with me. The general discussion board was fairly busy, partly to resolve some technical problems and to point out 'deliberate' mistakes, and partly to ask me to explain certain aspects more clearly. Despite these limitations, the students commented to an external reviewer of the course that they found learning online to be 'very flexible, you can learn how you want to learn' and perhaps surprisingly both the students and I remarked that we had better access to each other than when we met regularly on campus (Barker, 2010).

Through access to the discussion board, the students commented that it 'does seem like you get slightly more interaction with him'. For the first two years, I archived the discussion board anonymously and used this as a basis for a frequently asked questions section. Perhaps this wasn't a good idea, as it gave the students less reason to interact with me and I felt that the course became 'a bit dead'. This may have been more apparent to me, as the tutor, than to the students, since I had seen its presentation several times whereas they were coming to it fresh. However, I did feel that it could be improved by allowing the students to interact with other humans (other members of their cohort, me and sometimes other e-moderators) as well as a machine.

Running alongside the course, I therefore introduced weekly podcasts and a series of four e-tivities in 2006. Perhaps I should really call these quasi-e-tivities for they differed substantially in two ways from the model that Gilly Salmon had introduced me to. First, the students mostly already knew each other quite well from campus meetings, so one could argue that the first two steps of the e-tivities were less important. However, this is not totally true: I still found that the students were challenged by having to form consensuses online and indeed were still somewhat shy about introducing themselves. Perhaps they didn't know each other as well as I might have assumed! Second, the students could have worked largely offline (in the coffee shop or wherever); they didn't really *have* to work online. Despite this, for the first three e-tivities they did seem to work mainly online. The fourth and last e-tivity, as I'll go on to discuss, was more substantive both in scope and in credit, and it is not perhaps surprising that, whilst students usually collated their contributions online, they found it easier to physically meet to organize their work. I should also note that this module is quite short: it only counts for about a sixth of their total workload in a given semester. Furthermore, the e-tivites are not a major part of the module, having said that, when re-writing this module I will change the balance away from e-lectures towards a more Web 2.0 – interactive – style.

The first e-tivity effectively amalgamated the first two steps that Gilly suggests – so this was about 'access, motivation, and socialization'. I felt it was important to explain what these e-tivities are about – and why students should join in. This first e-tivity was not dependent upon understanding the course – it was about ice-breaking. The students were split into groups (about five students each) for the e-tivities. Interestingly, because I was teaching the course online, I was able to accommodate two cohorts of students studying different degrees at different levels by giving them slightly different pathways and assessments through the course. Although there could have been some beneficial reciprocal scaffolding in combining members from each cohort in a group, I felt that this would have been detrimental for the more advanced students and perhaps more difficult to assess fairly (Holton and Clark, 2006). This first e-tivity started soon after the course began and the cohort settled down. As an e-moderator, during the first couple of weeks of the course, I've found it necessary to encourage everyone to join in. Some are keen to do so and seem well organized, others find it difficult to get round to logging in. Through the VLE, I keep an eye on metrics such as the number of times students are logging into the site, and, where necessary, contact individuals by e-mail to encourage them to get started. On the group discussion boards, I try to give encouragement and guidance in this first e-tivity as to how they are progressing, and how to reach a group decision – such as a name for their group.

The second e-tivity that followed was more to do with information exchange (Stage 3). I asked the groups to find the longest continuous optical fibre communication link using information from the internet. I was able to follow this up with a supplementary question towards the end of the e-tivity, asking them what limited the length. This is not difficult, although it did point up how poor the online searching skills of many students are. Giving the students feedback, through voice (see about my podcasts later), I was able to engender some competition to find the longest fibre. (It's currently over 7000 km by the way!) The third e-tivity at first sight was similar: I asked them what limited the speed (bit-rate) of information down a fibre. Actually, this is much more subtle and it meant that not only did they have to discover new information on the internet, they also had to construct an understanding of the contribution of the various factors that might limit the speed. My role during these e-tivities was somewhat different to that in e-tivity 1. The members of the groups were not really inhibited about contributing – although encouragement to reach a group decision was still required to a lesser extent. My role now was to be more critical – in a constructive way – of the information they discovered and their interpretation of it.

The final e-tivity formed a mini-project. This year, I asked them to write an e-lecture for next year's course on an aspect of the subject that was currently only covered in a passing way. This formed the summative assessment for the final section of the course. Apart from setting the subject for this mini-project/e-tivity, I had very little interaction with the groups; my main role here was assessing the final outcome.

As well as the e-tivities giving more collaboration and interaction between the student and the tutor and, indeed, the other students, podcasts were introduced. I had no model for these, but what has evolved is a model in which podcasts complement the e-lectures (and, to some extent, the e-tivities). The e-lectures are relatively difficult to prepare and update and indeed I have only done this where the subject has evolved and left them inaccurate. I felt that the podcasts ('Profcasts' as Gilly named them) needed to provide context and feel to be *of the moment*. I was not too worried about the quality, if they were a bit rough around the edges, they would sound more spontaneous! I might start a podcast commenting on the weather, or the current performance of the local football team, to demonstrate that the podcast was fresh – perhaps making the students realize that I'd recorded it especially for them. I would then spend a few minutes talking about something contemporary. Often this was a development in internet technology, perhaps a news item. A sub-sea breakage in an optical fibre internet cable, which cut off much of India for a couple of weeks, was a great opportunity for students to realize the importance of the technology. Interestingly, it also enables them to talk to their (non-engineering) friends about what is otherwise a rather abstract subject. I then gave them some feedback on their performance or/and made suggestions about what they should be doing in the coming week, through the podcast. I linked the podcasts and the e-tivities at this point. It was useful to be able to give hints on the e-tivities – partly to give more reason for the students to listen to the podcasts, but also to stop them following dead ends in their investigations. I could also fuel that competition that I mentioned between groups, saying, for example, that Group 4 had found an optical link that was twice as long as that discovered by Group 2. To end the Profcast, I'd usually inject some humour. A rap for this purpose made me famous, causing my appearance in the *Times Higher Education* newspaper and on local television. I rather hoped that the students might also listen to the end (rather like the 'and finally' items at the end of news broadcasts!) if there was something enjoyable to look forward to. The podcasts were therefore informal, some would say unnecessary, but they gave life to a course and motivation to the students.

If we think of the five-stage model as 'scaffolding' and as support for learning as ideas are introduced, then almost all aspects of the course may be included. Engineering academics may often consider the 'push' technology of lectures without the 'pull' components of self-motivated learning. In the types of scaffolding that I have introduced, it is interesting to consider how e-tivities and podcasts may fit into this spectrum from push to pull.

PUSH (conventional teaching) – hard scaffolding	e-lectures video clips and animations
Interactive – mainly reciprocal scaffolding	e-tivities and discussion boards
Soft scaffolding	podcasts
PULL – self-motivated learning	website links and background reading formative quizzes lists of desired learning outcomes

The response from the students has been very positive. The continuous involvement of the students motivates them to study and keep up with their peers. The overall marks have increased by more than 10 per cent with virtually no one failing. The many positive comments that I've received have included, 'Glad I did the course', 'Great course – new style yet effective', 'Final report really did test understanding', but perhaps my favourite was simply, 'It actually works!'

With the success of the e-tivities in promoting a deeper understanding of the course, and the podcasts interacting with the e-tivities to provide feedback and motivation, I feel that it would be beneficial to give these a greater involvement when developing future courses of this kind.

Do you get the idea?

Acknowledgements

Thanks to Drs Alejandro Armellini and Palitha Edirisingha from Beyond Distance at Leicester, UK, for the developments in Table 3.1.

Many thanks to Dr Alejandro Armellini for his contribution to Table 3.2.

Thanks to Gabi Witthaus, Ming Nie and Jeff Stanford of the DUCKLING project (www.le.ac.uk/duckling) at the University of Leicester, UK, for their contributions to the section 'Asynchronous voice boards', pp. 87–97.

Chapter 4

E-moderating qualities and roles

This chapter considers the knowledge and skills that the best e-moderators probably have, and uses examples to explore and illustrate their roles. I say 'probably' because what makes for good teaching has been the subject of many debates over the centuries, and now fresh consideration continues in relation to online teaching. In the second decade of the twenty-first century, more students articulate their needs for online learning than ever before, as Berge's study found, 'students expect to see expertise from their instructors and the competency to teach online' (2007: 4), and indeed, evaluation of learning is increasingly judged on the 'learners' experience'.

My intention in this chapter is to explore the qualities of e-moderation and to place the e-moderating roles firmly and significantly within the online learning environment. This chapter includes recruiting e-moderators and key aspects of their roles.

You will find throughout this chapter, indeed throughout this, the third edition of the e-moderating story, hundreds of ideas and suggestions. I think the 80:20 rule applies! The 80:20 principle suggests that there may be an inherent imbalance between cause and effect, effort and reward and inputs and outputs. Of course the 80:20 principle is a very simple approximation of the value of work and effort but something that in straightened times we should at least consider! Do you know which 20 per cent of your online work has the most impact on your students' learning (Salmon, 2006)? My suggestion – try to find out. In the meanwhile, train your e-moderators and change the balance!

E-moderator competencies

In Table 4.1 I have shown the qualities and characteristics of successful e-moderators – the competencies they should acquire through training and experience.

Recruiting e-moderators

The e-moderators you recruit should of course be credible as members of the learning community.

I am going to assume that you will be looking for e-moderators who are able to understand their roles and willing to be trained online. They will need reasonably good keyboard skills, and some experience of using networked computers. However, given those requirements, you will find that good e-moderators come from many different backgrounds, with very varied learning and teaching experiences. If they do not need to meet face-to-face with their course participants, you can select them on the basis of their suitability rather than their geographic location.

I suggest that you try to recruit e-moderators with the qualities from columns 1–2 of Table 4.1. If there are few people available with these abilities, I suggest you focus on selecting applicants who show empathy and flexibility in working online, plus willingness to be trained as e-moderators. Before asking them to work online, I train them in the competencies described in columns 3–4 in Table 4.1. I would expect e-moderators to be developing the skills in columns 5–6 by the time they had been working online with their participants for about one year.

Proponents of emotional intelligence promote controversial ideas, but they do suggest that a great deal more is going on in learning processes than what is covered by cognitive capabilities. Emotional intelligence includes aspects such as motivation and intuitiveness (which act as goal drivers) together with resilience and conscientiousness (which curb excesses in the drivers). Especially important for e-moderating are self-awareness, interpersonal sensitivity and the ability to influence. There is evidence that people who display higher levels of emotional competence have greater success in relations with others (on and offline) and superior performance. In particular, emotional intelligence is related to leadership competencies, so we always look for some evidence of emotional intelligence when we recruit e-moderators (Dulewicz and Higgs, 2002).

E-moderators do not need to be subject experts as such, but instead have the ability to 'recognize communication styles and learning patterns from other cultures' (Simons, 2002: 126). Knight's summary of the move towards online facilitation is instructive: 'It is ironic that what some take to be dehumanising technology may actually need teachers to be more empathetic and considerate' (Knight, 2002: 122). At the recruitment stage you need to look for people with at least some sympathy with this view!

Choosing e-moderators

You may like to consider the mode of recruiting for e-moderators, if you are able to choose them from scratch or are lucky enough to be able to make choices. Emily, the Human Resources Manager from All Things in Moderation Ltd, a company that offers e-moderating training, writes:

As the main bulk of work for an e-moderator is carried out online, then it seems illogical to test a candidate's suitability in a traditional face-to-face interview. Online interviews can minimize the discrimination sometimes associated with selecting face-to-face. The cost of travelling to a specific place is saved for both the candidate and the interviewer. The candidate can choose the best time to reply to the questions, reducing their stress levels and therefore providing better answers for the recruiter to assess.

Whatever mode of recruitment is chosen, it is important that a good job description and person specification are sent to the candidate in advance.

I think it is best to undertake online recruiting for e-moderators wherever possible, as it demonstrates straight away if the candidates are confident with the technology and online written communication. Selecting through internet-based means allows us to recruit e-moderators throughout the world. We have found that online interviews identify:

- *Written communication styles* (for example, you can identify their confidence, effectiveness, patience and enthusiasm, which can be different to their verbal communication).
- *Time management skills* (how will the candidates combine e-moderating duties with their other work/home commitments? Did they provide the answers by the deadline?).
- *Understanding and answering questions concisely* (do they save time, are they likely to give students a chance? Can they control, engage in and pace a discussion?).
- *The candidates' comfort in using e-mails and the internet* (essential for running an online course or practical exercises).
- *Their flexibility* (are they willing to adapt to a new interview context and working environment?).

Table 4.1 E-moderator competencies

Quality/ characteristic	Recruit		Train		Develop	
	1. Confident	2. Constructive	3. Developmental	4. Facilitating	5. Knowledge sharing	6. Creative
A Understanding of online process	Personal experience as an online learner, flexibility in approaches to teaching and learning. Empathy with the challenges of becoming an online learner	Able to build online trust and purpose for others. Understand the potential of online learning and groups	Ability to develop and enable others, act as catalyst, foster discussion, summarize, restate, challenge, monitor understanding and misunderstanding, take feedback	Know when to control groups, when to let go, how to bring in non-participants, know how to pace discussion and use time online, understand the five-stage scaffolding process and how to use it	Able to explore ideas, develop arguments, promote valuable threads, close off unproductive threads, choose when to archive	Able to use a range of approaches from structured activities (e-tivities) to freewheeling discussions, and to evaluate and judge success of these
B Technical skills	Operational understanding of software in use, reasonable keyboard skills, able to read fairly comfortably on screen, good, regular, mobile access to the internet	Able to appreciate the basic structures of online conferencing, and the web and internet's potential for learning	Know how to use special features of software for e-moderators, e.g. controlling, weaving, archiving. Know how to 'scale up' without consuming inordinate amounts of personal time, by using the software productively	Able to use special features of software to explore learner's use, e.g. message history, summarizing, archiving	Able to create links between other features of learning programmes, introduce online resources without diverting participants from interaction	Able to use software facilities to create and manipulate conferences and e-tivities and to generate an online learning environment; able to use alternative software and platforms

C Online communication skills	Courteous and respectful in online (written) communication, able to pace and use time appropriately	Able to write concise, energizing, personable online messages. Able to create 'presence' and 'visibility' in virtual environments	Able to engage with people online (not the machine or the software), respond to messages appropriately, be appropriately 'visible' online, elicit and manage students' expectations	Able to interact through e-mail and conferencing, and achieve interaction between others, be a role model. Able to gradually increase the number of participants dealt with successfully online, without huge amounts of extra personal time	Able to value diversity with cultural sensitivity; explore differences and meanings	Able to communicate comfortably without visual cues, able to diagnose and solve problems and opportunities online, use humour online, use and work with emotion online, handle conflict constructively
D Content expertise	Knowledge and experience to share, willingness to add own contributions	Able to encourage sound contributions from others, know of useful online resources for their topic	Able to trigger debates by posing intriguing questions. Know when to intervene, when to hold back	Carry authority by awarding marks fairly to students for their participation, contributions and learning outcomes	Know about valuable resources (e.g. on the web) and use them as sparks in e-tivities	Able to enliven conferences through use of multi-media and electronic resources, able to give creative feedback and build on participants' ideas
E Personal characteristics	Determination and motivation to become an e-moderator	Able to establish an online identity as e-moderator	Able to adapt to new teaching contexts, methods, audiences and roles	Show sensitivity to online relationships and communication	Show a positive attitude, commitment and enthusiasm for online learning	Know how to create *and sustain* a useful, relevant online learning community

The issues I have found important are:

a) How many questions do you want to ask and how much information do you want to receive (interviewee and interviewer workload!)?

b) Should they reply on e-mail or as an attachment? (If an attachment, then this shows they are able to use a word processor – is this important?)

c) How long should they have to answer (same day, three days, one week)? This should relate to the requirements of the job – how often will they need to log on?

d) Will they be e-moderating on a course that is entirely online or will there be some face-to-face or verbal contact with students? (If the teaching/training is blended, then it may be necessary to include a traditional face-to-face interview or phone call.)

e) If other interactive technologies are likely to be deployed such as virtual worlds, it's a good idea to meet avatar–avatar.

f) If podcasting is to be deployed, then suggest that they send you a short MP3 voice file describing some aspect of the topic or their proposed role.

Of course, it's possible that someone other than the candidate could answer the questions! However, if you ensure that the online interviews are part of a larger recruitment and selection process, this is unlikely. A well-designed (online) induction and training should follow successful selection for the job. For ongoing development, mentoring online is effective. Emily

Many e-moderator recruits come from face-to-face teaching where they may have relied quite heavily on personal charisma to stimulate and hold their students' interest. Others still see online as about delivering materials to students. It is a big change to make! Even those recruits who are used to developing distance learning materials need to explore how online conferencing can underpin and extend their teaching. If they are used to being considered an 'expert' in their subject, they may find the levelling effect and informality of conferencing very challenging to start with. It may be best to encourage such staff to undertake 'question and answer' or information exchange conferences until they become more comfortable with the characteristics of online discussion groups.

Stepping down from the 'spotlight' and into the e-world can be hard. However, lecturers and trainers used to being successful leaders in classroom situations have the basic skills and knowledge to become e-moderators, including introducing topics, engaging participants, and running plenary and feedback discussions.

Similarly, students used to the paradigm of teacher as the instructor may expect a great deal of input from the e-moderator. This can be very time-consuming and unsatisfactory for both. The e-moderator must explain his or her role at the start, to reduce the chances of unreasonable expectations arising, and gradually move to facilitation and enabling of learning.

Key issues for e-moderators

A number of issues come up time and time again for e-moderating. Understanding them may make the difference between a happy and successful e-moderating experience and a miserable one. These issues include the appropriate numbers of participants that make up a successful e-tivity or discussion forum, the use of time online, coming to grips with the asynchronicity and complexity of conference messaging and the development of professional online communities. What follows is a brief exploration of these, which I hope will help those of you soon to encounter these in the real online situation.

Group size

What is the right number of participants in an online discussion for it to be successful (for all)? Is there a critical mass, in the physical sciences sense, so that with too few participants success eludes even the best e-moderator? The right number for any conference depends fundamentally on its purpose. Six participants and an e-moderator, for example, may lead to all contributing and a collaborative outcome for an online activity. Or one thousand participants could pose questions to an online expert, and all read the answers. They might then join in smaller groups – perhaps of 20 each – to put their own views.

As you know, starting off with good welcoming messages helps very much. After that, part of the e-moderator's role is to try to orchestrate appropriate participation for the purpose. It is always necessary to keep track of what is happening to ensure participants do not disappear for avoidable reasons! Most conferencing software systems offer features such as 'message history' to help you track numbers and participation. Good e-moderating always includes weaving, summarizing and feedback. These are difficult to do with more than 20 active participants.

I have found that one of the best ways of building up the right numbers for a conference is to work with the energy that naturally builds up online (for whatever reason). You can certainly expect spurts of increased online activity to be associated with offline purposes, such as assessed assignments, the start of a new section on a course, periods just before face-to-face meetings or the run up to the exam. There may also be unexpected reasons for increased online activity (e.g., a relevant news event or even a problem such as delayed arrival of course materials) and e-moderators can turn this to their advantage. When a conference or online activity starts to wane, it is best to close it and start something fresh.

Asynchronicity

The nature of asynchronicity makes it harder for e-moderators to create positive group experiences and excitement, rhythm, engagement and focus, compared with face-to-face groups. It is not impossible, though! E-moderators need to acquire the key ability to create clear goals and appropriate challenges, through a vision of the learning outcomes and very short focused steps, good timely feedback and appropriate motivation (Salmon, 2002a).

Experienced e-moderator and trainer of e-moderators David Shepherd wrote to me:

When training e-moderators to create online activities (which we call e-tivities), we have noticed that they have a tendency to ask a whole series of complex questions in one message. Such a strategy may work well in face-to-face situations, where the facilitator can pick up on any response and manage the discussion by moving on to the questions in turn. But online, all participants could (in theory at least) respond to all questions, asynchronously, in any order.

Four questions, for example, will present participants with the decision on whether to respond with one message for all four questions or to provide four separate messages over time – one for each question. In a group of many participants some will decide on one of these strategies and others on another – resulting in a complex mix of messages for the e-moderator to cope with. Summarizing and responding become a real challenge, and many of the participants will lose track of the discussions and 'flow'.

By setting out four e-tivities from the onset (one for each question or task), the e-moderator anticipates the difficulty, provides the participants with clear guidance on where to post each message, and how to respond to others. The participant is given a clear process to follow and the e-moderator can see that it will take some time for the participant to work through the four tasks. Weaving and summarizing are easier to achieve effectively. Result? Happier participants who respond, and are more motivated to contribute. David

In order to learn from online conferences, participants need to be able to select, organize, elaborate and explore new knowledge and understanding in relationship to existing knowledge. Much of this can be supported not only by appropriate interactive and supportive design of conferences (Salmon, 2002a) but also by appropriate interventions by the e-moderator, including excellent threading, weaving and summarizing and the removal of irrelevant messages (Schwan, Straub and Hesse, 2002). One strategy is to reduce the number of messages; another is to ensure very good reply structures.

Here are some examples from the All Things in Moderation e-convenors:

Ah! So it's that old enemy 'time' again?

Annie writes: I think the concept of time changes in online courses, and we don't realize how long and how much time we need to set aside . . . 'how much time does a student have to invest in a task for us to consider that it is "enough" time?'

Bob writes: I am a very social person and when I started doing my online studies, I was surprised to discover how quickly and deeply one builds up relationships with people online, especially once you start discovering common interests. And it takes up time.

The e-convenor weaves:

Do you find that time does indeed become different online – somehow expanding your commitment such that you habitually spend more time than anticipated (I own up to being guilty)? If so, is this partly perhaps a by-product of what Bob describes – the feeling of being part of a community (if the group has successfully bonded) such that you feel somehow impelled to keep returning – perhaps beyond 'enough' time for the task in hand? If we're on to something here, what might the implications be? (Is Carla's earlier remark that 'students appreciate that the e-tivities start and finish at fixed times' in effect rather wishful thinking?) So what do you think about the real as opposed to the notional demands of time online?

Ken

VLEs and learning diaries! A thought for the day.

Anita writes: As a trainer I don't believe that a virtual environment can completely take the place of face-to-face contact but for many aspects of learning it is an ideal forum for debate and a sharing of information and opinions.

Brian writes: I think a blend of face-to-face and online is the right way to go.

Christa writes: Students often 'demand' online environments use for distributing notes & PowerPoint presentations, perhaps sometimes to the detriment of teaching. Few of my colleagues go beyond document distribution: some use the announcements section to email the class directly, but it's part of my job to broaden the use of online where it can be fruitful for both staff & students.

Derek writes: I haven't really strayed past document distribution and group email. I mentioned in my Arrival's message that I tutor a Maths module via blended learning, last semester being my first. The students told me they found Maths a subject less suitable to this type of learning. I want to improve my skills and hopefully develop ways to help the students better.

The e-convenor's weave:

So . . . everyone, quite a few thoughts there, based on some mixed experience of VLEs as learning tools. A sense that there are real possible advantages, coupled with perhaps potential disadvantages. Obvious advantages for distributing material, but a lurking sense that there is unrealised potential, if only we could unlock it.

Since all the texts are available for any participant (or researcher) to view online, the sequencing of messages, when viewed after a discussion is completed, looks rather more ordered than during the build-up. Yet trying to understand them afterwards is rather like following the moves of a chess or bridge game, after it is over. When participants start using online group conferencing, this apparent confusion causes a wide range of responses. It can elicit quite uncomfortable, confused reactions from participants and severe anxiety in a few. Although many people are now familiar with e-mail, they are not used to the complexity of many-to-many conferencing online, with its huge range of potential posting times and variety of response and counter-response. E-moderators can help, as one noted in his reflections:

This is a very difficult but rewarding area. More effort is needed to keep even paced and also even-tempered at times. A conversation can be spread over several days without all the intervening gestures and interruptions of real conversation. This can lead to great misunderstanding. Thus to be reflective and not 'dash' off replies is important. To seek an even written style would hopefully bring some peace to bear, but the delay in reply which may be the result sometimes, of other commitments, can be annoying for colleagues. A welcoming and encouraging tone is vital, as being on the end of a computer can be very lonely.

An e-moderator can ensure that all participants are familiar with the best the software has to offer and help them to be comfortable in the online environment to start with. A key e-moderating role is to build a clear structure by breaking responses, if they get too busy, into sub-topics or sub-groups, and by regularly archiving, weaving and summaries.

PB

Time

Nearly every participant, new or experienced, teacher or learner, worries about how much time it takes to be online. You will find the concept of time is emotive and value-laden for both e-moderators and participants (Salmon, 2002a). The key issue is that the advantages of 'any time/any place' learning and teaching mean that time is not bounded and contained as it is when attending an online synchronous seminar or a real classroom session. Although a face-to-face tutorial may last two hours, it has a clear start and finish time and is rarely interrupted by anything else. The participants are either there or they are not, and if they are, they cannot be doing much besides. Online is not like that. It has a reputation for 'eating time'. Genuine fears and concerns do exist, and must be addressed.

'Finding the time' is a continuous theme. Many participants report 'lack of time' as a key reason for non-participation either in a timely fashion or at all. However, something more fundamental is probably happening (Tsui, 2002). 'Time' is a social construct, and not something that can be 'managed' by someone else. We are so used to living our lives in cycles, but working online disrupts our carefully constructed if tentative feeling of control of our lives. This is not a plea for clocks on the home page of the VLE! It is worth structuring your course to provide participants with rhythm, enticement, flow and pace to their online study. The technology should also offer quick and easy ways for e-moderators of completing weaving, summaries, archiving and effective presentation of plenary results. Most VLEs don't do this as well as we would like at present.

Asynchronous internet time is quite different from the cycles and seasons that we are used to in our every day life. Time and place normally provide an 'embedding and situating space for human activity. Human orientation, human interaction and human cognition are all processes deeply and extricably tied in with the time and context in which they take place . . . An understanding comfortable enough to enhance a person's inclination to act and interact' (Sorensen, 2002: 193). Therefore, interacting with others online and without being in the same place and at the same time requires a change in perspective. Working online involves shifting time about and changing patterns of how you work with colleagues and participants. Ways of e-moderating need rethinking, almost a reinvention, to accommodate remote asynchronous internet time.

> There is no denying how useful clock time can be, but it is clear that it is entangled in our everyday lives . . . with the time of consciousness and memory.
>
> (Lippincott, Eco, Gombrich, et al., 2000: 11–12)

My research on the original OU online courses revealed that the participants' experience of online time is one of the most important factors in determining their rate of participation and completion of internet-based courses. Both learners and e-moderators have difficulty in grasping hold of internet time. Strong feelings can be evoked, and confusion can occur. Without an understanding of internet time, important aspects of personal pacing are quickly lost in asynchronous courses, together with motivation, satisfaction and self-determination. The design and support needed to create feelings of tying time into collaborative activity and of being in a 'shared space' are two of the most important e-moderating tasks. Participants put it this way:

I need to become capable of thinking 'cyber-clock-wise' – I don't know how to explain this, but learning traditionally is a different kind of mental process, not only as far as your role and motivation are concerned, but as far as 'mental data management' is concerned: realizing you are in an asynchronous environment, your classroom is somewhere out there, people are spread all over the planet, and things are happening simultaneously you're involved in multiple actions . . . It's not something Mr Stone Age Man was born with, but it's fun after you've done a bit of evolution. ;-) FF

Once upon a time . . . before I was an e-moderator . . . my alarm clock had only one setting . . . now it has many! RA

Time takes on a new dimension online. Working asynchronously involves a radical rethink – not only of learning or teaching time but also of other aspects of life. Most people find this very difficult indeed to start with. Failing to get to grips with internet time can result in the feeling of falling into a 'deep well' (and certainly failure to complete the course, discussion or programme). By providing a clear indication of an expectation of active contribution and by pacing and structuring the online activity, we can help participants to make the adjustments to their lives and dramatically increase completion rates in e-learning.

The first few weeks of being online is a critical period for group forming and confidence building. One e-moderator said:

> Currently I'm e-moderating an online course with 15 participants so I go in twice a day. Once around midday and then again after 8 pm. I know when I need to join in – after around 20 posts (not before!). In other words I based my approach on the participants' postings, not on the clock time. This strategy wouldn't work for everyone but I like to monitor the activity closely in the first three weeks for indicators of technical/social/and psychological well-being. BB

In my experience, online courses, even those that are well structured, tend to result in more time than usual being spent thinking about time itself, and the choices there are to make. Some participants try to control their time from the start, as the first participant below demonstrates:

> Will it take me longer to do more but lightly, or do less but more depth? I've spent 15 minutes thinking about this! AH

> I did not pace myself terribly well, wanted to go everywhere and read everything (can't bear to miss out) and found that rest of my life was in fair disarray by week 4! HS

Participants simply will not all log in on the day and time that the course plan intends! A few will come a little early and may race ahead. Some will come late. At least a week is needed for everyone to be ready for the more productive work.

Participants in online learning are involved in a variety of communities of learning and practice at the same time, and have a myriad of other responsibilities. Some of these may be similar in values, beliefs and norms of behaviour to those of the course groups and some may not. You need to build enticement, inclusiveness and pacing to make your experience stand out.

You may decide to offer a regular time beat, by providing a framework that starts and finishes at predictable times, and actions that occur regularly, such as the e-moderator's summaries. In addition, you can promote interest and motivation through underlying rhythm. Engaging in authentic tasks and working with others can provide this idea of rhythm. 'Overfilling' an e-tivity with many online resources is the enemy of active engagement online. Such pacing needs to appear in the e-tivities because participants will not meet often 'by chance' online to coordinate them for themselves.

Train everyone involved in Netspeak! For example, long messages take time to read and respond to (but may be more worthwhile than short ones). Summarizing, archiving and weaving are the key skills for the e-moderator. They save participants time, and enable participation in new ways. Furthermore, the more successful an e-moderator is, the more likely he or she will be overwhelmed by success in terms of many student messages – our own little Catch-22!

It is important to specify what you expect e-moderators and participants to do and by when, and not to leave this open ended. It is of course also important to design for the numbers involved in a conference, and be realistic about how much an e-moderator can do. Online novice learners and e-moderators will need much longer to do everything than experienced participants. Ensure that you use the most trained – and probably the most expensive – people (e.g. academics, faculty, experienced e-moderators) to do what they do best. Use less trained and experienced people, perhaps cheaper, for other tasks (e.g. use alumni as social hosts or to run helplines shared with other departments or schools). When choosing media and activities, make sure the time online is used for what it's good for rather than to force-fit activities online. At the same time, reduce offline activities for participants by as much as you are providing online activities for them, so that looking after both sets does not overwhelm e-moderators. Be explicit about who is going to do what online, how much time you expect them to devote to it and what their payment rate will be. Ask them to do one or two important online activities in a time-bounded way, with deadlines, until they gain experience. Develop and share a process of working together in e-moderating teams and in providing cover and breaks from online commitments. Develop, and publish for all to see, your 'online office hours' and tell participants how much time e-moderators are being paid for so that there's a reasonable level of expectation about the frequency of online visits.

Networking

Online, as you know, there are three kinds of key players – the participants (students, learners, trainees), the academics (perhaps represented by resource material) and the e-moderators. Researchers, theorists and other experts or practitioners can be brought in occasionally, too. It is exciting for participants to have access to expert views, though they may 'go quiet' and let the expert dominate, therefore it is best to keep such sessions down to a week or two. Craft knowledge can be passed on through anecdotes and stories without one individual 'holding the floor'. Some younger or less experienced participants may need to be explicitly drawn in and valued.

By learning through well e-moderated conferencing, each participant can construct his or her understanding according to previous experience and may make this explicit and available for others through the conference messages. The new information can be 'encoded' and learnt by other individuals through linking it to their previous knowledge. The emphasis that constructivism places on creating challenging learning environments means that continued efforts are needed to go into training e-moderators and inducting students and to ensure that they understand the importance of online knowledge construction.

With our present understanding of how to develop and disseminate knowledge online, e-moderators need credibility in the field of study. When professional knowledge is shared in face-to-face meetings, it has been easy to recognize others as 'one of us'. The e-moderator should therefore establish his or her credentials as a like-minded and experienced professional – and probably needs to work a little harder at this online than in a face-to-face group. E-moderators need to develop good working relationships with librarians – who have now transformed themselves into ICT resource providers.

E-moderating with synchronous technologies

The most basic kind of synchronous networking is the text-based chat session that anyone can join. Google has a text chat within its suite, MSN Messenging and Skype are popular examples. The software shows each participant who else is online at that time, and messages can be addressed to one, some or all of those 'present'. These messages appear almost instantaneously on the screens of all participants, inviting immediate responses. Sound and vision can also be added offering a learning environment more like that of a telephone conference call, or a videoconferencing session. The newest web-based virtual worlds also work in real-time so are also synchronous. Recent years have bought a range of web-based virtual classrooms such as Wimba, Adobe and Elluminate, and offered us an excellent low-cost way of presentation and discussion synchronously through text and voice whilst viewing slides or other resources.

These technologies allow for real-time communication: participants are online together at the same time and speaking or writing to one another immediately. Synchronous events for learning need planning and an e-moderator is essential to avert chaos and guide participants towards desired outcomes. They can add a sense of presence and immediacy that is attractive to participants, some of whom find they can engage and get to know others. Many find that being online together is fun, so long as the experience is short, say an hour maximum.

The role of the e-moderator in online synchronous discussion reflects some of the qualities of the asynchronous e-moderator, especially to focus the conference at the beginning, keep it roughly on track and summarize it. Achieving full participation through ensuring everyone 'takes a turn' is also an important e-moderating role. Virtual classroom software offers special rights to the e-moderator, who can use the technology to control turn taking.

If you are involved in this kind of e-moderating, the usual 'rules' apply. You need to be familiar and comfortable with the applications and aware of their strengths and weaknesses as learning tools. Participants soon spot a teacher who is unfamiliar with the equipment. As always, good preparation for the event is essential. You need to allow time to get ready for the online session and for follow up. Critical success factors are good clear structure to the session, the quality of the visual materials, the clarity of the objectives and roles of the participants and ensuring everyone participates. Some virtual classrooms offer easy links out to websites and various interactive tools, which, if appropriately structured, can be very successful. If your participants can see you, you may need to brush up on your presentation skills! You should also plan to follow up the synchronous online event with a record or action plan, perhaps using e-mail, asynchronous conferencing or post.

The use of synchronous conferencing through the internet offers participants the feeling of immediate contact, motivation and some fun, which is especially valuable if they are studying largely alone and at a distance, or where there's a need for them to experience a wide range of learning opportunities.

Terese Bird of the Beyond Distance Research Alliance at the University of Leicester tells us of her experience of her team's co-ordination of an eight-day online academic conference called the Learning Futures Festival *Online* 2010:

E-moderating a global academic conference with a synchronous virtual classroom

The Learning Futures Festival Online

From January 7 to 14 in 2010, the Beyond Distance Research Alliance at University of Leicester held their annual academic conference, the fifth in a series. Unlike its predecessors, which lasted one or two days and took place in Leicester or as a combination of online and face-to-face meetings, the 2010 Festival lasted eight days and was held entirely online. The topic was the future for learning and was discussed from a wide variety of perspectives. Three technologies were utilizsed: a 3D virtual world (Second Life), a VLE for asynchronous discussions and resource provision, and a virtual classroom and conferencing facility called Elluminate *Live!*®.

The synchronous schedule took place using the web classroom software Elluminate *Live!* and ran throughout the day and into the evening (GMT). Daily sessions included an opening address, a keynote speaker, three selected 'paper' presenters, and lots of workshops.

There were 231 delegates registered for the online Futures Festival, with an average of 30 taking part in each of the synchronous web sessions. Some sessions exceeded 50 active delegates. Delegates took part from 22 countries and from every continent except Antarctica. Due to extremely heavy snow in Leicester, many snowbound local university people logged in from home. We had a 'control centre' from our 'Media Zoo' research lab in Leicester, and some of our colleagues emerged as outstanding 'anchor' men and women – but there were rarely more than six people physically present together at any one time. Presenters participated from a total of 33 different locations.

Elluminate *Live!* provided an easy-to-use and stable environment for the conference. One or more presenters could speak, be seen, and display presentation slides, websites, or other programmes running on their computers or alternatively could type or draw on the 'whiteboard' – the software's shared space for typing, writing, and drawing. Delegates could watch, listen and contribute synchronous text or their voices for questions and debate. It often became very busy. . .

Elluminate *Live!* deploys a browser with Java, and requires the delegate to run a setup in advance. Delegates needed headphones or speakers to listen and a microphone to speak. We offered practice sessions in advance of the conference, which some delegates took up. In most cases, however, people just asked for and received help at the time they needed it. Only one person was put off by the difficulty in activating Java due to her institution's IT policy.

Each session was assigned an e-moderator who had previously been in contact with the presenter, was familiar with the topic and planned approach and acted as 'master of ceremonies'. The e-moderator welcomed delegates, introduced the speaker, watched the chat box for questions arising from the delegates, noted questions and comments and brought them to the presenter's attention, and led at question times.

E-moderators were issued with a 'Learning Futures Moderator Guide' which outlined the principles of synchronous moderating and practice. They rehearsed and practised on their colleagues in advance!

E-moderators endeavoured to set a friendly, relaxed, yet professional tone to create an inviting environment for discussion and learning. E-moderators found it important to begin sessions on time and spend a few minutes checking that remote delegates could hear and see ('Click the smiley face if you can hear') and that they knew what to expect in the session and what tools they might need. Some moderators made use of the 15 minutes prior to start of session to greet early arriving delegates and invite them to try out the software tools and introduce themselves to each other.

Handling questions

We found that it was best to agree in advance with the presenter to speak for no longer than 15–20 minutes before stopping for questions. This helped the presenter stay in touch with the discussion in the chat box, which otherwise could run off on its own tangent, rather independently. Delegates typed questions into the chat box, or clicked on the 'raise hand' icon which indicated to the moderator that the delegates wished to speak into his/her microphone to ask the question, and would thus be personally invited to speak. Having a second e-moderator was helpful, even essential for groups larger than about 20. The second e-moderator could carefully watch the chat box and note questions or issues to address to the presenter, which is difficult to do when many are quickly commenting.

We found that many presenters defaulted to using Elluminate *Live!* in a teacher-centred way, mainly delivering the material and then taking questions. Some presenters, however, creatively employed well-structured collaborative activities, asking questions and inviting delegates to type responses or draw on the whiteboard, and discussing the results. Because (with the exception of the presenter showing himself or herself on webcam) delegates do not see each other, it is hard to pick up cues as to others' comprehension and reaction. Presenters found they could compensate by using the polling feature, asking multiple-choice or yes–no questions and displaying results for discussion on the whiteboard. Delegates used emoticons (smiley face, confused-face, applause icon) to signal their reactions; savvy presenters encouraged this and responded accordingly.

The technical moderation

As with all web-conferencing software, better bandwidth produces better transmission, so we attempted to have all presenters speak from a computer that was hard-wired rather than wirelessly connected to the internet. Having at least one technical supporter on hand for every session was essential. The technical supporter kept headphones on to monitor transmission of the session and deal with problems if they arose. Broadcasting the presenter's image with a webcam is great for creating a shared feeling of 'being there', but it may strain the transmission, so if sound began to break up, the webcam was either turned off or switched to a lower-resolution setting. All delegates who could take the microphone were encouraged to wear headphones, as ordinary speakers usually created feedback.

Feedback

Delegates' feedback was overwhelmingly positive about the synchronous web conference sessions. One person wrote, 'I found it more interactive than a face-to-face conference. There were more questions from the delegates via Elluminate and comments in the chat.' Another was more wary of the chat box: 'This was my first online conference and by the end of it I was really enjoying it . . . I still have mixed feelings about the chat box. It seemed useful for delegates, but at the same time I saw it distracting some speakers. In these instances I felt it was as "naughty" as whispering during a live conference.'

By using email, Twitter and phone, a handful of delegates reported some difficulties enabling Java or getting sound to work; these were quickly remedied by technical supporters. We found that early distribution of clear instructions prior to registration would have solved even those issues. Next time!

The flexibility of web-based conferences is illustrated by the fact that 83 per cent of survey delegates reported that they participated in the festival by fitting it around other commitments. One person summed up the flexibility and resource-saving aspects of this kind of conferencing by writing, 'This has been a very worthwhile experience and you are all to be commended for setting such an environment up during an age of CO_2 emissions awareness, global warming and intense pressure on staff at universities to work hard, work long and work productively. I do not think I could, in this time of financial constraint, have attended the conference were it a physical one happening on the Leicester Campus – but I got in to your virtual conference with ease and in between my personal workload peaks. So efficient, effective, and very attractive.'

And next. . .

We are now planning a Futures Festival with a partner university in Australia in 2011 – where we can have 24-hour synchronicity!

New topics online

An e-moderator working with the unfamiliar describes her achievement.

Helen Perkins, Head of School for Early Years and Childhood Studies at Solihull College in the UK, shows us how important careful and appropriate e-moderator intervention is in working with participants unused to online learning.

I have used a variety of functions available on our VLE (MOODLE) in developing students' confidence knowledge and skills in writing a research project.

I have the challenge of teaching research methodology and skills to Level 3 BTEC National Diploma students. The students have successfully completed many other assignments for their programme, however, the research module seems to hold a particular dread for them. The research model challenges them because, unlike other assignments where the title is given to them, in research they have to select their own area of interest. In addition they then have to grapple with unfamiliar terminology and concepts such as literature reviews, qualitative and quantitative data, validity and reliability to name a few that send even the most able into a spin.

Each year I reflect on how to allay fears, avoid melt downs and create confident researchers ready for their next step to university.

The VLE has made a real difference. I use a range of the facilities to develop the skills and confidence over time. We begin with a discussion board on suggested topics. This gets us talking, initially in the classroom and then over the week I see them talking and supporting each other. They find others in the group who share their interest and so the discussion develops into defining and refining a research question. In the past, meeting only once a week, choosing the topic used to take four to five weeks. The VLE allows this debate to go on outside of the classroom; this cohort had the topics agreed in the first week. This means we can move on to what research *is* much more quickly.

One of the big challenges for the group is to understand the research language and terminology. We use MOODLE tools to create quizzes to match and sort terms with definitions; the students can practise this as many times as they need to and have the information available anywhere there is internet access. As a tutor I can monitor their progress and address any repeated errors. One student told me she used her i-phone to complete the quizzes on the bus!

Once we get into the business of reviewing literature, the students upload a draft, I am then able to give feedback before the next session which means that the students can work on the piece and are ready to hand in a completed piece of work and pass first time rather than the demoralizing resubmission and refer cycle I have encountered in life before VLE.

As students get more confident in using the VLE, realizing that the feedback is more expedient, my role becomes that of moderator, valuing their contributions, encouraging them to look deeper. The students take ownership of the forum; they begin to support each other using the discussion forum, directing peers to articles they have read, programmes they have seen, offering support to get questionnaires completed. My role becomes that of e-moderator. I only need interject as an equal pointing them to relevant research or ideas.

In summary, I use a broad range of the functions building the students' knowledge, skills, confidence and competence until they really don't need me at all! Last year, we had 100 per cent pass rate and 95 per cent achieve a distinction – I can't really ask for more . . . but I will!

Celebrate!

We need to mobilize and deploy the brains and commitment of teachers and trainers of all kinds in the service of e-moderating. We also need to raise the profile of e-moderators, and recognize and reward their valuable work. E-moderating is somewhat less visible (sometimes almost invisible if done well) and therefore special efforts need to go into celebrating good practice! I hope the exploration of roles and qualities in this chapter is of use to you and will enable you to recruit and train for very productive online teaching and learning.

Chapter 5

Developing e-moderators

The main message of this chapter and the next is simple and direct: online learners (whether students or staff in development) benefit from a proper introduction to, and familiarization with, networked-based discussion, as a way of working and learning together. This is critically important whether your plans are to provide entirely remotely mediated groups or combined with other modes.

This chapter is about the process of creating e-moderators through training online in all their roles. In the first and second editions of this book I used as my main example the online training programme developed in the OU Business School in the 1990s. Although it all happened a long time ago in internet terms, the experience still feels useful and valid for now. Chapter 6 goes on to describe later developments of e-moderating training.

Staff development's role in educational change

There are some key issues that are strongly emerging. Technology adoption lies with the lecturer, teacher or tutor but they act within the much wider institutional and disciplinary context (Salmon, Edirisingha, Mobbs, Mobbs and Dennett, 2008). Russell (2009) finds that engagement in her fellowship programme decreases individualized and discipline-specific uses of learning technology and increases shared, collaborative, cross-disciplinary uses that relate to institutional and departmental contexts. There are important lessons here for those of us involved in evaluating institutional change programmes.

Any significant initiative aimed at changing teaching methods or the introduction of technology into teaching and learning should include effective e-moderator support and training, otherwise its outcomes are likely to be meagre and unsuccessful. Even where technological infrastructure and support are strong, and when worthwhile learning applications are developed, without development of staff for the role nothing is likely to happen beyond pilot schemes. In the medium term, the costs of training and support for participants can be higher than the provision of the technology; therefore it is worthwhile giving the training of e-moderators due consideration and adequate planning. Even in well-supported and well-developed distance environments, students' expectations of their e-moderators may be higher than the real experience. There is still much to be done!

If you are feeling enthusiastic about developing online learning or any form of e-blend, please be aware that a fair bit of rethinking of course methodologies, and of training and support for e-moderators, is needed for success. There are examples where, despite early adoption of online, courses reverted to old technologies. This is often due to the lack of support and development of teaching staff, or failure to manage the necessary organizational changes appropriately, or an inability to train sufficient e-moderators for expansion and development. E-moderating is not a set of skills any of us is born with, nor one that we have learnt vicariously through observing teachers while we ourselves were learning. As yet there are comparatively few online mentors to guide us through step by step. Maybe in the future, adults will draw on their childhood online experiences and try to emulate the examples of good e-moderators who changed the direction of their lives! But, meanwhile, e-moderators must be trained.

Because the pace of change is fast, few of us can allow for long apprenticeship through learning, supporting and then teaching in the online environment. It is likely that pressures will build up – either because student numbers are large or you want to be sure of early success – and gradual change may prove too slow. Critically, you must know what you are training for, and, as in any planning of learning activities, what competencies or outcomes you are seeking. Table 4.1 in Chapter 4 gives you a suggested list on which you can build, bearing in mind your discipline, your students and your context.

Training and development needs to take into account the contentious issue of how much time e-moderators can be expected to work online. The time required depends on what they are doing, of course, but you can be absolutely certain that if they are untrained they will take longer and do it less well. As I have said, teaching online needs careful planning and preparation, otherwise the stories will continue of e-moderators being overloaded, underpaid and burnt out by the work.

I've noticed a wide variety of reactions from colleagues in universities and colleges around the world to the introduction of virtual learning environments and other new technologies, ranging from wild enthusiasm from some to strategic undermining by others. Some faculty members are still looking for contractual positions regarding their use of information and communication technologies, so the major moves towards online in many different contexts rely on goodwill and the support available to reskill. Barriers and opportunities include complex intrinsic and extrinsic factors.

Most teachers and trainers, especially those in higher education, learnt to teach largely through apprenticeship in their disciplines. Their practice consists of complex sets of values, attitudes and behaviours, many of them largely 'taken as read'. Nowadays, there are many people admirably trying to offer them the chance to be 'trained in new technologies for teaching and learning'. However, such attempts to address the reskilling of academic staff through half-day workshops in the use of the VLE are unlikely to do more than scratch the surface, and they may also convince faculty that teaching online is mainly about learning to use a computer program. Indeed several studies confirm that 'no amount of hands-on . . . training can replace the practical application of technology to the teaching and learning process'.

The CARPE DIEM work at Leicester and elsewhere has proven time and time again that there is great value in working together in teams around the design and delivery of simple online e-tivities and scaffolding (Salmon et al., 2008).

Focusing training on use of the features of the technological system is unlikely to do more than make the slightest dent in the long apprenticeship in practical and theoretical knowledge or competence in the teaching profession, much of which is acquired rather mysteriously, or at least informally. Another strong tendency has been to teach a great deal about teaching theory and hence 'put off' large numbers of potential e-moderators who want practical guides. The innovators and the early adopters persist with more or less good grace, although some 'burn out' or become demoralized in the attempt. For some of the others, the battle is lost early on, and they can become convinced that satisfactory knowledge transmission and construction has to happen face-to-face. However, if early in the process participants are enabled to be active online participants for themselves, they see the benefits and are motivated to acquire the skills (see Chapter 6 for a recent example of engaged development of e-moderation).

They then need a 'very safe online environment' where they feel free to express their ideas and concerns, challenge and ask questions. E-moderators trained in this way perceive the work involved in teaching online very differently. Their positive perception is reflected in the way in which they relate to students online, and ultimately in their self-value and professionalism. Providing such training is a non-trivial task.

Essentially I am arguing here that there is a new form of literacy, based around the acquisition of e-moderating skills, that goes well beyond training in the platform. To create e-moderators we need to scale up the acquisition of such skills, and if we are to do so, potential e-moderators must be placed in real but virtual situations as early as possible (Bennett and Marsh, 2002). Bennett and Barp (2008) and Bennett and Santy (2009) advocate peer observation online to augment the training of staff who have not had an opportunity to acquire e-moderating skills.

Downgrading the human role and upgrading the technological impact by suggesting that we now need to consider the 'human factors' misses the key point. What we know of learning is that if we want people to change what they actually do, we need to offer experiences that shuttle backwards and forwards between what they already know, and what they are prepared to develop, between specific details and their implications in wider contexts, and between practice and reflection (Harvey and Knight, 1996).

First, teachers and trainers, new and experienced and at all levels of education, need to acquire new skills in creating, managing and promoting students in participation in interactive conferencing online (Barajas and Gannaway, 2007; Smet, van Keer and Valcke, 2008). These skills are more important but harder to acquire than technical ability in a particular platform. Second, key attention needs to be given to enable them to gain confidence and professionalism and continue to develop (Underhill and McDonald, 2010; Michinov, Brunot, Le Bohec, Juhel and Delaval, 2010). The approach to acquiring the skills initially and continuing to develop should be the medium itself, and it depends on the support of experienced facilitators: the people I call e-convenors, the e-moderators of the e-moderators, the trainers of the trainers.

I should add just one word about the importance of stable, reliable and appropriate technologies in the support, training and development of faculty and tutors, at least beyond the natural innovators. Just as with infants for whom sensitization to a potential allergen early in their development may lead to major and sometimes incurable problems later on, so is the impact of foisting a poor platform or a weakly supported technology on an unsuspecting audience. At the slightest indication of trouble later, they'll be convinced that 'e-learning doesn't work'!

When I wrote the first edition of this book, I argued that e-moderating training was about changes to pedagogy. Since then it has become fashionable to assert that teaching, not technology, is the 'solution' to working online. I guess that's progress! However, it's too simplistic. To develop effective and efficient e-moderators, we need to create training that provides an online environment where the sense of emotional identity, the shifting of time, the experience of the context with all its foibles, can all be experienced. Most trainee e-moderators are happiest undertaking their online training with others from their disciplines, and hence are able to make strong practical links between theory, practice and skills. It is important to try to model (rather than teach) the desired skills, offer real practical experience and many opportunities for challenge, collaboration and reflection.

Training of e-moderators in the Open University Business School

I want to summarize the large-scale well-researched online training in e-moderating in the Open University Business School (OUBS), 1996–99, which I ran with my colleague Ken Giles. The five-stage model provided a 'scaffold' or guide for training up e-moderators from novice to expert status. I hope that this account of our experience will be of value to you if you are facing similar training requirements whether on a small or large scale, in whatever discipline.

In building the first online training programme during the winter of 1995–96 we were faced with a fairly major task. Human and financial resources were limited. There was very little experience of working online beyond early adopters and enthusiasts, at that time. We wanted to deploy the five-stage model as a basis, as it was founded on 'grounded principles' (see Chapter 2). We expected up to 200 participants, spread over most of Western Europe – it turned out that 187 registered for the first round of training. They were appointed to work as part-time tutors for the Open University Business School from home and most had full-time management or academic jobs outside the OU. We could assume that they had basic computer literacy although very few had more advanced skills. E-moderating online was but one aspect among many of the teaching strategy and of their role as tutors for the MBA courses. Online had to be meaningful and worthwhile for both the students and their e-moderators if it was to be judged to be a success.

We wanted to indicate to our participants that online was essentially a distance medium of communication and to demonstrate that the training objectives could be achieved at a distance. We therefore considered that the training programme itself should use online discussion groups and be accessed from tutors' own networked computers. At the end of the last century, this was a much bigger challenge than it is now and created considerable anxiety. The tutors' first need was to be able to log in using their particular configuration of hardware from their home base, rather than using someone else's configuration via a different access point. The tutors truly needed to experience, much as their own students would, the pitfalls and the potential of online if they were to e-moderate effectively. A further very real reason for using online for the training was that to offer intensive face-to-face training would have stretched our human resources and provision of training facilities to the limit. Furthermore we wanted the training to focus on pedagogical knowledge, built up through personal and collective reflection on practice, rather than on acquiring a technical grasp of the hardware and software.

We were reluctant to ground the training in any form of text-based instructional materials, although this was common throughout the OU, because of the risk of these materials being divorced from the construction of the online knowledge and skills. However, it rapidly became obvious that a booklet, showing exactly what the screen should look like at each point in the procedure, was essential, probably because at that point in time it was truly the main way that people learnt. We produced a printed booklet for the second and subsequent versions of the training. To prepare the booklet, we had to create the online programme first, then print exact copies of the screens and key messages. This booklet supported those who wanted a paper manual (most at that time!). It also enabled them to work offline if they wished, and they didn't need to print pages for themselves.

Our training programme needed to be intrinsically motivating and lead to competent practice. The task was therefore to create a programme that, while providing the development of essential basic skills (such as confidence and competence in using the software), represented as closely as possible the realities of teaching and learning online.

We decided the following:

- An average tutor would be expected to devote some ten hours to the online e-moderating training programme.
- The design would be based on the five-stage model previously developed.
- A core of online e-moderators (online trainers of the online trainers) would be selected and trained to e-moderate the individual training conferences within the programme.
- Evaluation and action research would be based on tracking the trainees through the stages in the programme by a series of online conferences and questionnaires of a quantitative and qualitative nature and through monitoring the work of the trainees online after the training finished and the tutors commenced working with students.
- A small fee and a sum for telephone expenses (it was in the era of chargeable dial-up access!), and a certificate of completion, would be provided which the trainees could claim on completion of their exit questionnaires.

Training programme design

We planned for a wide range of prior knowledge and/or experience of online among the participants. Each would have his or her own 'map' of the topic.

The programme needed to include training in declarative knowledge (what is this icon?), procedural knowledge (how do I send a message?), as well as more strategic knowledge (what can I do with my e-moderating skills?). However, we planned that participants would acquire these various kinds of knowledge in an integrated way. The online training programme would not only be about acquiring new skills but would also help participants to explore their attitudes to online working and its meaning for their own teaching.

We designed the programme to create 'microworlds' in which the participants could interact with each other, with the e-moderators of the training conference (who we called convenors) and with the software, before progressing to the next stage. We hoped that our participants would gradually build up their knowledge and software skills, particularly in the use of computer conferencing for management learning. We made them aware of the goals all the way through the training. They were advised of appropriate ways of undertaking the tasks but could also construct their own approach. We tried to enable them to use the software as a matter of routine while we raised their awareness of the teaching and learning aspects. The importance ascribed in constructivism to the building of relationships between new and existing knowledge (Bruner, 1986) led us to a careful choice of images and titles for conferences, and the use of familiar metaphors for explaining aspects of online working.

Helping participants to control their frustration is a key aspect of learning to use online. We tried to achieve a balance between a trainee struggling with too much complexity and being given enough involvement in the task. We attempted to give more help when participants got into difficulties and less as they gained proficiency. In practice some participants needed almost no help and others huge amounts. It did not prove possible to predict who needed extra help until they asked for it. So it was important to provide a continuously available source of help.

Evaluation

Engaging in reflective and interactive online activities, especially those leading to explaining, justifying and evaluating problem solutions, is a very important learning process. Schön (1983) pointed out that people change their everyday practice by having reflective conversations, they frame their understanding of a situation in the light of experience, and they try out actions and then reinterpret or reframe the situation in the light of the consequences of that action. Schön also argued that through reflection a practitioner could surface and critique understandings that have grown up around a specialized practice and make sense of a situation for him or herself. We think this applies to online training too.

We wished to find ways of enabling reflection on online practice to happen within the training programme, at each of the five levels. We therefore decided to introduce a set of simple motivational goals, by requiring our participants to reflect 'deliberately' on learning at each stage. They were encouraged to take part, to post at least one message at each of the five levels, to contribute to the 'reflections' conferences, to complete their exit questionnaires – and only then to ask for their certificate of completion, training payments and expenses.

The training programme was developed and updated year by year. By 1999, over 400 trainees had taken part, with nearly all commenting on their experience of the training through the reflections conferences and exit questionnaires. We also monitored the work of the e-moderators with their students and made adjustments to the training. The examples that follow are from the 1999 version of the online training in Open University Business School. The model has since been used on a global basis for training e-moderators (see Chapter 6).

Open University Business School training programme

We based the five levels of the online tutor development on the five-stage model described in Chapter 2, Figure 2.1. At every level, the simplest possible set of instructions accompanied activities in the online environment. The printed booklet accompanying the training programme offered a list of conferences to aid navigation, copies of what the screen should look like to the trainee at various stages and a print-out of key online instructions; for example, how to post a CV (résumé), how to send messages.

When a trainee logged on, she or he saw five icons, representing the five levels of the training programme (see Figure 5.1). In addition, a Lifebelt (or help) icon was available which contained virus prevention software, downloadable manuals, FAQs about the software, Code of Practice for use of the system, helpdesk phone numbers and even a 'lifeguard' to e-mail if necessary.

This was our first message to participants:

WELCOME!

Each stage will offer you skills with a range of activities designed to enable you to practise those skills. For the early stages the programme we will give you quite a lot of help, but for the final stages we will only give limited guidance! By the end of the programme you should have the skills required to work with your students in a productive way.

It is strongly recommended that you work through one stage before moving on to the next. Please visit the 'Reflections' conference at each level before closing that level and moving on to the next. We will use these for evaluating the training and research into conferencing.

Aims and objectives of this training programme

The aims of the programme are to:

- provide you with the technical skills to access and use the FirstClass system and to undertake a range of tasks online;
- provide you with the experience and confidence to use the FirstClass system as a key resource in teaching and learning online;
- enable you to become an active member of the OUBS online community, participating in and contributing to School, programme and course conferences.

The introductory message for each of the five stages in the training explains the purpose of that stage. Now click on the Welcome icon and announce your arrival! OUBS Convenor

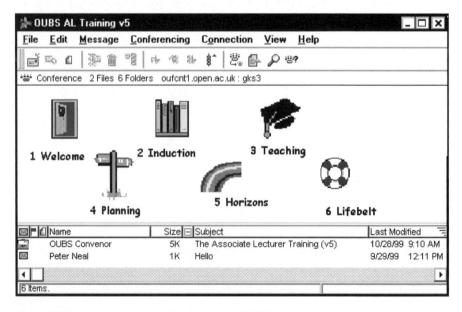

Figure 5.1 Desktop screen of online training in OUBS

Level one: welcome

The purpose of this level is to ensure that participants can find a conference, find, read and send messages, discover who else is taking part and give a little information about themselves.

The new trainee's first task is to visit the 'arrivals' conference, where they find instructions on posting a simple message to announce their arrival. Most participants succeeded in achieving this task on their first, or sometimes their second, log in. However, their relief or jubilation at having 'made it' is often obvious:

> I was preparing to sneak in by the back door but feel so much better having spotted several other 'started before but life got in the way' messages. JI
>
> I have arrived but not sure if I have landed – if you know what I mean! PP
>
> Present but probably not correct! DB
>
> Ho there – my first action is to print everything because I can't remember anything but the fact that I can't remember anything and have to do something creative to cope – like printing a whole load of instructions. RM

These efforts were rewarded by a personal 'congratulations and welcome' message from the online trainer (whom we called convenor in this context). At this stage the convenor also pointed the new trainee to any sources of help and attempted to assuage any worries or grievances. Many participants remember the importance of their individual welcome into the online environment when questioned months or even years later, so we feel it is always worthwhile.

At level one we also invited participants to explore the difference between e-mail and conferencing. Even at that time, trainee e-moderators presented with fairly well-developed e-mail skills. It is important to explain the differences to build on their prior knowledge and expertise. Finally we explained how to look at the résumés of other participants in the training, and invited them to post their own. We emphasized the importance of posting a few details about oneself early in the training, since we found that every participant felt more comfortable if they had a little knowledge about people they were working with right from the start.

Finally, the last task at level one was to post a message to reflect on their experiences so far. Here is our invitation message:

Reflections on level one

Please ensure that you have completed all the tasks at this level. Then send a message to this conference reflecting on:

The key learning points from your initial experiences in the training. After you have completed your reflections message, please close all the windows from Level 1, and click onto Level 2 Induction' (the bookshelf icon). OUBS Convenor

Most participants responded, establishing, we think, a small amount of reflection from the start of their journey into conference e-moderation. Here are some examples of their messages:

Things often look simple, and can also be simplified, but below the surface there's a lot more than meets the eye. TD

Hey, this isn't so bad. I thought it would be much more complicated given my not so literate computer skills! AL

My overwhelming sense of achievement at leaving this message is diminished by the entirely predictable instability of virtual communications. I feel like I've been trying to send smoke signals in a force 9 wind. DB

Good first session as people's online personalities emerge. It takes longer than I would have expected to read the threads/postings – would not dream of not trying to at least scan them all in case I missed a particularly good one. ;-) Perceive myself to be 'falling behind' which is providing a frisson of worry – at what point does 'asynchronous' become 'forget it'? 8-) A useful insight into what students may feel at times – the gamekeeper turned poacher. PD

I've found the first session a bit strange. It has brought forth an array of responses, attitudes and approaches from colleagues. As my usual teaching style is probably relatively structured, I've been surprised at how an apparently 'structured' set of e-tivities can lead to what (at first blush) seemed such an unstructured set of responses. PR

Level two: induction

Level two, equivalent to Stage 2 in the model, enabled participants to learn about protocols and how to relate to others through this medium, and to acquire useful software skills.

Participants worked through exercises aimed at analysing a mock discussion among students who are conferencing about a television programme. The 'participants' are making all the classic mistakes (lack of titles to messages, advertising, messages in the wrong conference, failure to re-title messages when replying and changing topics, 'parental responses' rather than collegiate and attempts at domination of the discussion). The discussion has a 'real' (virtual) feel about it. Participants are invited to view each message and consider how well or otherwise it contributes to the discussion. Feedback suggests that this is a very successful exercise for trainee e-moderators.

One trainee found this exercise particularly helpful:

> I think this exercise is an excellent one for its richness. It has a provocative title to get you into it, but sorting out the 'good' from the 'bad' proves a little too difficult for me. I would rather view it as an interesting insight into the different motivations these students may have for using online conferencing. On the other hand almost all the participants could be prompted to keep brushing up their netiquette! Great learning, thanks. ML

In addition, participants were invited to explore appropriate communication styles online by sending a 'postcard'. We have found that this simple metaphor enables participants to practise giving straightforward information in short messages. It also results in some sharing of information about themselves and some fun! Here is our message:

> *Send us a postcard, please!*
> It takes time to develop a style of your own online – usually somewhere between writing and speaking. It needs to be brief – more than one screenful is rarely appropriate, but informative without being indecipherable or offensive to anyone who might read it. This is not meant to put you off in any way!
>
> Some people suggest that writing conference messages is a bit like writing a postcard. This is your chance to try it!

> Use this conference to send a message to your colleague of maximum one screenful. This could give some information about you, or perhaps seek information from others. OUBS Convenor

The postcard messages offered fascinating insights into our participants, who typically mention their location and often why they're working online instead of doing something else!

> As I sit here on a Friday evening in dark decided wintry Brussels I can imagine the perfect golfing day – warm and sunny with a little breeze.
>   Never mind for those of you who know Brussels you will know this scene is sadly a very rare actual occurrence – but it has the benefit that you are not often distracted in reality! 'Au revoir' and 'bon weekend'. Best regards. KD
>
> The beauty of this postcard for me is that I don't have to hunt around for a stamp! Usually I forget to buy them. Here in Hampton (West London) it's a glorious sunny morning – postcard weather even. Just off to the Tate Gallery for a cultural fix and then a look at the Millennium Wheel on the South Bank. Regards PB
>
> Not sure 'I wish you were here' in my study staring at a screen. Life is for living – can you be living focused at a screen, yes I know 'virtual reality' is supposed to be the answer. Can you really experience life by accessing a screen? EP
>
> Fellow holiday-makers, I am sitting here in rainy Dublin, the Celtic tiger looks more like a drowned rat and I am faced with the familiar dilemma of what spurious candyfloss I can use to fill the blank space of a post card. Missing you already AN

Participants visited the reflection conference at level two before they moved on, which asked:

> What key learning points from your progress on the training so far would you pass on to your students?

Here is an example response:

> Amazingly enough it's all beginning to fall into place. My confidence in using FirstClass (which I have never used before) is increasing rapidly and I'm not so scared of pressing the wrong button. I have learnt a lot about setting up conferences and keeping them going etc. I find that the contributions from others online, both experienced and new ones, is really useful as there is a wealth of experience out there. This would be my advice to my students – try it – it's amazing! Thanks. FH

Level three: teaching

Level three, equivalent to Stage 3 in the model, was concerned with giving and receiving information. We have found that participants liked to gain and share information around their professional task of teaching online. We also focused on exercises that showed them how to set up their own online conferences. We included an essential practice area, and we offered exercises and discussions on the role of the e-moderator including practice in opening conferences and the weaving of conference messages together. Participants were invited to post examples of their own opening messages and to comment on those of their fellow participants. Among the most important skills to be learnt at this stage were summarizing, archiving and weaving.

Participants visited the reflections conference before exiting level three, and again we ask them:

> What key learning points from your progress on the training so far would you pass on to colleagues from a teaching perspective?

By this stage, some excitement and trepidation about conferencing 'for real' was occurring, but there is also evidence of some real learning. Here are some examples of level three reflections. One participant detailed his new insights into e-moderating:

> Lurking
>
> I agree that lurking (still looking for a more neutral term) needs investigating as colleagues suggest but note that you can check who has

read a message by going to 'History'. This may allow you to identify those who are not picking up the messages (e.g. in a tutorial group) which might justify a phone call. The person may have technical problems, or may be looking in the wrong place. Still lurking is better than not participating at all!

Weaving

HP certainly sums it up well for me: you do have the option of setting up another sub-conference so those who want to wander off can do so in parallel with the main topic in hand. Summarizing the main points so far that are on track and adding a few pertinent questions would also help. I guess one of the best preparations for a flagging discussion is to keep a few things up your sleeve, so that if/when things flag you have something new/interesting to add in to give it a boost.

Summarizing

I will need to be more encouraging about the contributions individually, select a title that would stand out more to enable late comers to catch up without having to read all the 'red flags' and end with a question if I were 'going live'. Wouldn't you agree . . .? J. :-) JS

Other participants compare e-moderating to facilitating face-to-face groups:

For me, opening, weaving, e-moderating are, in many ways, just like getting a discussion going in a face-to-face setting. The skills required are the same, only the medium is a little different. Someone once told me that an online discussion group is much like having a party in a dark living room. No one can see one another, but everyone hears what is being said. There are those who whisper in the corners (go off-conference, 1-to-1 e-mail) where others can't hear, but for the most part, one can only make sense of what is going on by paying good attention. This may be a dying art – and there are times I believe that. Enjoy EM

I think conferencing can be a valuable learning tool – capturing immediate reactions and ideas, which are often, very stimulating and which often get lost in assignments and face-to-face seminars – a virtual learning organization! AA

Level four: knowledge construction

Level four is equivalent to Stage 4 of the model. We found that stimulating participants to discuss how they will use online with their students worked best at this level. We provided a discussion forum so that participants could 'meet' and 'discuss' issues with those from their own course or programme. We also attached some texts for them to consider. This gave practice in downloading attached documents (still important at that time) as well as giving them ideas to explore. As always a reflections conference was provided at this level to encourage them to consider their progress.

Participants recognize that they need to get real experience in working with students:

I feel confident enough to get started, but am fully aware I will continue to learn, and probably learn a lot, through actual doing. BF

I feel quite comfortable with this. I used the old CoSy conferencing in my student days and absolutely loved it. It was really helpful in my studies and a very useful contact with other students (especially those on the same course but not necessarily in my tutor group), and other tutors other than my own. It gave me a far broader view than I would ever have achieved otherwise. I hope I can pass this enthusiasm on to my students, and get as many of them as possible involved in using computer conferencing as part of their studies. I guess central to this will be my role in providing the right environment in the conference for lively and useful discussion and support for novice participants, so that they can see a real advantage in using it. JB

I've derived great benefit from reading everybody else's reflections. It has truly widened my appreciation not only of the potential of the medium but also of its role in teaching and learning online. I'm ready and raring to do it for real but realize that I will need to 'stand back' and encourage the knowledge flow. JH

I've found computer conferencing an easy and effective method of engaging in debate as a student. Having completed this training I am about to find out what it is like on the other side of the modem as a tutor! I'm determined to build a sense of community with my group and perhaps encourage those who are less willing to contribute face-to-face to do so over the electronic system. (I wonder, however, just how intimidating it is for those who are not as computer literate as I am?) I'll have to ask my group. JP

Level five: development

This level is equivalent to Stage 5 of the model. Here we explored the use of the web in teaching, both to build up participants' confidence and to enable them to consider how they might embed web resources in their own e-moderating. At the time, this was still a very new idea! Participants shared their favourite search engines and sites for their discipline.

The exit questionnaire provided simple feedback to us about the participants' experience of the whole programme and has enabled us to make incremental adjustments and improvements over the years. Quantitative and qualitative feedback from the exit questionnaire helped us to confirm and develop the exercises and approaches throughout the five levels. Participants very consistently confirmed that the five-stage model of training worked for them. Creating motivation at level one was probably the most complex challenge along with the encouragement of participants to keep working through each of the levels until they reached level five. However, from level two onwards, confidence grew in almost every trainee and many were very appreciative of learning or reinforcing online communication skills and information exchange at levels two and three. Several commented that these are basic life and business skills that were not otherwise taught in this way. Although everyone now has much more experience in working through the web for teaching and everyday life, there are still few courses of this kind. At level four, participants really appreciated the focus on e-moderating and considerable anticipation was generated. By level five, nearly all participants were very keen indeed to try out their new skills on their participants!

The vast majority of participants appreciated the highly structured, staged approach to training and learning software and e-moderating skills in an integrated way. A small minority, however, continued to ask for a software 'manual'. They often expressed this as an 'idiot's' guide to the system – a request that still sometimes comes my way in 2010. Regrettably, it is not easy to simplify an interactive and complex system sufficiently for these people. We encouraged such groups to download the instructions that they seek. Another small minority is happy with the training programme taking place entirely online, but wish to take their own route through the training exercises and conferences. We allowed for this, of course, although we found that a lower percentage of this group completes the programme.

Most concerns about working online were somewhat alleviated by the time participants completed the programme and most considered investment in their training 'good value' for the use of their precious time. However, those worries that remained are typically about the use of their time when working online with students, suggesting that expectations, reward and recognition in the use of e-moderating time must always be given careful consideration.

I have two fears: 1) my students not using it very much; and 2) it will be used a lot by my students and it will take up too much time! MD

Some students may be accessing conferences through an employer's system. And time. Could this encourage excessive inputs and unreasonable demands on the e-moderator's time? PB

And a word of caution. It all gets so engrossing that it is easy to forget that it is way past bedtime again! People at the office will be wondering why I always seem so tired. NH

Most participants felt they had achieved and accomplished personal development by level five and were very pleased to have completed the programme. Completing participants frequently said they believed such a training programme should be compulsory for e-moderators before they are 'let loose' on student conferences. They expressed very tangible progress compared to their first tentative messages at level one. Some were by then already working with their students online. Some were very enthusiastic. We encouraged staff to reflect on their whole range of feelings at the end of the process, and to recognize who or what had contributed most to their learning. Most participants expressed a mixture of relief and regret.

Mixed feelings here because the e-moderators course is ending. . . . Happy because the light is finally emerging, the feeling of managing to pull through and survive the 6 weeks course is beyond speech. . .

Thankful . . . so used to reading many of your postings: fun one, serious one, deep and profound one, encouraging one, refreshing. . . . I am learning soooooooooo much from all of you! What a powerful collective learning process I witness! When paths cross, life changes. . .

Excited . . . to share with the colleagues the good news of an e-tivity and the gold mine in it for learning. Carefulness . . . mindful of the pitfalls and possible traps for implementing an e-tivity for engineering modules.

Regret . . . I didn't respond to many of your questions and comments; some I have not thought through, some make me smile and delighted, some I simply can't find the messages again after being interrupted, . . . If only time allowed. . .

Christine, Ken, and Len . . . Thanks for showing me how to be a good e-moderator. I have enjoyed and learnt very much from the course. LC

Now, what am i to do with my life
When i need not log-on to my e-tivities?
But, should i accidentally do so
(post a message or respond to one)
Will I find that there's no soul there
to acknowledge, encourage, and say a kind word or two?
What's life i wonder. . .
In post-e-tivity!
NE

Many thanks all.
Have enjoyed the ride.
Special thanks to you e convenors Keith, Larry & Carole.
Have learnt much by doing the work!.
And especially seeing how you model the skills. Great job!
MD

This is the future. I have seen it and it works (sometimes). BA

Using online reminds me of the time I learnt to drive a car, I was very proud I could drive, but now I am much more interested in the places I can visit in the car. I have a feeling this is going to be similar. HF

The convenors' summaries acted well as closures to the tutors' online learning experience. E-moderators can offer encouragement to participants to continue to implement their new knowledge and understandings along with their farewell messages:

E-moderation – the next step
Congratulations to all of you who have completed this 5 week e-moderation course.

While you have all learnt much along your personal learning journeys, this course is only the first step. In your discussions, you have already identified some of the aspects of your work that could be modified to support better both yourselves and your students.

Some things that may need to be reviewed include:

1. *Induction* – how will your students know what is expected of them?
2. *Assessment* – how are you going to ensure your assessment processes are valid and reliable, fair and authentic and that you are not absolutely overwhelmed with work?
3. *Collaboration* – how will you 'sell' this concept to your students? When will you use collaborative learning activities to achieve maximum impact?
4. *Motivation* – how will you design your programme to ensure all students participate where required?
5. *Organizational support* – how will you promote the changes in the way you wish to work to your senior managers, policy makers and funding sources? Sometimes a new way of working challenges the accepted practices in an educational institute. Engage a 'champion' who will press your case for change at appropriate occasions.
6. *Collegial support* – how will you maintain your interest and enthusiasm for this new way of working? You need friends and supporters to share new ideas and to test new approaches. Think about how you can maintain the enthusiasm and momentum that this course has already generated.

Best wishes, good luck and farewell, your e-convenor Christine

Monitoring the work of trained e-moderators

New and experienced e-moderators benefit from feedback and support in order to develop and professionalize their roles. There are many benefits in sharing both resources and understanding

The Open University has always had policies and extensive systems to monitor the quality of its tutors' performance. It provides them with feedback and offers development where necessary. Until the advent of large-scale working online, this monitoring took the form of visits to face-to-face tutorials, day schools and residential schools by full-time academic staff, and the systematic and very large-scale monitoring of correspondence tuition, based on a peer review system. Drawing on the experience and procedures for these, we devised and implemented a system of monitoring of online e-moderation for the Business School. This system involved a series of virtual 'visits' to each conference by peer or colleague tutors who had fully and successfully completed the online training. They provided reports on their view of conferences that they visited and commented whenever they found good practice in e-moderation. They also alerted managers to problems or lack of participation. There is a direct correlation between active e-moderation and successful completion of the online training. The monitoring system has been gradually built up and refined over the first few years, and was extended to other courses and faculties.

An online community of tutors has also emerged, centred on discussion and information conferences known as the 'SCR' (Senior Common Room). The exchange of good practice, support, collaboration – and the flattening of communications with the full-time course team and the part-time tutors – was welcome. We did not anticipate the importance and strength of these communications devices at first but they have proved an unexpected bonus. There is little doubt that the training has produced new cohorts of tutors comfortable with communicating electronically. This has an almost immeasurable impact on the sense of professional community that this generated. I recommend to everyone that they set up an easily accessed but 'e-moderators only' online conference for sharing and exploring good practice.

To gradually build up appropriate and consistent e-moderating practice in your own context, you do need to set up monitoring of your e-moderators' work. You may, like us, wish to base this on a peer review system. It is tempting to revert to visiting face-to-face sessions, where these are feasible, but it is better to review and monitor the work of e-moderators online. I suggest you make sure that the reviewers are fully comfortable and competent themselves as e-moderators, so they don't apply old paradigms of teaching and learning to the new environment! Of course, another important way of determining the success of the work of the e-moderators is to explore the responses of the participants. Chapter 7 provides some ideas for success factors for participants.

Chapter 6

Further development of e-moderators

Here is the programme offered by All Things In Moderation (ATIM) Ltd., a company that specializes in training e-moderators worldwide and has conducted a large number of online courses since it started in 2000. The examples given here are from 2010. We have also used it in adapted form at the University of Leicester where it is known as the 'Barefoot e-moderators' course.

Tutors who take part, as learners, in short online e-moderating courses acquire basic skills that enable them to maximize the benefits of their designs and moderate effectively in collaborative learning contexts. As part of these courses, participants encounter relevant literature on task-based course design and management of online groups. These courses give tutors valuable 'learner experience' in online learning and provide a solid starting point for pedagogical change. Tutors can easily transfer e-moderating skills and techniques into their own practice (Armellini and Aiyegbayo, 2010).

We need to move towards 'aligning' our assessment with our online teaching approaches. Biggs's framework (2003) suggests a form of matching between learning outcomes, assessment, teaching methods and activities.

Since the first few Open University Business School tutor development training started, some 14 years have gone by. Many lifecycles in learning and technology terms! The five-stage model has informed e-learning and development practice across many levels from school pupils, corporate training to postgraduate research students, and especially in online and blended learning in higher and professional education. It has served disciplines ranging from arts to science and practice-based subjects such as nursing and management. But, fortunately, it has also hung onto the branch where its first application began – providing a development experience for teachers, tutors, trainer, instructors on all kinds of journeys to be becoming wonderful e-moderators.

In the year 2000 with a colleague, David Shepherd, I set up a small dot.com, called All Things in Moderation to offer the five-stage online e-moderator experience to anyone wishing to take part. We recruited, trained and developed our own e-convenors (because there were very few around at that time). There are two main ways that we engage with potential e-moderators: we run regular open courses on which individuals and small groups register, and we also set up and license the well-rehearsed programme for organizations – often universities – and provide the e-convening to ensure its a success. Around 2,000 individuals from around the world have now successfully taken part and completed e-moderating, receiving their participation certificates, through at least six different VLEs. We have worked with individuals and partners around the world and the short programmes have been completed in Spanish and German as well as English. We know for sure we have learnt very much more from them than they ever could from us – but it's been a great privilege and a joy to be able to influence the online knowledge construction world in a positive way.

So I thought you might like to see where it's got to! What follows is based on Version 6 of 'E-moderating' which was first delivered through the Janison VLE in June 2010 to a group of nine individuals from four countries with a variety of roles. David himself was the e-convenor.

Developing e-moderation skills in 2010: an example

David (the e-convenor) writes:

> My aim of any interaction or intervention is to help the participants to develop into self-sufficient competent e-moderators, I check this out just before I post a message. If I can't see a positive outcome I do not post! My first aim is to have everyone engaged and participating with the minimum of information using the skills they already have of engaging with the internet. I assume participants have the skills to order books from Amazon!
>
> We invite participants via email with a short enticing paragraph and access details saying that the course will be open for about four days before the official start date. It is usual for about half the participants in each group

to make contact and post a message before the start date. One or two participants usually do not appear online until day two of the course!

I interact with the participants who log-on early, those that appear on time and follow up those who haven't turned up at all with a brief 'Is everything OK?' email.

This is what they see when they log on:

E-moderating v6	Welcome
Information	Welcome to the E-moderating course. We begin in earnest on Monday, 7th June. This is the first of my regular course blogs.
▶**Enconvenors Blog**	
Announcements	
Course Wiki	
Course content	The software you are using (Janison) works best using the Internet Explorer browser. Please use the left-hand menu to look around the course before Monday to get an idea of its content and shape, and have a play to see what is on offer. You can't do any harm! Let your mouse hover over the various icons, buttons and hotlinks to see what they do.
Main menu	
Introduction	
Week one	
Week two	
Week three	
Week four	
Resources	
Group conferences	Although the course starts formally on Monday with Week 1, feel free to announce your arrival earlier. To do so, click on 'Introduction' in the left-hand navigation bar. Read through until you come to 'Lesson 8 Arrivals' where you can post your first course message...
Blue group	
Red group	
Accessories	
Forum	
Chat	
Utilities	
Your Info	
Your Group	
⚇	David, Your e-convenor.

Figure 6.1 The menu for the e-moderating course and extract from the e-convenor's blog

Once logged on participants see a navigation bar on the left of an easy-to-use webpage together with a welcome message from the e-convenor's blog, explaining that the blog will be updated regularly pointing out useful discussions. Participants need help to find the best contributions once discussions build up and several are active. We direct participants to start by opening the 'Main Menu' to see what's in store for them and then to look through the 'Introduction'.

We do not explain what the 'Announcements' and 'Course WIKI' are about, as explanations are clear when they are opened.

Week one

When opening the main menu, participants find a brief paragraph about each part of the course (we are inducting our participants with the navigation, structure and content our of course!). Here are examples of the paragraphs for the Introduction and Week one.

The main menu gives a brief overview for participants to confirm they have joined the right course and provides a 'feel' of what they have let themselves in for. By displaying dates we may trigger participants' memories of their own timetables. Occasionally participants will let me know by email if they may have some clashes with trips away from their place of work and seek advice.

The Introduction menu provides access to basic information about the course, including the five-stage model diagram. We have several aims:

Introduction
Welcome to the course from Gilly Salmon, author of the recommended book 'E-moderating' and other useful bits of information.

Week one – Getting together (7th–13th June)
For your participants to become involved in any online course they first have to arrive into your online environment. Access can be difficult for some people.

Access makes demands on participants – of their technical ability and their motivation. Whatever the problem the e-moderator is expected to be able to solve it! Getting acquainted with the course, the e-moderator, and each other, takes a little time.

And, of course, there are those that can gain access easily and become impatient waiting for others to join in.

Figure 6.2 An early message

- to answer most of the questions that are likely to be asked at the start of the course;
- to get the participant familiar with the navigation method employed, without having to explain it;
- to draw the participant into positive action – posting a message – through the use of the arrivals e-tivity.

The first e-tivity enables the participants to become acquainted with posting a message on this platform, getting a response from the e-convenor for motivation purposes and from fellow participants – which is much more inspiring! They also start to read the messages from other participants. The Arrivals task doesn't require the participant to look for information anywhere and thus avoids delaying their responses.

The e-convenors role is to check that everyone who has enrolled has arrived and to provide a friendly environment for the initial postings. From feedback collected through end of course evaluations, we know that some participants see this process as a little trivial, but if necessary we point out that we are modelling ways they can work with their own students, who may be less confident or familiar with VLEs.

To this point, our participants are becoming inducted into the technical environment by using it, are able to read pages on the VLE and are gaining confidence in navigation. They are also being introduced to the course, the e-convenor and their fellow participants. We are modelling the first two stages of the five-stage model. We use several methods of navigation to offer immediate confidence to participants so they can focus on the course itself without niggling concerns about the online environment. Feedback on this stage results in participants reporting that the online environment and navigation is easy.

In the first week we aim to encourage communication, providing a discussion on motivation which helps to build skills at taking part in conferencing, familiarity with asynchronous discussion processes, the ability to make their own contributions and encouragement to the less experienced to join in. We also suggest that participants tackle one e-tivity per day and respond daily to the postings of their online group.

In addition, we actively encourage online interaction, team and trust building, by addressing a number of aspects of socialization; getting acquainted with the e-convenor, the VLE, the contents of the course and fellow participants.

For example, e-tivity 1 is called 'Getting acquainted with the e-convenor'. It demonstrates the importance of being able to post a private message and getting a quick response. It also gives an opportunity for participants to privately flag up any special concerns or needs.

Note here that we introduce without saying so, the special structure of the e-tivities (Salmon, 2002a). We introduce a 'spark to start the dialogue' (which could include a video, podcast or a graphic, but in this case doesn't!) from the purpose, task and response of the interactive activity. We undertake to model what our participants can immediately do with their own students – and they tell us that this works for them!

Figure 6.3 shows you an example of an e-tivity. Each e-tivity in the course (there are over 20) follows the same structure, as this makes for easy reading and avoids the confusion of using too many differing formats. We also use a variant of the e-tivity – a discussion which comprises a brief introduction to gain interest and the purpose (outcome) for the discussion.

Most participants explore their own experience and share personal insights and experiences. The e-convenor has the opportunity of sharing his or hers too – a little self-disclosure at this stage is levelling and good for trust building.

Getting acquainted with the e-convenor

Making it easy for participants to make contact encourages them to do so.

We have already made contact with you – through the course advertising material, the registration process and the simple message to tell you the URL for this course, your ID and password. We asked you for a straightforward contribution to 'Arrivals' as your first input and you have probably contributed and responded to other participants' contributions. Notice that some participants will arrive early and for those there is little to respond to; others arrive later and may be overwhelmed by the number of messages to read!

By now you will be getting an idea of how this course is structured. But there may be things you wish to tell the e-convenor but do not want to make them public. So here we offer an early opportunity to make personal contact. This in turn provides your e-convenor with an opportunity to reply and be supportive.

E-tivity 1.2

Purpose: to make contact with the e-convenor.

Task: Send me (David Shepherd – email david@atimod.com) a short message. You might like to say which of the competencies in the e-moderating book (or in Resources – accessible from the sidebar) you wish to focus on developing during this course. I'll aim to reply within 24 hours.

Now move on to *Lesson 3 – Getting acquainted with your fellow participants*

Figure 6.3 The e-tivity 'Getting acquainted with the e-convenor'

This week's discussion (to which you can contribute throughout the week) provides an opportunity to identify the problems of motivation that participants in online courses experience and how the e-moderator can help to overcome them.

This week's discussion: Motivation

Purpose: to discuss your own experiences online and how your motivation has been encouraged or not, and thus enable us to develop a valuable list of does and don'ts.

Figure 6.4 The first discussion

In the course described here the first week's e-tivities generate over 200 contributions. There was indication of strong motivation and socialization taking place.

At the end of each week we invite participants to reflect by articulating on the forum just what they have got out of taking part during the week. Their postings also provide opportunities for the e-convenor to reflect on how well they are doing and checking that everyone has completed on time.

By the end of week one

The e-moderating course is offered entirely asynchronously and is open 24/7. Towards the end of the first week participants are reminded via the e-convenor's blog of the continuous availability as a way of enabling latecomers to make their contributions.

Most participants are fully contributing by the end of week one. Where a group of people are taking part from one work-based location, we find they tend to log in less at weekends. We know that one participant who has not arrived and is not contributing by the end of week one is unlikely to arrive at all, and in any case would not be fully absorbed.

During this 'getting comfortable and meeting others' period, we do not know what else is going on in the participants' worlds – they may be experiencing distractions at work, at home, or with their families. Over time, always take a non-judgemental approach to chasing them!

We are sensitive to the participants' situations even though we don't know what they are. Some participants would like to see pictures of their fellow students as they claim it helps them to get to know them quicker. Some participants do not wish to post their pictures, others will post a picture of a celebrity! We don't think that a picture is important since we feel that we want them to engage with words.

By the end of the first week all participants have gained access and are visibly motivated, but are rarely reported feeling 'stretched'. There are varying levels of their engagement with others, which is a process that continues throughout the course.

Week two

In week two we step up a gear and are more demanding of our participants; we move on from encouraging participants to engage and making them comfortable. The e-tivities demand more of them and this is matched by my giving constructive feedback on their contributions. I continue to model the three skills of encouraging, summarizing and weaving.

I also gently start to give feedback. During week two typical examples include:

- commenting on the length of contributions (those with too many points will be less likely to get responses);
- commenting on inappropriate use of language;
- for participants whose English is less developed, I encourage them by saying that if I can understand them, their English is good enough!
- insisting on motivating (or at least informative) titles including simply not allowing 'Re:re:re';
- encouraging feedback to fellow participants.

During week two we focus on Stage 3 – information exchange. Here is a typical e-tivity (see Figure 6.5).

The information exchange e-tivity has the added purpose of providing material for the summarizing and weaving e-tivities later in the week.

We also run, in parallel, a discussion about time (by now most participants recognize there are challenging issues for interaction with the use of asynchrous time for learning and development). They are learning about the challenge of time for themselves by taking part – the expectation for many before taking this course is that online courses can be fitted in 'when doing their emails'.

One online task (e-tivity) that has stayed with us from our Open University days (see Chapter 5) is the problem of the angry student who finds himself as a sole contributor to discussions. Participants are invited to respond to an example.

Responses tend to default into two categories:

- Encouragement through direct persuasion in a personal email to the angry student.
- Encouragement through direct persuasion in a forum posting to the non-participants.

How to exchange information

Purpose: to initiate and encourage the exchange of information.

Task: Post a message in *E-tivity 2.2 – How to exchange information* asking for some information (and be prepared to give some information to others in the group who will be doing the same) about any topic that you find relevant. Make sure that you create a new thread, thus providing the structure for others to respond.

Respond: to any topic that attracts you, first as if you were a participant in a group led by the writer of the message, second (in the same message), comment on why you were enticed to respond and where appropriate how it might be improved.

You may need to visit the conference several times during this e-tivity.

Success will be achieved if you are given some information that you didn't know before.

Figure 6.5 'How to exchange information' e-tivity

These solutions provide opportunities for the e-moderator to explore the many reasons that could lie behind this apparently easy to address problem. This e-tivity is an excellent example of the simply described situation providing a great deal of interactive learning.

We use areas of the discussion in the forum, where the e-convenor has not yet undertaken weaving or summarizing, to enable participants to carry out these skills for themselves – we know that practice is very important.

In giving feedback on their efforts, I revert a little to being a tutor by responding constructively to participants' summaries and weaves, suggesting imaginative approaches about how to get discussions flowing. I post feedback immediately after the first two participants have posted their efforts so that others will learn before they respond to the e-tivity. This is a great way of building group learning by seeing not only the efforts of others but also the e-convenor's comments.

Week three

For week three, we again move up another gear, directing addressing e-moderator development skills for Stage 4 of the model: knowledge construction. We offer a group activity that reveals the challenges of un-moderated groups, and an opportunity to design a simple e-tivity. These e-tivities serve to illustrate, the continuing need for good personal organization, use of time and the need for clearly set out processes (see *E-tivities*, Salmon, 2002a for more).

Group activities are complex for any group at Stage 4 of the model. Groups need very clear planned processes and e-moderation to be able to successfully undertake productive knowledge construction. We draw participants' attention to the skills that they need to employ and remind them that they have been developing them over the first two weeks. We offer a simple step-by-step process they can follow to build a practical working activity (Jacques and Salmon, 2007).

Getting the balance between enough information to carry out the activity and overloading with too much detail is quite a challenge. We constantly make the knowledge construction processes easier to comprehend so that participants can concentrate on understanding how groups can work. We also offer the important taster for designing an e-tivity for this stage, and often participants choose to undertake our later three-week e-tivity course for much more practice.

Week four

By week four, most groups of participants have built up around 600 messages. Their messages are all available to them to view, which serves as a record of their achievements and visibly shows them their progress in developing skills – over three short weeks! It seems to be a waste if this superb record is not put to use.

This week is about self-assessment and developing plans to follow after the course has ended.

Here are two – the first focusing on inputs and the second on outcomes (see Figure 6.6).

In the following posting we can see how the group comes to the aid of a participant who they feels she has been a little hard on herself, demonstrating the skills of encouraging that had been developed over the four weeks of the course.

Self Assessment – Marie Howard – Fri, 2 Jul 2010, 14:26

My assessment – I think that I have done really badly on the quantity of participation . . . I think that I am quite snappy in the length of the postings. I did get some reaction from my postings but I think this is just because you are all really kind. . .

E-tivity 4.3 Developing participant skills

Purpose: to encourage group process development.

Task: Reflect on this week's discussion, or that of any other week, and comment on the skills that you have seen used. What did you see that contributed to the discussion and what do you suggest to improve its success?

Respond: by identifying any lessons you've drawn that you'd wish to pass on to a beginning e-moderator.

E-tivity 4.4 Assess your own contributions

Purpose: to assess your own contributions.

Task: Look through the contributions you have made throughout this course, apply some of the criteria. Draw some conclusions about the effect of the contributions you have made and post them in the forum for others to consider.

Respond: by reading through fellow participants' contributions and identifying the key skills you would wish to pass on to your own participants.

Figure 6.6 'Assessing' and 'developing' e-tivities

I think that being really clear is important for the participant and for the e-moderator – there is just a few words and sentences available to convey the entire message – not like face-to-face where you can paraphrase again and again . . . The thing with online communication is that you read and respond really quickly and it could be that sometimes you get it wrong!!

Re: Self Assesment/online communication more time to think. . . – Alex Cable – Fri, 2 Jul 2010, 18:04

Marie,

I do not think that 'The thing with online communication is that you read and respond really quickly and it could be that sometimes you get it wrong!!'

Maybe I did not understand what you try to say. But I think that with online communication we have much more time to think and answer.

Alex

Self Assesment/online communication more time to think. . . – Marie Howard – Fri, 2 Jul 2010, 23:57

Maybe I should have said you have less information to respond to and this can impact the output.

Self Assesment/online communication more time to think. . . – Jane Smyth – Fri, 2 Jul 2010, 19:48

Hi Marie,
   I agree with Alex that I think that generally you can have more time online to think about how you wish to respond or what you want to write, but of course it depends whether time is really tight and you just want to get it done (which I've found myself at times)!
   Also, I think you're being hard on yourself! I've found many of your postings insightful and useful – and I'm not just being kind!

Self Assesment/online communication more time to think. . . – David Shepherd (Course Director) – Sat, 3 Jul 2010, 21:45

I agree with Jane, your postings have been thoughtful and very useful. You have stimulated my own thinking about 'managing' communities.
   I hope we can maintain contact.
   David

Re: Self Assesment/online communication more time to think. . . – Marie Howard – Sun, 4 Jul 2010, 01:37

Thank you David – yes I think that it is a really interesting parallel in the community forums space that is still in developing stages. Yes I look forward to talking to you more about this area of work and perhaps working together on developments. I will keep you updated.
   Marie

And after taking the opportunity to assess their own progress, we then invite participants to develop a plan. After due reflection some opt for further practice, some for getting "stuck in" and others for more knowledge.

When the course is over I review what I have done. Figure 6.7 shows what happened in my example course. First the activity levels of the nine participants are provided and then how they compare against my own.

Activity	Total postings	Of which – My postings	Average number postings per participant	My postings as a % of total	Number of my postings giving feedback to individuals on their weaves, e-tivity design and development plan
Arrivals	46	12	4	26	
Week one	161	26	15	16	
Week two	195	35	16	17	9
Week three	147	18	15	12	9
Week four	171	22	16	13	9
Totals	720	113	66	16	27

Figure 6.7 Activity on one e-moderating development course (June–July 2010)

Additionally I responded to 24 emails and posted nine blog entries. Figure 6.7 is fairly typical of activity levels of the All Things in Moderation Ltd. courses.

The design of each e-tivity encourages two postings per participant, with 25 e-tivities this would suggest that the nine participants on this course could be expected to post ($9 \times 2 \times 25$) messages = 450. With encouragement and feedback from the e-convenor some 607 (720 − 113) messages were posted, approximately 30 per cent more than the original estimate.

The volume of the e-convenor's postings declines over the four weeks of the course. As participants gather confidence they are encouraged more by the responses of their fellow participants and the e-convenor can focus on giving specific individual feedback.

Early activity by the e-moderator aims at encouraging participation. Much of the later activity by the e-convenor is focused on giving specific feedback on participants' weaves, e-tivity designs and development plans. This shows that the volume of e-moderator intervention drops significantly as confidence increases within the participants. Much of my activity is:

- reading every post;
- deciding whether to intervene;
- only choosing to do so if my interventions add to participant learning.

This facilitative approach provides the space and time for participants to respond to each other. Any significant points that are missed can be picked up by adding to a summary. But the e-moderator should not remain silent as this is noticed in an environment where much motivation is derived from participants getting a response to their postings. I maintain a presence by using the blog facility.

The success of a course is achieved by a combination of course design and skilled e-convening. The design provides the context for discussions and activity relieving the e-convenor of the task of working out what to do next, so that s/he can focus their expertise on the specific needs of the individual participants or the group process. The bonus of increased communication between participants brings added learning within the course. We observe that a greater level of interaction occurs than in similar available in face-to-face situations – where the conversation moves quickly on and many contributions forming in the heads of participants never get an airing.

We'll leave the last word to the participants on this course

Stage 1 participant comments
I need to learn about how to motivate participants more. I think this comes with experience though, and learning new tactics.

Accessing the system regularly is critical – it helps to keep focused on the course. Motivating participants and retaining their attention is fundamental.

I am reluctant to say 'extremely well-covered' because the course has uncovered the need for much more practice on my behalf! This is a reflection on my level of skill, not the course. The course very clearly allowed us to explore this and learn about all sorts of tips and techniques. A question I should post is, does the moderator have a check list that, if not covered by the participants, is elicited in some way?

Stage 2 participant comments
I need to better plan my time when online. Sometimes it is very easy to spend too much time but not using it effectively.

Time management – making a conscious effort to go online regularly is so important. If you do not keep the socialisation going on a regular basis, encouraging comments, feedback – I would easily see how you could fade away from the course.

Stage 3 participant comments
Information Exchange was an extremely good skill to learn on this course and it was great to see how others did it also

Stage 4 participant comments
I would feel competent on the opening – but the weaving and closing I am not so sure about.

Feel I need more practice with opening, weaving and closing skills – especially weaving.

I think continuous practice on the course will help me to develop these skills.

Stage 5 participant comments
Great skills to be able to learn on this course and I learnt a lot from the contributions of others.

It is important for me to continue to develop my skills as an e-moderator so that I can enable the development of participants.

I think further development or confidence will come from positive feedback from participants on my courses.

Yes, I will mirror until I feel the confidence to take the stabilisers off, if you know what I mean.

Chapter 7

Learning experiences

The continuous and radical changes underway are a result not only of the widespread diffusion of technologies but, most importantly, also of the changes in the way learners arrive at knowing something and learn using tools, relationships and interactions. Frequently, participants' expectations of online learning are high, but some become disillusioned and disengaged. As more students are taught, with fewer resources, their expectations of online continue to rise. In addition, participants in online programmes are becoming ever more diverse, in terms of their ages, backgrounds, locations and needs

Daniel, Kanwar and Uvalić-Trumbić (2008) undertook a meta-analysis of 600 papers on distance education. To summarize, although students asked for more contact with their teachers, the actual impact on their performance was increased as a result of fostering interaction between peers. For me, I continue to be driven by the critical importance of the engagement with others in all types of online environments to move towards not only quality learning, not just quality enhancement, but also new ideas and achievements.

E-moderators could fall into the trap of thinking of online as one experience, whereas each participant can and will respond according to his or her individual needs. In this chapter I explore, with case studies and examples, the needs of special groups such as novices to computing and people with disabilities as well as attempting to explain some behaviours such as 'lurking'.

The relatively few 'early adopters' are likely to tolerate technology that does not always work and be willing to take risks – they will believe that the benefits outweigh the difficulties (Norman, 2010). However, most participants fall into the 95 per cent category of late or later adopters of the technology. These people will be pragmatic and realistic, looking for convenience and reliability, and their tolerance will be low. Most will not want their learning to be disrupted. Would you?

Even where organizations have had online learning environments for years, few students start to learn online with much experience of communicating with each other and their tutors through computers. Training for e-moderators and some form of scaffolding for learning online are important for students.

Even those participants who are very familiar and comfortable with e-mail need some support in understanding the collaborative and collegiate environments offered by conferencing. Some students need help with appreciating the shift in the teaching and learning approach that accompanies increased use of online. In Stage 1 in the five-stage model there is a strong element of deferred gratification. Skills that are promoted and developed through online working may well be important study and work skills for the future. Participants need to become literate in online communication: this is going back to writing and reading, involving extensive use of typed text. They need to develop new skills of acquiring and managing information and knowledge obtained in the online environment – and applied elsewhere. Learners need the ability to select items from masses of data to inform their judgements. They need to learn flexibility in using varied resources. They need to function in global communities. They need to maintain their motivation without constantly meeting in learning groups, and without encountering the professor in the corridor. While induction into online working will not meet all these needs at a stroke, it can lay the foundation for the development of such skills.

In learning computing skills, two main types of knowledge are needed: 'declarative knowledge' or 'facts' (e.g. what icons exist on the screen), and 'procedural knowledge' (e.g. how to undertake tasks with the keyboard or mouse). In learning to undertake a series of tasks, learners need to memorize basic sequences and gradually build up associations with prior knowledge before starting to undertake these procedures almost automatically, as they do when driving a vehicle. Then they can hope to benefit from online networking's collaborative learning potential.

It's rarely necessary to undertake separate induction to the online environment – this can send the wrong message about the learning addressing computing skills! It's better to design and deliver for the gradual emergence of skills and then move towards competency. In this way you can take account of the need of online novices to learn the skills and procedures of the software, and how to operate online successfully and productively. This process requires a stage to be undertaken *online* and integrated with interaction and knowledge-based tasks rather than through more traditional teaching or training.

Perhaps even more challenging is the complexity of working online. Designing and delivering e-learning is an increasingly complex and inclusive area of activity. Conceptions of learning have become much more sophisticated and diverse, and learners have greater involvement in shaping the learning environment.

Learning approaches

All e-moderators need to develop a clear sense of their 'audience', as well as the purposes of groups whose work they are facilitating in the online environment. When e-moderating online, it is easy to have a standard image in your mind of 'the students', but the best e-moderators obtain a sense of the composite needs of the group, along with those of a variety of individuals.

Online learning needs to be tailored to appeal to all approaches (and to preferences changing as a result of experiences) to avoid the need for offering a hugely expensive variety of learning materials and methods. In face-to-face groups, most communication involves talking and listening, so those students who learn aurally are well accommodated. However, at present, most online platforms operate mostly through reading and writing. It is likely therefore that online conferencing will appeal to those more comfortable with the written word. This places at a disadvantage those for whom writing (or typing) is a problem, or who are working in something other than their first language. Students working online who are using English, but not as their first language, may prefer to read and compose offline and take their time. They also need reassurance that minor mistakes are made by everyone in conference messages and so long as the sense is clear, these are unimportant.

E-moderators need to keep these various preferences and their dynamics in mind and plan their work accordingly. In particular, a clear mixture of engagement in immediately relevant activities and the opportunity to reflect on messages and contribute some are both important. Activities can either be entirely online, begun face-to-face and extended online, or prepared for online and continued face-to-face. An array of tasks can be provided and groups can be split into smaller learning sets. Such variations are likely to meet a wide variety of learning styles and preferences. Most importantly, scaffolding engagement with the learning materials and with the group is most likely to result in full engagement and completion for all types of participants (Hmelo-Silver, Duncan and Chinn, 2006).

Widening access

Many educational organizations (and indeed their governments) hope that online offers a new approach and a widening of access to non-traditional customers and clients. Many teachers have had the vision that online courses will empower individuals and groups. Students used to encountering passive learning methods such as lectures may display resentment of the substantial cognitive energy required for involvement in networked learning. However, we can observe many millions of people on the web learning informally from and with others, teaching themselves the technology with minimal training. Professor Sugata Mitra's work certainly shows that kids can self-teach in groups to a remarkable extent, given free access to a networked computer (see, for example, Mitra, 2010). We need to capture and tap into such motivations.

Assessment and feedback processes

Formative and summative assessment and feedback deeply affect the quality of student–teacher interaction. There is no doubt about it: assessment and feedback are critical drivers of student learning, and their satisfaction. Undertaking assessment is hugely demanding in terms of staff time and resources. Throughout this book you will by now have noticed the emphasis on interaction between people including the e-moderator, and, critically, the e-moderators' responsibility for setting up conferences so that feedback is easy, quick and effective. That's a great start, don't you think?

To be clear – assessing students' learning that took place fully or partly online is not radically different from assessing learning through any other mode. The same principles apply – a constructive alignment between the learning and authenticity about what is assessed is the key to fairness and effectiveness (Macdonald, 2003). Students inevitably benefit from the building up of assessment through assignments, in the same way as their confidence and abilities grow through scaffolded tasks and interaction (Armellini and Aiyegbayo, 2010).

After participants start to build their confidence in working together through the online conferences, all kinds of potential for giving and receiving feedback emerges. Nicol (2007) insists that students can thus be empowered towards self-assessment and self-regulation. Formative assessment needs participants to develop these skills.

E-moderators can look to build on participants' ability to give and receive effective feedback and become more self-supporting rather than always provide expert feedback themselves (Nicol, 2007). The principles from the REAP project are pertinent to working through online mediation and highly relevant to scaffolding and the five-stage model approach. I reproduce them here for convenience but do urge you to look through the resources on the REAP website.

Assessment design should:

'empower'
Engage students actively in identifying or formulating criteria
Facilitate opportunities for self-assessment and reflection
Deliver feedback that helps students self-correct
Provide opportunities for feedback dialogue (peer and tutor-student)
Encourage positive motivational beliefs and self-esteem
Provide opportunities to apply what is learned in new tasks
Yield information that teachers can use to help shape teaching.

'engage'
Capture sufficient study time and effort in and out of class
Distribute students' effort evenly across topics and weeks
Engage students in deep not just shallow learning activity
Communicates clear and high expectations to students.

(www.reap.ac.uk)

Michael Bromby, a Reader in Law at Glasgow Caledonian University, takes an innovative approach to integrating work on Problem Based Learning (PBL) (Bromby, 2009) through asynchronous discussion boards, with assessment of his students' achievements and feedback to them from the tutors.

Students were divided into independent groups of six to seven to work collaboratively on a problem scenario, each group using a private discussion board on the institution's VLE, Blackboard.

Within each group, one participant was nominated as having feedback responsibilities to the other groups – the role circulated among group members each week to allow all students to play it at least once. This inter-group communication took place in an additional open access discussion board that could be viewed by all students within the cohort.

Students can gain 10 per cent of the module mark through their contribution to discussions over the entire session and a further 10 per cent for the quality of their work in producing a summary report for one allocated week.

The summary report was designed to share the group findings and reduce the need for tutors as e-moderators to indicate plausible alternative pathways that each group could have explored. It encouraged the independent, self-directed, enquiry-based approach that PBL attempts to promote. Indeed, feedback showed that most students read this feedback, with benefit. One student said:

I was surprised to find that the scenario summaries were not all identical and people from different groups had come up with points our group had failed to consider. It allowed me to widen my knowledge.

During the week's discussion, the tutor as e-moderator was able to give feedback, usually in private, to individuals, particularly if discussions were going off-track or contained significant factual errors. The tutor could also advise the entire group (usually regarding their collective direction, questions and responses) in the open access forum for posting summaries, and in the forum could even advise the entire cohort, generally in response to the range of opinions and decisions in the summaries. As the feedback from the tutor was in the written form on the discussion boards, rather than verbal feedback in a classroom situation, students felt more able to reflect and respond to the tutor's feedback with further comments or questions.

Thus feedback was used collectively: the shared summaries allowed students to take control of their own learning, produce reports that were read by their peers and build a community of shared learning.

I've been working with partner institutions in different legal jurisdictions (such as Australia, USA, England, South Africa) to broaden students' considerations of the PBL problem scenarios by involving students from other countries where their legal system may pose different problems or indeed solutions.

For the foreseeable future, most participants will want to achieve qualifications, accreditation or awards, so more formal assessment in some form or other will be necessary. Most learners crave teachers' responses to their coursework and their examinations. Learners see the quality and quantity of feedback on their work as an important part of their relationships with their professors and educational provider. Where the use of online is integral to a course or programme, the assessment should reflect the skills participants are using and developing to learn (Macdonald, Weller and Mason, 2002; Weller, 2002a).

I do not recommend that you try to 'drive' online discussion from or to assessment too directly. If you are using the five-stage model you will find that directly contriving activity to 'force' participation adds almost no value and may be detrimental. However, the more context-sensitive, authentic, relevant, applicable, engaging assessment assignments can be, the more aligned they become with the learning (Reushle and Mitchell, 2009; Reeves, Herrington and Oliver, 2002). For example, working online lends itself especially to collaboration and/or tasks and presentations such as exhibitions and portfolios and to problem-based inquiries and action research. When providing cases, illustrations and examples to be used in assignments, it's important to represent the context in the way that the knowledge will be used in the real world. It is also excellent practice to encourage participants to quote each other's messages with careful attribution in assignments.

As you have seen throughout this book, the use of e-moderated online learning directly addresses the broadening acceptance and understanding of learning as a socially mediated and constructed process (Billet, 2009 a, b; Woo and Reeves, 2007) and of knowledge as personal and not 'fixed'.

Reflection on practice has been the focus of important research into learning and has come once again to the fore with the opportunities offered by asynchronous conferencing. The results from such studies reveal a degree of convergence: that good online discussions foster effective collaborative learning and deep reflection if suitably structured and e-moderated (Ellis, Goodyear, O'Hara and Prosser, 2007).

To date, some assessment procedures are still based on the transmission model of information. This means that unless issues of evaluation and assessment are tackled as the use of online for learning continues to increase, the gap between how students learn and how they are assessed may widen. Some students already comment on the irony of spending most of their learning time communicating through their computer, but taking their examination in a formal setting with only a pen and paper for company. As e-moderators become more comfortable with their online teaching roles, they will start to look closely at online assessment and evaluation, and will not wish their time and their students' time to be constrained by old assessment methods. Highly networked organizations such as professional associations are already waking up to the huge potential of 'any time, any place' assessment.

You may want to try assessing at each stage of the five-stage model to see whether the learning and development of your participants are showing progress. This kind of assessment has been tried at Caledonian Business School:

We see several pockets of developing assessment practice based on sound constructivist approaches and utilizing research-based models. Where module teams attempt explicit implementation of the five-stage model of online learning, they often then wish to assess along similar lines. For example, in one honours marketing module students are allocated 20 per cent of their coursework mark for their ability to facilitate, as well as contribute to, online discussions on each other's seminar papers. The assessment criteria issued to students show the clear influence of the model:

Assessment criteria:

1. Motivation and online socialization skills demonstrated through regular and frequent contributions.
2. Knowledge and understanding demonstrated through sharing of relevant information.

3. Ability to draw out, compare and reflect on applications of knowledge in a variety of contexts, demonstrated by the quality of message contributions.
4. Ability to evaluate and synthesize others' contributions on the discussion board, and post messages accordingly, hence demonstrating personal development and learning.

Gillian Roberts

Online learning offers more opportunities for students to write for themselves to benefit their own learning and also for each other (rather than 'writing for the tutor'). Through networking students can make their writing easily available for review and assessment. As a start, suggest to participants that they should use conference messages in their assignments and that they will be given credit for their ability to use and integrate messages in their work. You might like to try a peer review process of students' written work, even if their essays, assignments or exercises are afterwards handed in for marking by a teacher or assessor. If you try such a process, ensure that the criteria for judgements are made explicit from the start and based on learning outcomes. Digital portfolios can be tools for both learning and assessment although many academics are still trying to work out whether they truly add to learning – or maybe it's a challenge associated with learning design (Lopez-Fernandez and Rodriguez-Illera, 2008; Tochel, Haig, Hesketh, Cadzow, Beggs, Colthart and Peacock, 2009).

More universities are innovating in online assessment, usually based on campus networks using commercial software. Several pioneers have addressed important concerns (Badge and Scott, 2009). These include issues of access and security, plagiarism and cheating (is this work really my student's?), the time and costs of setting up (efficiency gains), dealing with bias, fairness and anxiety, and test design and implementation of systems. It is likely that students, as customers, will drive this sensitive but important area further towards online provision in the future. A corollary will be the need for the valid assessment of the performance of large numbers of learners at low cost.

Most higher educational organizations use some form of electronic plagiarism detection as feedback to e-moderators and participants. It's a good idea to have some discussion around these in the conference to ensure that students understand the concept of plagiarism and that the monitoring software can give feedback and improve assignments (Badge and Scott, 2009; Gullifer and Tyson, 2010).

Disability awareness for e-moderators

From the early days, it was clear that online messages appear to others as an individual's thoughts, without them knowing much at all about the writer's age, race, appearance, gender and disability. Participants with a disability appreciate that they can go online at more or less any time and in any place, obviating the need for travel and physical access. Instead, they are valued for their thoughts and contributions. The challenge for e-moderators is to be aware of the issues involved.

In the spirit of wide diversity and empowerment, it is good that online participants with additional needs are not usually obvious. It is normally impossible to tell from the messages in a conference that a participant or an e-moderator has restricted vision, hearing or mobility, unless that person wishes to write about it. People who have problems with their speech or hearing are not at a disadvantage in text-based messaging. Those who have problems with their vision or physical movement may well find that the keyboard and screen prevent them from doing as much as they would like. Dyslexic participants sometimes still have some difficulties online, even when using assistive technologies. However, it's best if the e-moderator knows about any special challenges that a participant has, since it often impacts on their participation.

Blind and visually impaired participants

Whereas many people with vision problems can learn to touch-type, they usually have problems in reading the screen. Windows software, for example, often requires precise placing of the mouse, even when keyboard commands are used wherever possible. An electronic screen-reader, which reads the text aloud at a steady pace and in a computer-generated voice, is valuable when long sections of text are onscreen, but sometimes of little help when there is a diagram. The same is true of speech recognition software (such as Dragon Dictate) that enables messages to be spoken, then converted into text by the computer. Recorded instructions may help, but it is sometimes difficult to navigate between sections or paragraphs.

Consideration of fonts used is also important, as some blind participants may find certain fonts problematic to read, such as italicized or decorative texts. Ariel or Comic Sans are usually considered to be the most straightforward fonts for most readers, including those with a disability such as dyslexia.

You will also need to ensure that any graphics or visuals are clearly labelled, as the user may not be able to see them clearly.

Physically disabled participants

Participants who cannot freely move their hands and arms find that they cannot use the keyboard at a reasonable speed, even when the stiffness of the keys has been varied to suit. Speech recognition software may be better or text prediction software that enables them to select whole words after the first few letters have been typed in. Exceptionally, participants may need single-switch devices to control modified computers and their peripherals.

Some physically disabled participants may use specialized ergonomic keyboards, which may be designed for single-handed use or with large keys for those with poor muscle control.

Dyslexic participants

Spelling and grammar checkers can be very helpful to dyslexic participants, particularly if their dyslexia is severe enough to put off non-dyslexic conference participants. The odd spelling or grammatical error worries nobody, but some participants will not be confident about making major errors online. Some dyslexic participants will prefer to produce their text using an assistive technology package, and then load their comments onto the blog or discussion pages. They will also find simple, clear fonts preferable to anything that is brightly coloured or has flashing images or text. A glossary of common terms being used during the conference may also be particularly helpful for this group of participants – this could be made available as a text file.

Good practice for dyslexic participants will also benefit any overseas visitors who may not be confident in their use of written English.

Assistive technologies

You need to have some awareness of the assistive technologies that participants may be using to support their online learning. The diversity of conditions and disabilities and the range of technologies that are available to support learning are too huge an area for an e-moderator to master in a short period of time. But you can personalize the experience and direct the participants to seek appropriate advice and help. When you become aware that a participant has a disability challenge, try to find out how well the software or platform used for learning works for them. For example, a participant with a visual impairment might be using a piece of software to enlarge the size of fonts on their screen. The question for the e-moderator is does the discussion threads in a discussion forum respond appropriately to the software that the learner uses to enlarge the screen.

More on visual challenges

A visually impaired tutor took part in the Open University Business School online e-moderator training (see Chapter 5) and appeared on my first list of lurkers that I followed up by telephone. I discovered he was waiting for special software to be installed and was meanwhile having the messages read to him.

He soon secured software that produced an audio version of them and took part later in the training with very few problems. He proved to be an effective and active e-moderator on OUBS conferences. The learning point for me here was that I should not assume lurking necessarily meant laziness – participating might take longer for some people with visual impairment, but they can still gain and contribute.

Blind participants can adapt online software through Braille printouts of messages or through using speech synthesis. They cannot use a mouse so need to become adept at keyboard commands. An experienced intermediary is needed to train and support blind participants to the point of competence and independence. When changes are made to the system, blind participants must be notified early so that they can arrange for specific adaptations and training, in advance. Manuals and instructions need to be recorded onto audio by experienced readers able to describe in words items such as flow charts, diagrams and the like.

In constructing conferences, consider the font and style and how they might look on a variety of screens, in different browsers and to different people. This will help those with partial visual impairment, but will also be of benefit to all participants.

More on hearing challenges

A deaf colleague wrote to me on e-mail of his encounters with online networking:

> Conferencing was for me a hugely liberating experience. I started working in industry in 1973, when the 'managerial communications' model was through using the telephone. My then MD was someone of good heart and intentions who thought I would never be able to 'be a manager' because I was excluded from the information community of the company. Not his terms but that's what he meant. So I was placed into special projects, away in an alcove, where I could work on my own.
>
> I arrived at the OU in 1986 just as the CoSy conferencing system was getting implemented. It was a secret known to a few – I heard about it by grapevine over the photocopier. I joined and nothing was the same again.
>
> Liberation came for me in several linked forms. First was the sense of 'connectedness' – the world expanded beyond my desk. I didn't have to get up and physically see someone in order to make contact. The relief from a sense of embattled isolation was immense. Second was the

increased meaning in communications because I could find out more about the context of what was going on. Not just answer a specific question but get a sense of why some things were seen as problems or opportunities. That meant having a 'relatively' relaxed sense of the 'social' or off-topic communications that frame the on-topic discussions. This is quite important in giving a sense of communicative competence.

Third is another aspect of communicative competence. The ability to 'say'. This can be difficult for deaf people as communication face-to-face needs an awareness of the social turn-taking codes of communications and these can be very subtle. Hesitate and you are excluded. So conferencing can unleash the power of 'speech' for a deaf person. It did a lot for my confidence in other situations too.

Here is where an e-moderator can play a part, by fostering an appropriate online communication code so that all can find a way to take turns.

A factor that didn't apply for me but does for other deaf people (especially for those whose first language is signing) is that literacy can be a problem. English can be very much the second language for some people and written English a particular trial. So conferencing isn't necessarily a panacea for the deaf . . . Maybe some awareness by e-moderators of strange and sudden pitfalls with written language can help.

Finally conferencing – and associated e-mail facilities – put the initiative with a deaf person. Not being dependent on others to initiate or negotiate contacts is once again a liberating experience. Freedom can be rather frightening, so for me the e-moderator's role in creating 'safe spaces' is very important (1999).

My piece was of course written before the great explosion of communication pathways and in the age of blogs, facebook, Twitter, Blackberry, iPhone and Youtube I would not now use the term 'conferencing' as shorthand for the totality of the experiences I talk about.

I suspect that part of the response would parallel the comments of Tim Harford ('The Undercover Economist') on the claims that new communication technologies encourage more dispersed work patterns and will lead to the downgrading of urban centres. Harford says that a key feature of the new communication possibilities is to make it easier and more productive to have face-to-face meetings, so people who live in concentrated population areas still have an advantage. So while the communication revolution has empowered many people it has empowered even more those who had advantages in the old order of things.

If so this still leaves a lot of work for moderators of 'conferences' – for people learning at a distance who still have to put in an effort to reproduce the added value people get from face-to-face interactions in (say) a campus based university population.

I also have comments on the barriers a deaf person has seen erected to easy communication over the last decade or so such as increased use of video and audio clips on website and blog pages for example.

(Bevan, originally written 1999, updated May 2010)

Of course if you choose to use some voice conferences or podcasting (see Chapter 3), you'll need to transcribe voice into text if anyone needs it.

Claudine SchWeber of the University of Maryland University College, outside Washington, DC, who has experience of e-moderating in innovative ways, sees e-moderating as 'guiding a discussion and fostering interaction among students rather than between students and instructors'. This can be a challenge, because as Dr SchWeber points out, the tendency in a question and answer session online, much like some onsite classes, is for the students to respond to the instructor rather than to each other.

University of Maryland University College case study

The Maryland experience suggests the importance of purposeful and explorative nature of collaborative working online. The best activity was through an online case analysis where students commented, reacted and referred to each other's work. This case study shows how potentially contentious and emotive issues can be surfaced and explored productively online through supportive groups.

The key e-moderating activity in this example was setting up appropriate and challenging questions to ask online and the gradual sequencing and release of appropriate material. The case dealt with an engineering company's branch located in the West Indies, far away from the headquarters somewhere in Europe. It involved issues of management and supervision, superior and subordinate relations, race, age, perception, organizational culture, feedback, trust, diversity, new and experienced staff, home country and expatriate relations – and a surprise ending. What a great way of gradually introducing material into an asynchronous environment! They started out with four guiding questions on which students were asked to comment by a given date:

1. What are the perceptual issues? How did these impact the situation and affect the outcome?
2. What are the cultural/diversity issues? How did these affect the relationship between B and R, and R to the rest of the unit?
3. What are the performance appraisal and retention issues? What motivational and job satisfaction issues played a role here? How might B have handled the situation if he knew about relevant management theory?
4. What are the trust, communication, and feedback issues here? What strategies did the men ignore? What might have been done? Then, the question that brought it home: assume Y has been fired and you have been brought in to replace him. What might you do in the next two weeks? Why?

Even before the due date, the class became intensively involved in the questions and in what they might do as a replacement for Y. Some of the students were originally from countries outside of the United States and from ethnic and racial minorities. Their reaction to the expatriates and locals situation in the case was intense, highly engaged and from their personal perspective, as these excerpts show:

Trust was an issue from the very beginning. As I am a (member of) minority myself, I am glad that X left the company. I wish he had done it sooner. I did see it coming though. What gives anyone the right to imply that they know a race of people without ever walking in that race's shoes?

Our views, while similar in affront (for the most part), differ when it comes to agreeing with R's decision. Under the circumstances it would be difficult not to share his anger. I still believe, however, that he blew it.

On your question 'What gives anyone the right to imply that they know a race of people without ever walking in that race shoes' – how do you feel about X's written comments 'bashing' (others)? And, you made several comments about the expatriates, suggesting they all behaved like Y. The case study gives no evidence of this.

The online discussion, commentary, reaction and referrals went on for about a week, as those who joined in later got involved in some section of the comments. Dr SchWeber pointed out that this had never, ever occurred in a face-to-face class; not with the same intensity, not with that frequency of response to each other (several people made several comments), not in the students' willingness to disagree (as noted above) on controversial topics such as race, nor in their apparent ability to look at the conceptual issues and the theory that might apply.

One dramatic difference from the face-to-face class was that there was an ongoing transcript, so students could join in at any point and comment on points made earlier (which they did), or refer to each other's recommendations. For example, one student said, 'A's recommendation to hire J as a consultant is a good point because. . .'. That kept the dialogue going, somewhat like a ball on an elastic that keeps bouncing back in and going out again. Dr SchWeber eventually met the students and when the case was brought up, everyone was much more subdued and discussion did not take much time. Faculty colleagues who looked in later on the discussion said that they had never seen such a fine and thorough discussion of this particular case.

Gender and e-moderating

Access by women to networked computers has reached a similar level to that by men. Others are concerned that online discussions may be dominated in some of the same ways that occur in face-to-face groups. E-moderators should always focus on individuals' contributions to conferences, rather than their offline gender or identity.

I have not found very much evidence or huge differences in the published literature on gender and retention or achievement in e-learning environments, nor had any serious difficulties with gender differences in my own courses. Maybe it's not being studied or maybe it's not there! There is some evidence that women respond particularly well to structured internet environments (Chuang, Hawng and Tsai, 2008 and also see the interesting example of the use of Facebook by Arabic students in Shen and Khalifa, 2009).

For e-moderators, it is important to be sensitive to any individual or group that appears to be disadvantaged or not participating online. While it is difficult to police harassment and inappropriate behaviour on public listservers and the like, these cannot be allowed in any kind of educational environment. Harassment of any kind online must be stopped immediately, as it is on campuses and in corporate environments, to ensure equality of learning opportunity for all. In particular, e-moderators should regularly consider the tone of their messages and their online behaviour (and be open to monitoring from their peers), to ensure that no exploitation of their more powerful position occurs, even inadvertently.

In addition, personal communication style has an impact. This exchange, from an e-moderating training course, shows that sensitivity in communication is always needed.

Hi Lurkerperson.

I hope this finds you well. I'm sorry we haven't heard from you yet. We really would welcome your contribution to the discussions that are taking place. Don't you think that it's a little unfair that other students are making the effort and taking the time to contribute and you're not? SO GET YOUR BUTT IN GEAR AND SAY SOMETHING. TR

And the response:

My goodness, if anyone wrote to me like this I would be horrified, not my language at all. While it could work wonders for some people it would alienate me enormously! Derek's style would motivate me much more, for example, 'I notice that you have not logged into the course yet. If you are having technical difficulties or problems with the software please contact me and I will offer any assistance I can. The course is off to a good start and many of your fellow participants have started to post assignments. Please explore the software, post your work and have fun. Thanks for your participation; I'm looking forward to reading your work.' I liked the positive approach and particularly encouragement to have fun – it seemed so warm and human. Isn't it interesting how cultures, and sometimes sexes, tend to use different approaches to motivating people. Working with people from different parts of the world don't we have to be aware of sensitivities? Many years ago I saw a foreigner to me make an impassioned plea to a British academia audience which failed because the speaker used emotional reasons when the audience expected logical arguments. It made a big impression on me because I realized how I could totally fail to get my messages over to other people if I used the culturally inappropriate style of argument and motivation. SC

E-moderators and lurkers

Since the kind of participation I am describing here derives from social constructivist ideas, the key notion is that participation (i.e. active and frequent engagement) is not only a positive contribution to the group but also essential for learning (Duffy and Kirkley, 2004; Bax and Pegrum, 2009).

Stephen Bax's study of lurking offers us some rather new insights. For example, he asserts that:

online lurkers have no direct equivalent in the offline world, so it is unsafe to rely too heavily on intuitions derived from offline experiences. A lurker is not simply the silent student daydreaming at the back of the class. Because a lurker must, by definition, log into an online environment in order to lurk, such behaviour is deliberate, targeted and . . . potentially invisible to other community members. Thus, online lurking has its own unique characteristics and motivations, and . . . be understood in its own terms.

(Bax and Pegrum, 2009: 149)

In practice then, lurking – or what some might call vicarious learning – is a complex process.

In the exit questionnaire from the Open University Business School e-moderator training described in Chapter 5, I asked the participants their level of engagement with the training programme and their maintenance of interest throughout. This question was intended to elicit a crude notion of whether participants have, by the end of the five-stage programme, become active participants and whether the software has facilitated this. However, the question was typically answered in a more sophisticated and expansive way than I originally expected. Although over three-quarters of the participants reported 'active participation' online, half also point out the value of 'passive' participation, that is, browsing, 'listening' or lurking. Late starters in the programme are more likely to report 'passive' engagement than early starters (who perhaps had more opportunities to complete the online activities). This suggests that timing (and considerable amounts of time) to get used to communicating online is very important. The OUBS's participation figures showed a very wide range of response to online, from willingness to spend huge amounts of time and mental energy to a need to be online but to 'browse' before actively contributing. The OUBS therefore re-labelled 'lurking' as 'browsing' in an attempt to recognize this need in some individuals and to remove the negative connotations. If, however, the majority of members of a conference are browsing, it is time for a rethink and redesign of the purpose and activities of the conference. There is no doubt that the more active participants become upset with browsers, and managing the interface between contributing and browsing is a key e-moderating task.

A face-to-face facilitator is often able to ascertain from body language why a learner is listening rather than contributing. The listeners form the audience and they may be nodding agreement, applauding or sleeping! The e-moderator cannot look at the audience and determine its reaction in the same way.

Online communication involves commitment on the part of the contributor of various kinds, hence the importance of the five-stage scaffold to enable increasing trust, motivation and purposefulness. Silence on the part of participants seems much 'heavier' online than in face-to-face contexts (Mathiasen and Rattleff, 2002). It is important that the e-moderator creates the feeling of 'presence' too, without unnecessary interventions (Wheeler, 2007). Some browsers visit but leave no trace of their presence other than in the message history. Try to establish why they are browsing, if necessary contacting them by e-mail or telephone.

Are lurkers learning? It looks as though many are, and some are unabashed about this:

> As a confirmed lurker, I have found the conferences stimulating and broadening. It is seldom possible to access views from such a wide range of backgrounds. There are individual contributors whom I will always seek out in particular where I have found their solutions to questions of benefit. NH

From the Open University Business School conferences, we noticed three main types:

1. The freeloader

> It has come to my attention that we have a large number of lurkers and freeloaders in this conference (don't take offence – just my way with words). I am not saying that a lurker is a bad person but I am saying that a lurker is using my contribution and giving me nothing in return. And that makes me feel some grievance. My experience of such things is that *what you get out* is in proportion to *what you put in*. So feel free to contribute!! PN

2. The sponge

> In fact, in lurking in this particular area, I am getting good tuition both in the use of the medium and in the vocabulary (jargon, if you like) of an area of knowledge that is new to me and into which I would hesitate to insert a contribution. AB

3. Lurkers with skills or access problems

> I'm lost. Please help me. I just can't remember how to post a reply
> to the right conference that will get me help. I'm in a loop. I'm really
> upset about the combative tone of the active people in the course
> conferences – I'm really not here as a thief you know! GK

Learners generally browse before they are ready to contribute – and, as you
have seen from the model in Chapter 2, this happens in different ways and at
different paces. Sometimes a participant would have posted a message but did
not because what the participant wanted to contribute had already been said
by another member of the conference. Often they contribute on a topic or at
a level with which they feel comfortable, perhaps in a different conference.
However, most participants are put off by a conference that is constantly
dominated by one or two individuals (including sometimes the e-moderator!).
The names of such over-keen individuals get spotted and other participants
fall away. E-moderators need to watch carefully for this happening, as groups
often find dominant individuals more difficult to deal with online than they
might face-to-face. The solution is to encourage dominant individuals into
e-mail or to set up conferences of their own and create increased structure in
your learning conferences.

In sum, I hope this chapter has convinced you of the importance for all
e-moderators to understand the variety of issues and needs that each participant
will bring to his or her online conference, and help you to create a more
productive and level online world. Valuing every contribution is essential.
Doing so is likely to engender the best possible response from anyone who is
or feels disadvantaged, whatever the reason, and provides for the twenty-first-
century focus of enhancing learning for everyone.

Chapter 8

Future
e-moderating

In this chapter I hope to raise your awareness of the need for imaginative e-moderation to embrace a range of new directions. The most successful educators of the future will not be those who keep up with the race to put content on the web, but those who can predict and act on the less obvious, weaker signals coming from the environment, and then work out how to enable productive, happy e-moderating for learning. I consider here what these opportunities might be. I believe that even a rough and ready chart is better than no map at all. I highlight a few key areas that will have an impact on the work of e-moderators: the changing education environment and the nature of future online participants and communities. I risk a view of the up-and-coming technologies, and throw out a challenge to those responsible for providing us with the tools of our trade, the platform creators and manufacturers. Each area has a developing body of literature for you to explore. I hope I shall stimulate you to create your own map of the future for e-moderating in your own context.

Scenarios

When the first edition of this book was published and we greeted the new millennium, futurists predicted four key discontinuities that we would experience in this century. They relate to time and space, mind and body, real and virtual experiences, and humans and technologies (Martell, 2000; Burn and Loch, 2003). Ten years later, their influence on educational institutions is still strongly debated – but we can be sure there is a serious shake-up going on, some say a 'revolution' (Bonk, 2009; Beck, 2009; Hunt, Bromage and Tomkinson, 2006; Avila and Léger, 2005; Altbach, Reisberg and Rumbley, 2009; Amirault and Visser, 2009; Bennett, Maton and Kervin, 2008; Collins and Halverson, 2010; Helsper and Eynon, 2010; Turney, Robinson, Lee and Soutar, 2009; Snavely, 2008). And of course there are many critics (for a good example see Carr, 2010). Every week yet another 'break-through' in technology is reported but often without examining the impact on learning and education.

In this chapter I want to develop scenarios for possible futures for learning, with special reference to the impact on e-moderation. A scenario is a 'plausible and often simplified description of how the future may develop, based on a coherent and internally consistent set of assumptions about driving forces and key relationships' (sourced from word.net).

Using scenarios helps us to explore the increasingly puzzling and uncertain world in which we live and work, learn and teach. A scenario is a descriptive forecast of a landscape that an organization or institution might find itself in. Scenarios are not about forecasting the future but about looking at the possibilities – what we might think of as holding 'strategic conversations'.

Scenario planning helps us to make sense of the choices we face. It started in large organizations to help them understand their external environments, but scenarios can also be useful tools for all of us when we face uncertainty and complexity and grapple with what's happening within our own practice and disciplines. They help us to tap into our own judgements and explore our own visions as key resources to help us to prepare for uncharted territories. In this way we can avoid a simple 'solutions' approach and the risks of trivializing potentially significant decisions.

We can think of the scenario for the plot for a screenplay or as an aid to 'what would you do?' – decision-making. So in the case of the business world, scenarios usually include commercial, sociological, technical, economic, political, regulatory, ecological and other domains that make up the external environment of the business world. As such, they can help us to explore the virtual world that is imminent or just over the horizon and grapple with the implications. In constructing the scenarios, I've tried to consider elements close to our hearts such as learners' needs and expectations, assessment, research, teaching philosophies and learning technologies, and the role of e-moderators. I hope to promote our strategic conversations and ultimately enable us to work within the reality of what actually happens more happily and successfully. To accomplish our purpose, come with me on a starship voyage to a new planetary system as we boldly go.

Scenario 1: Planet Contentia

Landing on Contentia, where Content is king, you find technology as your gateway and delivery system for e-learning. Contentia dwellers attach high importance to targeted virtual learning environments (VLEs), content management systems, integrated learning management systems, multimedia, industry standards, DVDs, digital and cable television and high-capacity bandwidth.

Historically, the early years of the century on Contentia are known as 'the Dog's Breakfast era'. The telephone, cable, wireless and satellite companies competed to deliver as much information as any e-moderator and online learner could use. The war between open source and off-the-shelf solutions was finally resolved in favour of commercial interests, resulting in their considerable continued investment in e-learning. Combinations of technologies and widely used high-bandwidth access helped a little to move learners from watching and listening to slightly more interaction. Nowadays, rivalry between solutions providers is still strong, though two or three market leaders are emerging.

The predominant pedagogy on Contentia is that of the transmission model of teaching, where information is transferred from experts to novices. Content and 'push' are king and queen. There is a strong role for the observation of physical, location-based events (called Big Brother learning) using the latest technologies. Initially Big Brother learning was used for clinical practice, but it is now being deployed across a wide range of disciplines. Economies of scale and efficiency are reached through reduced interaction between teachers and learners compared with the lecture and question mode of teaching. Everyone is talking about the new plug-in that immediately senses who has written an article, for whom, when and what the commercial interests involved might be. Customers make choices on where to study from media profiles, online resource availability and league tables of various kinds.

In the second decade of the twenty-first century, the Open Educational resources movement with its sharing approach finally took a hold, driven by universities and governments worldwide. A few academics regretted the loss of their income from textbooks but ultimately, and rather quickly, the hold by commercial publishers disappeared and Universitiespedia took over the main provision of coded knowledge through vast online open repositories linked to popular mega access and distributors such as Uni-tube.

Diagnostic tests, delivered early in the learning process, determine which content is needed by which student. Assessment of students' learning is based on reproduction, comprehension and critique. Frequent automated testing is delivered in very small chunks through complex and structured questions. A popular feature is fast, sophisticated automated feedback on achievements and assignments, which also guides students' future learning directions.

The e-moderating role on Contentia is a combination of creator, e-librarian, e-lecturer and e-mentor. E-moderators are recruited especially for their content expertise, their advice on developing multimedia programmes and for building online libraries and pathways through resources.

E-moderators need to captivate big audiences. The internet and digital television spawn their own e-lecturing stars, and the most successful assume 'rock star' status. However, support for these elite few requires a very high level of research to go on in the background. Of course there are still a few lecturers campaigning actually to be with their students, rather than look at them on monitors. Some have joined the medical doctors' campaign for real patients. But they are fewer each year. We will remember them.

Recruitment of e-moderators for Contentia is from those at home with broadcasting and presenting, in love with the media, media wise and 'savvy', and with personal qualities indicating media 'presence'. Screen tests are set up for e-moderators. The select few are very good 'communicators' and happy to work with commercial media organizations and businesses. Training for Contentia e-moderators includes professional grooming for those showing particular aptitude. They receive media presentation and communication skills (putting yourself and your content across to the audience) and understanding of and insight into their audiences. They can earn big money.

Scenario 2: Planet Instantia

The pedagogy on Planet Instantia is usually called e-learning. Instantians use sophisticated learning object approaches, with information technology seen as a basic tool. Computer-based courses are offered from desks at work or in learning centres. Learners work and learn almost simultaneously, since every technological object is integrated with everything else. Flexibility and instantaneousness are the keywords.

The costs of travel, training facilities and trainers are slashed compared with those on Earth. The role of ambient intelligence in devices is seen as key on this planet. Every device that is connected to electricity is also connected to the internet, known as always on and always everywhere. Simply everything and everyone has an e-address. Hence educational providers are able to think both creatively and in a very integrated way about learning devices.

Individual learners assess the value of the learning experience, asking, 'Is this learning just for me, just in time, just for now and just enough (known as Tagmania)?' With the impact of the skills at work shortage and the rise in importance of corporate universities, professionals only join an organization that has its own special university. Bonus systems are linked to success at learning and application. The inclusion of e-career development is standard in salary packages.

The key feature of assessment on this planet is authenticity. Employers consider whether learning provision helps to recruit the right people for the organization. They also evaluate the speed and effectiveness of the learning provision by considering the extent to which organizational performances improve.

Assessment tasks are always related to specific work or professional needs, and are deeply embedded in the learning activities. Gaming technologies are used to create 'real life' scenarios that combine learning and assessment in seamless environments. There is a high level of tracking of outcomes, which are automatically transferred to employees' development accounts.

This planet has sometimes been accused of navel rather than star-gazing since the inhabitants spend much of their time exploring the core of the planet rather than considering its environment. Telescopes are no longer in use, for example. Seismology and geophysics have replaced astronomy. However, with the increase in effective links between e-learning, performance and knowledge management, an improved systemic approach has been achieved and the advocates of lifelong learning have begun to see the benefits of including Instantia in their universes.

On Instantia, e-moderators support autonomous learning (although many learners exist magically with little human contact to sustain them). Real e-moderators or virtual prepared responses (simulacra) are available 24 hours a day, both synchronously and asynchronously. E-moderators focus on skills development in employees (to enable them to learn in this way) and on ways of fostering the adoption of a strong in-house knowledge culture.

E-moderating talents are part of the package of competencies expected of human resource (HR) professionals on Instantia. They are recruited from within an organization's HR function, and are considered professionals. They come from a corporate training tradition. They are also skilled in needs assessment, and the tracking and measurement of learning outcomes (so act as a kind of learning accountant). Their professional training includes working in networks and information exchanges, and in developing professional practice. Their loyalty is to their profession, organization or community of practice rather than to the learner.

Scenario 3: Planet Nomadic

At first on Planet Nomadic the impact of smaller, faster and wireless technologies went well beyond mobile phones, and they were adopted by the most forward-looking universities. Consider teaching and learning in a world where democracy is promoted by net-based voting and where everyone carries one TB of digital storage in their signet rings! Learning devices were once carried, then worn and are now often embedded subcutaneously.

Some people think that part of our sense of identity is based on not only who we are, but also where we are and knowing our precise place in the world. Global positioning systems (GPS) using a network of satellites can fix someone's location on the planet to within a few metres. These devices first transformed exploration and the emergency services on Nomadic but as soon as everything in the physical world became tracked, tagged, barcoded and mapped, teaching and learning opportunities emerged. Location technology fixed learners in the physical world, while inviting them to operate in the virtual world (Leander, Phillips and Taylor, 2010). By connecting learners in a network of people with a physical sense of place, this finally took away the sense of isolation, although for a time during the second decade of the century, invisibility became a lifestyle choice.

On Nomadic there is less stability, less structure, less fixed time for work and leisure, retirement and education than on Earth, along with significantly more nodes for accessing learning. Planet Nomadic provides portable learning for mobile lifestyles. Learning on the Planet Nomadic is time-independent and individual. The learners are seen as electronic explorers and adventurers. The technology that originally merged GPS with telephony, to keep people safe and comfortable during walking weekends in Wales or Montana, now offers them access to their learning resources after the post-hike supper.

The explosion of opportunities for travelling learning resulted in hype and myth about mobility, similar to that about e-learning in the closing days of the twentieth century. The term 'learning location' soon replaced the term 'e-learning'. However, once the pedagogy was worked out and m-moderators had been trained, real benefits emerged. Learning is now truly any time, any place. Textual, visual and audible information becomes available as learners move closer to their m-moderators. Individuals choose based on their cognitive preferences and styles. Pacing and timing for distance learners are easier than on Earth, as learners carry 'place and pace' keepers with them.

There are few physical classrooms left. Terrestrial universities and corporate training facilities have disappeared; new e-universities have inherited the planet. Students calculate the cost of their courses based on airtime and connection, rather than attendance at class, or purchase of books, as on Earth.

English has become standard for learning. The *New Oxford Very Concise Internet Dictionary* is the all time best e-seller. (The Campaign for Full English Grammar gave up in 2007.) However, mobile learning is also popular to support modern language development. (Visit the country, live in the culture and access your course at the same time.)

Technologies are highly portable, individual, adaptable and intuitive to use (Sharples, Arnedillo-Sánchez and Vavoula, 2009). Mobile technologies are seen as essential communication and learning tools, rather than as disruptive, as at the turn of the century. Main technologies in use are tablets, personal digital assistants, sixteenth-generation mobile communicators, embedded satnavs, unfolding keyboards, blow-up screens, wireless and personal networks, low orbit satellites, national and international communications networks, infrared connections and dedicated e-book readers. All students have e-tablets and mobiles devices are ubiquitous for all – from the time they were given away with content by publishers. Breakthroughs occurred when safety was achieved in the use of mobile phones, and decreasing size matched increasing functionality and capability. PADs were worn in underwear for the first manned mission to Mars. Indeed, the latest fashions and jewellery always include a suitable pocket and security strap for the mobile.

The war between the PC or the television as a focus for home entertainment gateways was won some years ago, as set-top boxes for games and learning are now ubiquitous in children's bedrooms. Interactive games are the new chocolate buttons. 'Finish your homework and you can play the game', say parents. A few forward-looking educators combined complex games and learning, and scooped the learning market.

Paper-based books are considered very quaint indeed.

All universities, colleges and schools produce their own very cheap microprocessors, led by the UK Open University's new mission, and these are embedded in everything from shoes to furniture, buildings and regions. Planet Nomadic heralds the move away from generic software applications to providing focused key learning components geared towards an individual learner. Wearable components (WCs) have 'context awareness' and hence interact with the participants and their environment. They know when to switch themselves off and, importantly, regularly help to pace the learners, day by day, through their courses.

On Nomadic, students design, negotiate or choose their own assessments, often in collaboration with their assessment helpers. Assessment helpers are sometimes real people, peers or alumni, and sometimes programmes based on artificial intelligence. Assessment of learning is in small bites, based largely on projects and outcomes, and achieved incrementally. Every assessment event contributes to updating an individual's learning profile, and hence suggesting future learning needs. Interaction is evaluated using the latest computer-mediated tools. The great mobile phone exam scam of 2012 accelerated the demise of several struggling universities, and promoted the use of biotechnology to ensure authentication of students' own work. Biometrics ensure the security of learners' identities. Portfolio learners expect to transfer their learning credits easily from one institution to another. The shift away from memorization towards performance is welcomed by learners, universities and employers.

E-(M-)moderators are as mobile as their students are. Many are portfolio m-moderators and work for several educational institutions and providers, all over the world, at any one time. They have not only a highly developed awareness of the ways in which traditions of learning and expectations vary in different cultures, but also the ability to work across disciplines and levels of education. They can break activities and content down into tiny components that can be transmitted and studied in small chunks. They are fully comfortable with using online assessment, and confident in the technologies that ensure the students they are assessing are the same ones they are teaching. They can relate well to students without needing to meet with them, so the issue of plagiarism is less of a concern than on Earth. They focus on promoting the concepts of ownership of the learning process, active learning, independence, the ability to make judgements, self-motivation and high levels of autonomy. They provide and support resource-based learning, working with skilled technicians and e-librarians.

It has proved necessary to add an additional literacy skill – so that learners indicate whether they understand the difference between real, blended and virtual 3D environments.

On Nomadic e-moderators self-select if they feel 'the call', having first saturated themselves in the ways of learning on Nomadic. E-moderation is an outgrowth of enthusiasm for the e-mobile lifestyle and a love of helping people to learn. People graduate to e-moderation from being effective m-learners themselves, and there are few professional barriers between being an effective e-learner and becoming an e-moderator. Nomadic e-moderators move in and out of the work as fits their particular professional wishes and the needs of the moment. Training for e-moderators on Nomadic includes experiential learning, observation, apprenticeships, networking and learning on the job, as befits a mobile lifestyle.

Scenario 4: Planet Cafélattia

Communication and mediated networked computers can be used to build upon and amplify human talents for collaborative purposes. On Cafélattia hundreds of millions of people lend their computers for cooperative purposes. The impact can be positive or negative, used for inclusion of those disadvantaged, for learning or destructively (Rheingold, 2002). As a result, new global subcultures blossomed, new industries were born and older industries launched furious counter-attacks. This threw into relief the different needs of learners, and resulted in much increased merging and competing in educational provision. Much energy and money was wasted chasing rainbows.

On Cafélattia instant messaging is used for most communication and everyday transactions, with automatic language translation where necessary. Travelling is an indulgence, not a necessity.

What emerges on Cafélattia is the importance of peer-to-peer technologies for data, documents, music and knowledge sharing across offices, across campuses, from industry to universities, from professional associations to learning providers, and across disciplines and cultures. New information and knowledge are no longer the preserve of academics. Collaboration is commonplace, and integrated into everyday work and learning, but often in unexpected and unplanned ways.

On Planet Cafélattia, learning is built around learning communities and interaction, extending access beyond the bounds of time and space, but offering the promise of efficiency and widening access. Think of individuals as nodes on a network and evaluation as based on voting.

Some people still look back to the embryonic days of social networking as the Cloud built up – Remember Facebook and Twitter they say?– but most are entirely comfortable with the latest virtual worlds and their multiple avatars.

The key technology is the developed, entertaining, effective internet (beyond the browser!), to allow immediate and satisfying interaction between students and students, and between e-moderators and learners. Technologies are asynchronous and synchronous group systems to support a wide variety of environments for working and learning together. Rather than a place where millions of participants all connect to a handful of large sites, the internet has reclaimed its purpose as a place where everyone talks to everyone else, equal to equal. Peer-to-peer (P to P) technologies have survived their legal challenges and become acceptable. Groupware in use is specially developed for learning purposes, rather than based on messaging or corporate meeting software as on Earth. Both co- and remotely located learning communities (clicks and mortar) are of key importance, as well as interaction in 2D and 3D converged environments. Individuals utilize new forms of community, based on augmented awareness of their proximity to places of interest and each other. This is known as the Outernet Highway.

Although media cartels and government agencies sought to create and control online participation in the interests of ownership, in similar ways to the broadcast era of the turn of the millennium, e-moderators and learners maintained their power to create rather than consume. For example, the online 'free learners' movement fought cyberbattles over file sharing, copy protection and regulation of the radio waves. Most individuals are provided with free technology, since they are expected to connect into the global network for distributed computational tasks from time to time.

Learners connect through high bandwidth devices and systems. Face-to-face meetings are extremely unusual and considered old fashioned and non-green. Hence the technologies are seen only as mediating devices, promoting creativity and collaboration. Cafélattia learning appeals to a very wide range of people, including the increasing numbers and percentages of 'grey learners' who have a great deal to offer to others, a desire to learn through non-traditional means, and who have the time and resources to access networked technologies (Swindell, 2002).

The pedagogy is based on notions of a very strong social context for learning, with the model of acquisition, argumentation and application. Key activities for learners are finding and interacting with like-minded individuals anywhere on the planet (for example by gender, by interest, by profession), and being intellectually extended by dialogue and challenge from others. Learners express themselves freely through speech, text and, increasingly, moving images. The roles of reflection (an essential tool of expert learners), professional development and the sharing of tacit knowledge are of critical importance. Learning is contextualized and given authenticity by the learning group and the learning community (rather than by the university, as on Earth). On and offline resources are important, but electronic and structured information support and stimulate the learning group rather than replace the active, participative learning experience.

Assessment is based on complex problem solving and knowledge construction skills. It is learner-driven, highly contributory and negotiated with peers. Assessment is seen as non-restrictive, and an enhancement to and motivation for learning. Hence the level and scope of assessment are largely the product of interaction with other like-minded learners. Group and peer assessment has become the norm.

Equatorial (360 degree) assessment is common. Evaluation of contributions to text, interaction and complex problem solving is all automated.

E-moderators on Cafélattia think globally but are able to turn their ideas into local and contextualized action. They see the technologies as yet another environment for learning rather than as tools. They are experts at mentoring individuals online, and may be seen as companions in the democratic networked learning process, rather than teachers as such. They know when to take part, when to provide expert input, when to act as a peer and when to stay silent. They also have very highly developed skills in online group development for learning and in the use of online resources to stimulate groups. They know how to welcome and support learners into the online world and how to build effective online communities. They act as intelligent agents and facilitators. They have the ability to visualize others in their situations. They know how to allow a sense of humour and fun to manifest itself online. They know how to build gradually on the processes of exchanging information, and how to turn this into knowledge sharing and ultimately into knowledge construction.

Recruitment of e-moderators on Cafélattia comes from community workers and people mobilizers. They are teachers who are interested in e-community development. They value people for themselves and for their potential as self-developers. They are natural leaders who emerge 'on the job' as they themselves demonstrate their e-learning prowess and are encouraged by experienced and effective e-moderators to take up the work. Cafélattia e-moderator training is on the job as apprentices and as part of communities of practice. Like their e-learners, they are self-developers as they seek to improve their professional practice. As they dip in and out of e-moderating, so they seek ways to maintain and update their knowledge by drawing on sources of continuing professional development – particularly virtual and experiential ones.

What planet are you on?

It's likely that all the planets will have an element of reality, and there will be a variety of players and processes. Institutionally, we will probably see further combinations of these scenarios, such as universities with corporates or colleges partnering media companies. There are key branding and rebranding issues to consider. If elements of Nomadic come about, for example, where does that leave beautiful campus locations such as Bath in the UK or the Gold Coast of Australia? If Cafélattia gains a hold, where does it lead the high-profile research-based universities such as Oxbridge and Harvard? You may find that different groupings of people in your organization are excited by the possibilities of some planets and horrified by others. For example I've found that managers often favour Contentia and IT people Nomadic. Academics often like the constructivist Cafélattia and teachers Instantia with its shared resources approach. Where do you stand?

However, the patterns of the use of information and communication technologies cannot easily be determined, as the ways learners and explorers will use new forms of online learning offerings are unpredictable. Acceptable use and the meaning given to new technologies are a complex mix of distinctive and perplexing forms of rational and non-rational behaviour. The implementation of information and communication technologies is a process of 'taming' wild objects, and adapting them to the routines and rituals of everyday life (www.le.ac.uk/mediazoo). As the e-moderators increase their skills and add the magical human touch, the wildness can be changed in a more ecologically friendly direction!

I hope you will start your own strategic conversations, challenge these scenarios and develop new ones. I hope they will help you to see through the confusion, spot developments before they become trends, see patterns before they fully emerge, and grasp the relevant features of learning technologies that do truly reflect our needs, and those of our students. I hope they will help you find a suitable pathway through inflated claims (vendors?), unrealistic expectations (students and participants?) and unformed strategies (politicians?). Furthermore, exploring scenarios for e-learning and e-moderating is best done with other people – from other departments, faculties and universities. Even within our own organizations, dealing with complex scenarios and their future potential must be handled in multi-functional teams. We need to engage fully with the providers of the technologies themselves as well; in this way deeper understanding and dialogue will emerge. I believe you will be convinced that there is a very strong role for e-moderators in all these scenarios, but the way these responsibilities and privileges are discharged may be rather different from yesteryear.

So what will actually happen? To a large extent, it's up to you. Vision it and action it! When you approach each of these planets, check out the atmosphere for yourself before landing. Does it support life for your discipline? Where will the power come from to sustain you on this planet? Are you the first to walk on this planet? And do you want to be? If not, what can you learn from previous explorers? Either way, please make sure your experiences are available for others who follow you, both your successes and your failures. In this way, not only is knowledge built, but also a new explorers' e-moderating community.

Going boldly and successfully into the future inevitably involves organizational change. The gap-closing exercises probably involve many years, so we need tactics as well as strategy along the pathways. One way of helping, as education goes global, cyber and geo-located, would be to recognize a worldwide licence for e-moderating.

So as you can see, it's still teaching, but not as we've known it on Earth. Most of the skills we have already acquired are much needed, but there is more. In this way, the amazing and diverse planets will continue to be open to exploration not only by e-moderators but also by learners who will boldly go. . .

Part 2:

RESOURCES FOR PRACTITIONERS

The following provide a variety of resources for you to try out with your learners and e-moderators. All are rooted in research, development and practice. None are intended to be definitive, but they provide you with checklists to make your own or to use as the basis of resources for online or offline workshops and discussions.

1 Scaffolding online learning
2 Achieving online socialization
3 Achieving knowledge sharing and construction
4 Developing e-moderators
5 Costs
6 Summarizing and weaving
7 Taming online time
8 Promoting cultural understandings
9 Creating 'presence'
10 Housekeeping
11 Promoting active participation
12 Aligned student assessment
13 Evaluating online conferencing
14 E-moderating for synchronous conferencing
15 E-moderating for virtual worlds
16 E-moderating for podcasting
17 Monitoring e-moderating
18 Encouraging self-managing groups
19 Supporting online novices
20 Understanding lurking
21 Valuing online diversity
22 What's going on?
23 What will we call ourselves?
24 Communicating online

Resource I

Scaffolding online learning

You will find below a summary of advice relevant to each of the five stages of the model. For each stage, there are suggestions on the technical support you can provide, on helping participants to learn and on e-moderating.

Stage I: Access and motivation

Technical support

- Provide a helpline for password and access problems.
- Ensure new participants can read and know how to send messages as soon as they are online.
- Give great attention to precise detail in your written and onscreen instructions.
- Clarify the differences between 1:1 e-mail, group e-mail lists and discussion forums.

Motivating participants

- Recognize that taking part is an act of faith for most participants at this stage.
- Present (sell if necessary) the benefits of interacting with others for learning.
- Specify how group online learning will be used in the course or programme.
- Ensure the 'look and feel' of your system is friendly for all comers.

- Try to create fun, making working online together enticing and enjoyable.
- Assure novices that their fear and anxiety will be overcome by trying out online conferencing.

E-moderating

- Acknowledge that high levels of anxiety and lack of confidence in some participants may mean that some individual 'hand holding' is needed.
- Welcome participants individually.
- Constantly improve and update support materials.
- Keep the conference structure very clear and simple.
- Encourage participants to log on regularly, and do so yourself.

Stage 2: socialization

Technical support

- Explain carefully how to save time.
- Expect participants to critique the systems and suggest they know a better one – explain this one is effective and secure.
- Navigating around the conferences will be easier if you use meaningful names and icons to signify activity.
- Some participants may need reassurance from you about spelling and typos – all contributions are welcome.
- Don't alter the look of the forums too often.

Learning

- Enhance participants' confidence in using online learning by praising both their contributions and their efforts (not just outcomes).
- Offer ways for participants to benefit from reading about other people's experience and problems.
- Explain the importance of acknowledging others online and set an example yourself.
- Point out why it is usually better to keep messages short and purposeful.
- Explain the benefits to participants of their working at their own pace.
- Ensure that ways for individuals to establish their identities online are used but don't go over the top on this too soon.

E-moderating

- Check for any participants with relevant disabilities, however minor, and find out how you can help them.

- Use metaphors and straightforward explanation to provide bridges between familiar ways of communicating and interacting and online.
- Emphasize transferable skills and links to other experiences.
- Promote awareness of appropriate online communication styles.
- Encourage practice to reinforce developing skills.
- Allow lurking or browsing to start with, without making this a moral issue.
- Offer structured exercises and activities to participants, especially those involved in finding online others with similar interests.
- Help participants with navigation and selection of activities.
- Help participants to develop their own online identity.
- Allocate an online mentor to newcomers when possible.
- Aim to summarize and archive messages often, so that there are not more than 20 unread messages for any participant in any conference.
- Offer relevant and interesting e-tivities (Salmon, 2002a).
- Collect and monitor participation and feedback and change topics and structures of e-tivities if your first try doesn't appeal to participants.

Stage 3: information exchange

Technical support

- Offer advice and 'tips' for developing skills.
- Check that all basic skills are achieved.
- Encourage participants to see that the conferencing technology works and is simple to use.
- Provide information, for those who want it, about more sophisticated and advanced uses of the platform but avoid making early tasks and activities too complicated.

Learning

- Provide practical ways of sharing information online.
- Look for and build links with other media and processes in the course.

E-moderating

- Provide relevant and purposeful forums and tasks.
- Deal with requests for information.
- Deal very promptly with difficulties among participants, such as dominance, harassment, and perhaps excessive lurking.
- Offer tips and strategies for dealing with information overload.
- Provide a variety of forums to suit different student needs.

- Set up useful activities and tasks – especially those not so easily or productively undertaken offline.
- Provide links into suitable electronic resources – for example, web resources to use as stimuli for conferences.
- Remind participants of the protocols and guidelines if conferences get too busy or confused.
- Introduce structured e-tivities.

Stage 4: knowledge construction

Technical support

- Encourage participants to become more technically independent and to support each other.
- Ensure good use of forum titles and icons.
- Promote benefits of learning online through explaining its technical aspects – for example, its ease of use, asynchronicity and lack of dependence on a fixed location for each participant.
- Refer any persistent technical problems.
- Ensure that all e-moderators have access and the skills for setting up conferences, creating sub-conferences, summarizing messages and creating archives.

Learning

- Pose insightful questions and give participants time to reflect and respond.
- Encourage participants to contribute to the conferences, not merely read them.
- Ensure there is no domination of conferences by one or two individuals.
- Explore every opportunity for online collaboration with others.

E-moderating

- Be prepared to explain and clarify the e-moderating role to participants (especially if they are still expecting 'the answers' from you at this stage).
- Work on developing your design and delivery skills in e-moderating for knowledge construction.
- Share with other e-moderators insights into how to deal with online 'problem participants' and 'problem groups', in case you encounter them.
- Encourage full contribution and participation by students.
- Know when to stay silent for a few days.
- Be prepared to value every participant's contribution but weave, weave, weave, summarize, summarize, summarize.

- Be ready to hand out specific e-moderating tasks to participants, to give them a chance to experience e-moderating for themselves.
- Close off any unused or unproductive conferences and create new ones.
- Use structured e-tivities.

Stage 5: development

Technical

- Ensure that good links exist from conferences to the course resources, podcasts, library, etc.
- Ensure that selected participants can be given access to set up and e-moderate their own conferences.

Learning

- Enable participants to offer help to others or to become e-moderators.
- Provide opportunities for reflection on the what and how of learning online.
- Provide opportunities for development and progress.

E-moderating

- Expect and welcome challenges of all kinds (the system, the conferences, the conclusions).
- Ensure that appropriate evaluation, monitoring and reflection on your own practice occur.
- Encourage participants to reflect on their learning by providing conference areas to discuss the impact of online networking for learning.
- Explore comparisons with face-to-face learning.
- Look for those with good online skills and communication styles, and encourage them to support others.

Resource 2

Achieving online socialization

Colleagues sometimes feel that they would like to spend less time on Stage 2, the socialization part of the model, and get on with the 'real learning'! However, time and time again we have found that it is essential to undertake this stage successfully, in the interests of better participation later in the model. This resource tells you a bit more about Stage 2, and offers some ways of spending less time and effort, under certain circumstances.

There are three main components of Stage 2. They are:

- establishing a successful online team or group;
- introducing the knowledge domain and the approaches to the learning;
- the induction of the participants into and their use of the online environment itself.

For all three, it's insufficient to post information. Participants need to work with these ideas and truly get to know about each other to make them their own.

Component 1: establishing a successful group

E-tivities at this stage need to:

- enable individuals to create and work with their online identities;
- elicit, expose and begin to explore the diversity of cultures and expectations each participant brings to the learning;

- create a climate of, and ways of, everyone contributing actively;
- build an effective virtual team;
- establish an online culture and ways of behaving in this group at this time for this course.

Component 2: knowledge domain

E-tivities should:

- explore the nature and approach online of the overall discipline or domain of knowledge, its wider context and relevance to the participants, and its use and application in the online environment;
- establish how your topic will be handled and what is expected for their learning;
- determine how assessment and learning outcomes will be handled and their relationship to the online opportunities.

Component 3: online environment

Introduction to:

- the way pacing, timings, rhythm will work in this programme, what deadlines are essential, what flexibility there is;
- the nature of asynchronicity and its advantages, such as opportunities for reworking contributions and reflections, and whether any synchronous 'events' will be used, requiring attendance at a particular moment;
- key technical issues, especially enabling participants to get the most from the software without it getting in the way of the learning.

Use a variety of 'sparks' and approaches – for example, some use of short feedback by human voice or visual impact (Nie et al., 2010; Sutton-Brady, Scott, Taylor, Carabetta and Clark, 2009).

If you are e-moderating a group that is already well established as a team and familiar with the knowledge domain, but new to online, then you can undertake one e-tivity from components 1 and 2, and put most of your effort into Stage 3, helping the group to work successfully in the online environment.

If you have participants who are used to communicating online and have experienced earlier parts of a relevant learning programme, but are new to each other, then you can focus most of your Stage 2 e-tivities on enabling them to work effectively and virtually together.

If you have a well-established virtual group who are starting out on a new course, a new project or higher level work, then most of your Stage 2 energy can be put into exposing the team to the joys of using online in the service of new objectives or directions.

Resource 3

Achieving knowledge sharing and construction

It is at Stage 4, knowledge sharing and construction, that online conferencing has the most to offer teaching and learning. To achieve these, e-moderators need to do the following:

- Get technical questions out of the way early.
- Make clear what the e-moderator's role is, that is, to facilitate process and to collect and represent participants' views.
- Create a setting and an atmosphere where differences as well as similarities are appreciated, and where disagreements are seen as an opportunity to learn.
- Be an equal participant in the conference.
- Avoid directive interventions and 'right answer' responses.
- Encourage and support other participants in the e-moderating role.
- Stimulate the debate, offer ideas, and resources (rather than 'the answers').
- Provide 'sparks' (comments or stimulating questions that will prompt responses). (See Salmon, 2002a for more ideas.)
- Be prepared to collate carefully, add value, weave, summarize.
- Intervene at the right point in time in the debate and appreciate the delicate balance between 'holding back' and intervening.

- Share your range of experience but avoid overload or overwhelming participants.
- Make explicit to participants that their contributions are wanted and valued.
- Be careful to acknowledge and be inclusive of all contributions.
- Be clear to the group about what additional 'powers' you have as e-moderator, and the circumstances in which you would use them. (Some participants believe that e-moderators sneak around online.)
- Be very tolerant of natural twists and turns of discussion – it's unlikely to go the way you originally expected!
- Look for evidence of knowledge construction and reward it (rather than expecting specific outcomes).
- Accept variety and diversity in responses and reward these.
- Reward task accomplishments and effort rather than test for information recall.
- Assess co-operative, group, collaborative and team outcomes, rather than individual ones, wherever possible.

Resource 4

Developing e-moderators

- Ensure that the trainee e-moderators experience online learning as learners before they start e-moderating for real.
- Ensure that they undertake all or most of the programme in the online environment itself – make it a real experience.
- Keep the focus of the programme on skills.
- Keep the training as simple as such a focus will allow – don't over-complicate it.
- Provide an environment suited to participants with a wide range of prior experience of working online (or none).
- Check the training programme thoroughly before the programme goes live – use a novice ('reality checkers') for a final check rather than an expert.
- Make clear to the trainees how much time you expect them to spend on the programme.
- Make sure the training programme is accessible 'any time, any place'.
- Build in help with the software and the system as much as you can to control frustration.
- Enable trainees to acquire skills in using the software as they gradually build up their understanding of the online environment.
- When you are running your development programme, make absolutely sure that the people doing the e-moderating of the trainee e-moderators (we call them e-convenors) model exemplary skills.
- Include strategic knowledge (how will I work with my students?) as well as declarative knowledge and procedural knowledge (availability and capacity of the software and the system).

- Offer plenty of opportunity for the trainees to explore their attitudes to working online and its meaning for their own teaching, topics and disciplines.
- Ensure the trainees have opportunities to interact with each other.
- Make the participants aware of the goals of the programme all the way through it.
- Use familiar metaphors for explaining aspects of online and e-moderating.
- Try to spot trainees needing more help and offer it promptly.
- Build reflection on e-moderating practice into your skills development programme.
- Monitor the work of e-moderators and use feedback to improve your development programme.
- Ensure that ongoing development of trained e-moderators is available and build an online community of e-moderators' conferences after the development programme has been completed.

Resource 5

Costs

- Make clear decisions about roles and numbers of e-moderators that you will need and ensure they are trained in advance.
- Train and develop e-moderators online, rather than face-to-face.
- Establish early on how much e-moderators should expect to do, and what are reasonable expectations on the part of students.
- Set up good helpdesk and online support systems, and encourage competent students to support others, leaving more of your e-moderators' online time for learning related e-moderating.
- Use existing resources and online constructed knowledge as much as possible, and Open Educational Resources, rather than develop materials and/or pay for expensive third-party materials use.
- Develop systems for reuse, of online conferencing e-tivities and materials.
- Build up economies of scale as rapidly as possible – choose only systems that can be expanded cheaply.
- Learn about e-tivities.
- Promote student work groups.

Resource 6

Summarizing and weaving

Both techniques are effective regardless of the technology being employed – they work in asynchronous contexts (such as discussion boards, wikis, shared blogs) and synchronous ones (such as online classrooms, videoconferencing, virtual worlds). They also work in hybrid contexts, where an 'offline' reflection is needed to make sense of a real-time exchange – for example, turning a long sequence of Tweets or Facebook live feeds into a meaningful message.

Here is the outcome of an e-tivity on the e-moderating course that seeks to answer this question!

> Summarizing v. weaving. What's the difference?
>
> Terry: what is the difference between summaries and weaving?
>
> Vicky: I had some difficulty with this exercise, and I'm not really sure if I summarizing or weaving, or both.
>
> Ming: Regarding 'weaving'. I share the same apprehensions as Vicky . . . indicated, viz., it isn't necessarily trivial to establish a weave from apparently diverse threads.
>
> And the e-convenor
>
> Aha! So it seems we have a common problem people – the difference between summarising and weaving. Well basically a summary covers a much broader canvas – for instance, a *final* summary covers the whole thread. You wouldn't add your own thoughts to a final summary because the whole thing is ending, except to ask if it was an accurate reflection.

Weaving is what we do on the hoof in face-to-face (f2f) when we pull together two or three contributions and hold them up for inspection. I guess at the end of the day, one shades into the other, but weaving for me is short and sharp. It's 'Hey, let's look at this a bit closer. What are the implications?' (or something similar). Does this help to clarify the issue sufficiently for people to continue with the e-tivity? Is my analogy with what you do f2f valid/helpful? Or do you see a real difference? What think?

Does this help? Is it a useful illustration?

Ken

Table Resource 6.1 The differences between summarizing and weaving

Weaving	Summarizing
When a topic has not been exhausted or requires further elaboration.	When a topic has been sufficiently discussed and/or time is running out.
Looks forward by using these gaps in the discussion to generate more exchanges focused on filling those gaps.	*Looks back* and brings a discussion to a close by capturing the key points into a single message that latecomers can use or for revision.
Creative task that selects themes and rearranges them into a new statement, making connections that may not have been intended or seen by the writers.	Reproducing the material in shortened form, picking out the main points. The original meanings are not removed.
Be alert to possible themes arising from perhaps two or three messages where the e-moderator can draw out or highlight implications that may otherwise escape attention in the welter of messages.	Seek to be inclusive of all main themes that have arisen.
Seek opportunities to add value to participants' contributions.	Seek opportunities to add value to participants' contributions.
Don't weave just for the sake of it if the discussion is going well – only do so if you can add significant value.	Summarizing signals the close of a discussion – the summary can act as a spark for a new direction.
Use quotes clearly (model the way participants should acknowledge each other's contributions) and acknowledge relevant material, draw out a teaching point and invite a response from participants by means of an open question.	Quote and acknowledge relevant material, draw out teaching points, correct any misconceptions, links to course materials and concepts.
Give your weave message a very clear title that will stand out.	Give your summary message a very clear title that will stand out, archiving the original messages if appropriate.

How to summarize

- 'Collect' up all the contributions into one message (if your software allows you to do this) or cut and paste them into your word processor.
- Read through quickly and colour code the key themes.
- Create a list in the file for each of these, with titles.
- Identify the unifying themes.
- Identify the points of disagreement.
- Summarize by a sentence or bullet point or two for each of the themes, identifying points of agreement and disagreement, perhaps by giving examples, attributed to the originator.
- Add your positive and reinforcing feedback.
- Add your criticisms and point out omissions.
- Add your congratulations.
- Add your 'meta' (overall) comments or teaching points.
- If you wish to move on the discussion, ask specific but open-ended questions.
- Delete all the original data and create simple formatting for ease of reading.
- Post in the conference with a *clear title*, invite further comment.

And an example:

Latecomers' summary

We were asked to compose a brief message as if to a participant in one of our own courses – someone who has not yet contributed to our online sessions – to encourage them to take part.

What came across were warmth and encouragement/reassurance – and no big stick waving – as we couldn't always know what lay behind the seeming reluctance.

Everybody sought generally to reassure the latecomers by, for example:

Checking that all was OK (and prompting the latecomer to respond), stressing that their contribution would be valued, and offering help (private if necessary) if the student was experiencing any problems (Lauren, Brenda, Alexander, Alejandra, Neville, Joan).

Reassurance that using the VLE was not difficult (and hints and tips were there to use) and that it was good for keeping students informed and for tracking progress. Give it a go, was the message! (Marie-Claire, Una, Brenda, Pierre).

A new thread with an encouraging title – something like 'finding your way through the messages' – to stick out as something helpful that was not based on having read all the messages before. Reassurance that although the number of messages could appear daunting, there were ways to manage them – and advice was given as to how to do so (Heike, Karen, Pieter).

Fair summary? Nathan.

Resource 7

Taming online time

E-moderators tame time more successfully if they have:

- online development for their role;
- well-developed skills in weaving and summarizing;
- familiarity with reading and writing on screen;
- the ability to work flexibly and integrate working online with their everyday life;
- the reusability of resources and e-tivities;
- the e-moderators' ability to create 'presence'.

Technical issues

These issues help with use of online time:

- everyone's experience with the platform;
- quality and appropriateness of the technology for engagement and interaction;
- the levels and availability of technical support, mainly at Stage 1;
- the connectedness and mobility of the platform for use any time and any place;
- efficacy of platform in use for the mode of learning deployed.

Self-support

Self-support of participants depends on:

- deployment of the five-stage scaffold;
- level of excitement and motivation of participants;
- participants' socialization and emotional comfort with the online learning.

The impact of success

Full engagement by participants probably means more time for the e-moderators and depends on:

- numbers of participants;
- levels of contribution;
- levels of browsing and lurking.

Resource 8

Promoting cultural understandings

We rarely think about our own culture – the habitual ways in which we go about the business of living, learning and teaching in our daily lives in our particular society or discipline. We take it for granted. This resource is an encouragement to find out more about the implicit world of your participants before you begin to e-moderate – especially their ideas about working online and about the other participants – and then to remain alert to signs of cultural differences and expectations once you have started. Sensitivity and discretion may save you potential online embarrassment. Needless to say, none of the following should be taken as implying any criticism – it's just the way things are!

Styles of address, hierarchy and authority

The Anglo-American style of informality is itself culture-bound and may not be the norm elsewhere. Some societies preserve a greater degree of formality even in online environments. Cultural norms differ even across Western Europe. If, for instance, you are e-moderating a conference for German participants, you may experience greater formality and hierarchy online than you might expect in an Anglo-American setting. Titles may be used in addressing other participants and use of first names may not be much in evidence. However, academic institutions may be a little less formal than other organizations.

In general we suggest that as a wise precaution you ask participants what they would like to be called, and invite them to sign their messages accordingly.

Male and female

In some cultures, relationships between male and female are more constrained than in Westernized societies. In some the opinions of females may carry less weight than those of males, and females may appear inhibited or indeed be ignored in the presence of males. The e-moderator needs to be alert to ensuring everyone can contribute, and everyone's views are valued, and model these responses too.

Asking questions

Asking direct questions can sometimes be problematic. For instance, in traditional Chinese culture, asking questions (particularly of teachers and parents) is not generally encouraged. So being urged by the e-moderator to ask questions online may not translate naturally into action, and may need active and continuous – albeit sensitive – prompting and support. As a corollary, in some cultures, there can be an expectation that the teacher will 'tell' and the student will learn what the teacher says. A preoccupation with assessment and 'getting through the work' can follow. All of these may translate into an expectation of authority by the e-moderator on the part of the participants. It's impossible in a short time to change this. However, creating an atmosphere of equality and the e-moderator setting up structured opportunities will help.

Critiquing

Being asked to offer a critique of someone else's offering may be seen as being rude in some cultures. The person whose work is critiqued may feel slighted and in danger of losing face. Someone of lower status may be inhibited from offering an opinion other than a complimentary one. In the online environment, we try to enable gradual development and support for all participants, and then we encourage them to challenge. Some people may need more help than others in this way of working.

Opening up online

Personal disclosure online as part of socialization into the group, which some of us may take for granted if we are used to the Anglo-American style, is again not necessarily the norm in all cultures. And some will be more generally reticent about articulating their thoughts online. Really good e-tivities exploring cultural differences at Stage 2 will help lay the ground for the valuing of all contributions. Make it clear that people do not need to disclose personal information, and avoid posting your own information based on marital status or career achievements, since this may otherwise 'set the tone'.

Using names

Asking for preferred names for addressing participants can save great potential embarrassment. If you are used to the Western style of first name and then surname, you need to take especial care. Find out as much as you can from the course sponsor. Take the list of participants' names and annotate it with each preferred name as you learn it. Print off that list and keep it constantly by you whilst you are online. And try to gently insist that people sign their messages with their preferred name.

Genders can easily be confused too. Here's a recent example exchange from one of our e-moderating development courses:

JC writes: Val Richardson proudly added an example with his 6 year old granddaughter.

VR writes: Interesting gender assumption here!!!!! Juan, my name is English and it's Valerie. Val

JC writes: Sorry Val! Valery? Cultural misunderstanding. In Spanish sounds closer to Valentin.

PC (the e-moderator) writes: Hola Juan. Maybe I can give some assistance here. Val is a she, I've met her! You can find her introductory message in Week One Announcements Forum.

Resource 9

Creating 'presence'

Many online participants expect a great deal from their e-moderators, while e-moderators try to encourage online participants to be self-sufficient. Here are some strategies that create a feeling of 'presence' online, without the e-moderator having to be there 24 hours each day!

- Send out a personal e-mail letter to all participants before the course starts, indicating how often they can expect you to visit (usually once a day).
- Greet each participant by a welcome e-mail on his or her first arrival, as well as acknowledging his or her arrival in the conference.
- Ask for each participant to send a personal e-mail to the e-moderator as well as post a message in the conference, early in the course. This helps to check who has arrived and when, and makes it easy to respond individually.
- Mention each participant by name at some point in early summaries. Continue to mention individuals in your messages. This is very motivating and a fine way to acknowledge contributions.
- Run an e-tivity at Stage 1, exploring how participants expect to fit the conferencing into their daily lives, and self-disclose a little about yours.
- As the conferencing builds up and you find you have many messages to read on your arrival each day, focus on the last few messages in a thread rather than reading them chronologically.
- As participants become more self-sufficient and motivated (by Stage 3), avoid responding to each message but focus on setting up discussions

really well and then summarizing after a given length of time, adding your own teaching points then if appropriate.

- Be prepared to put a congratulatory message up and then an invitation to further action (such as, 'Very interesting points here, can I invite a summarizer', or maybe, 'please focus on ★★★ aspect now to build on the ideas').
- *E-tivities* (Salmon, 2002a) offers you more ideas for designing for effective and efficient use of e-moderator time.

Resource 10

Housekeeping

The conferencing environment needs to be looked after, in much the same way as your house, apartment or teaching environment, in order to keep it serviceable. These 'hygiene' factors will be invisible if they are working well. Without them, many conferences have foundered and your loftier or more creative teaching and learning online goals are unlikely to be achievable. Many studies have shown that small changes in housekeeping make a considerable difference!

Make these protocols clear to your e-moderators:

1. Decide whether forums or conferences and their sub-sets will be set up in advance, or whether you will allow topics and sub-conferences to 'emerge' over time – and housekeep accordingly, so that the conferences operate how participants expect.
2. Structured activities (e-tivities) need to be set up in advance of the participants' arrival (Salmon, 2002a).
3. Allow interesting and relevant topics to 'emerge' from participants at various times, create sub-conferences to support emergent topics, and delete dormant conferences to make virtual space for them.
4. E-moderators need to visit often (agree how often) and notify participants if they are likely to be offline for more than a week or so (lack of appearance online mystifies and disturbs other participants). Ask a colleague e-moderator to visit your conference whilst you are away. The more structured e-tivities you use, the less you need to visit.
5. With big conferences and large numbers, teams of e-moderators can work together to ensure regular responses to participants and maintenance of conferences.

6. Create and maintain good 'layout' of onscreen access conferences, very easy navigation around them, summarizing and the quick closing and deleting of inactive conferences to keep the screen as clear as possible.
7. Summarize, delete or archive messages so that no more than around 20 messages in any one conference or sub-conference are active at any one time. This avoids participants being overwhelmed upon visiting a conference after a few days.

Resource 11

Promoting active participation

I'm often asked, 'In what ways can e-moderators make learners participate online?' Well of course you can't make anyone do anything, but you can ensure the online environment is attractive and worthwhile for as many people as possible and reduce known 'turn-offs'. Here is a list of ideas from experienced e-moderators for you to consider. The ideas are divided into 'carrots' (encouragement) or 'sticks' (penalties for not participating).

Carrots

Sell benefits

- Promote the benefits of online at face-to-face meetings with demonstrations if possible.
- Get others to explain how they were once online novices and their satisfaction of achieving online communication and interaction skills.
- Ensure the benefits for learning are explained.
- Explain how easy online is.
- Explain the support available online.
- Explain that many people find online reduces panic as assessments and tests come nearer.
- Explain the opportunities for making contacts and friendships online.
- Explain online's role in providing confirmation of one's own ideas.
- Explain that it will help with everyday life skills – for example, e-business and e-commerce.

Add value to the learning methods

- Provide online feedback on students' progress. Feedback is critical to retention and achievement.
- Give recognition (public and private) to those successfully contributing online.
- Give plenty of opportunities for individuals to contribute and explore their own ideas and influence others through online networking.
- Ensure that online enhances understanding of course content.

Build contacts and communities

- E-moderate most carefully to ensure inclusion of all, lack of discrimination and celebration of diversity and effort.
- Ensure online enables the building of a community of peers (not only teacher–student contact).
- Ensure conferences give access to the knowledge of others in a distributed network.
- Give access to known experts in the field.
- Provide activities that are not available or possible except online – for example, large-scale but easy research.
- Provide specialist contact – for example, industry or interest groups.
- Provide conferences that enable individuals to 'keep up' with news about peers and competitors.
- Ensure everyone has a chance to contribute, that is, personal visibility.
- Ensure academics, instructors, teaching assistants log on as well as learners.
- Ensure social and friendship-building conferences are available.
- Provide ongoing online contact after the course is over.
- Provide for self-help groups and voluntary group working.
- Allow for lurking – give time for participants to develop.
- Keep the purpose of all conferences clear and focused and constantly reiterated throughout online activities or discussions.
- At Stage 4 (knowledge construction) provide for working through new problems, insist on valuing all contributions and no 'right' answer, creating and making meaning from all contributions, excellent e-moderating, sharing good practice.
- Provide online tutorials and support on course material that has proved difficult or challenging.
- Run online tutorial sessions before assessments or exams (watch them flock in!).

Personalize

- Ask participants to question themselves on what contributions and outcomes from the discussions really made a difference to them as individuals in their thinking, understanding, or practice
- Encourage the sharing of opinions, appropriately contributed, as well as experience.

Assessment

- Provide extra marks for participation or percentage of marks of total score.
- Consider peer endorsements based on quality of contributions to discussion.
- Monitor and publish longer-term performance, especially if working online leads to success on the course, linked to online participation of students.

Sticks (try to convert sticks into carrots)

Sticks to use

- Make other ways of achieving the same learning or assessment more difficult to undertake. In 'blended' situations, avoid making the face-to-face element easier to achieve.
- Insist on online participation having a direct relationship to assessment, that is, assessed components of course cannot be completed without online participation.
- Provide some pieces of information that participants can only access through online means.
- Ensure group working by making completion of projects impossible otherwise.
- Post relevant and useful information online for short periods only (i.e. an incentive to log on at a particular time).
- Set very clear and structured deadlines for submission of online work.

Sticks to avoid

- Discrimination of all kinds.
- Technical and access difficulties (for participants and e-moderators).
- Attacks from active contributors on lurkers.
- Marginalizing or lack of academic recognition or credit given for work online.
- Bullying of any kind (including by e-moderators).
- Exclusion from the course because of lack of online participation.

Resource 12

Aligned student assessment

Assessment should continue to indicate the constructivist and collaborative nature of working online (not just delivery) and should therefore be aligned with learning methods and integrated with the learning design as much as possible.

- Encourage participants to include messages in their assessed tasks from their participation in conferencing. This type of assessment feeds back into online skills development (true alignment!).
- Ask participants to work on a jointly produced 'product' which forms part of a submitted assessment. Marks may be rewarded in part for individual contributions and in part for the collaborative outcome.
- Give participants a chance to practise and demonstrate information literacy in using web-based resources and platforms of all kinds.
- Create some flexibility rather than standardization, in other words an acceptance that in constructivist courses there can be no 'true score'.
- Offer a variety of approaches to an assignment or examination answers, allowing scope for individual development or initiative, and for the most able students to add additional research findings.
- Increase freedom as the programme progresses.
- Use assignments to encourage reflection on the course e-tivities, and encourage participants to use their reflections as part of assessment tasks, perhaps revisiting, reworking or comparing and contrasting aspects of the conferencing.

- Try extended essays or portfolios rather than closed book proctored exams for the end of course assessment.
- If you have electronic submission of assessed elements, encourage exploitation of the media – for example, by submitting assignments in e-portfolios.
- Award marks for both content and presentation if you wish (but avoid participants spending all their time, say, on 'web design').
- Offer 'templates' for submission of work if appropriate. These make expectations of the students clearer, and marking easier and faster, but reduce creativity.
- Allow participants to continue to present their work for view and comment by others, indicating that only the final submission will be scored (perhaps using an 'unknown' marker at this stage).

See www.reap.ac.uk for more ideas.

By the way, you might be concerned about plagiarism. Martin Weller's experience with large-scale online assessment tells us, 'Tutors reported that verifying the students' work was not difficult, and that the prolonged interaction offered by such networked courses means they come to know their students to a greater extent than on traditional distance learning courses' (Weller, 2002b: 114; see also Badge and Scott, 2009).

Most higher educational organizations use some form of electronic plagiarism detection as feedback to e-moderators and participants. It's a good idea to have some discussion around these in the conferencing to ensure that students understand the concept of plagiarism and the nature of academic writing and citing. The monitoring software can then be used to give feedback and improve assignments (Gullifer and Tyson, 2010).

Resource 13

Evaluating online conferencing

Consider very carefully the objectives you want to use in evaluating your success with online interaction. Try to capture the learning experience – students will very readily tell you how it is for them.

It's difficult to hold for sufficient variables semester on semester, year on year, in a rapidly changing techno/pedagogical environment to be sure that technological innovations, or the improvement in learning design or e-moderating skills account for change in students' retention, completion or achievements. However, it's well worth keeping records over time – at Beyond Distance at Leicester we have been amazed at how some interventions really have had a rapid impact. You can see examples throughout this book – John Fothergill's case study on page 97 for example.

As I was writing this section, an e-mail came in from one of our psychology lecturers, talking about the power of the human voice for his distance learners. He said:

> not a single one of our dissertation students has needed an extension this year (this is unheard of and a very pleasant surprise!). All . . . have handed in their final dissertations on time. The only difference from previous years is that they have had access to the feedback podcasts on their draft dissertations.

The objectives may be different from ones you have used in the past:

- Be explicit from the start about your learning design strategies and the ideals and values behind your use of online teaching and learning and find ways of judging these.
- Explore the impact of conferencing on skills such as reflection on practice, meta-cognition and practical outcomes.
- Accept diversity of outcomes rather than demanding uniform learning.
- Consider whether knowledge is being created and disseminated rather than information merely communicated.
- Consider how well tasks and outcomes have been achieved.
- Consider the success of teams.
- Examine evidence of cross-boundary, cross-disciplinary achievements and complexity.

Evaluation questions

You may want to collect data from your conferences and forums for evaluation purposes. Make sure you respect the privacy of conference messages. Avoid dropping in unannounced, and seek permission if you want to quote a message from the conferences (the copyright belongs to the originator of each message, strictly speaking).

Here is a list of some questions you could explore:

- How many of your participants log on at least once, read and contribute? It used to be said that a third of conferencing students read and contribute, a third only read messages and a third neither read nor contribute because they never access the conferences. Is this true for you?
- What helps to motivate participants online, what do they enjoy and benefit from, what encourages them to contribute? Can you develop a control group for comparisons? When you change something online, try to measure the impact, which can be quite large.
- Do those that do not take part participate less in the course overall or are they choosing alternative means of communication? Do more of those who fail to take part drop out or achieve lower results?
- Who is relating to whom and in what way? What requests are there for setting up new conferences or other online activities?
- Do the conferences provide learning to those for whom it was intended? Or are they providing learning only to 'early adopters'? Are the benefits spread across all learners? Do some groups benefit more than others? Check whether there are improvements in student learning, as opposed to enthusiasm about the novelty of working with new media.
- What are the trade-offs on conferencing? What is not happening that did before?

- Does the five-stage model (Figure 2.1) hold true for your learners in your online course?
- Are costs shifted onto the students by working online? Is this worth it for them, and for you?
- Can you use message history and log-on facilities to spot and support students who are struggling?
- Are there differences in results between structured and unstructured, well and less well e-moderated conferences?
- How much time do participants spend online? How does this compare with your traditional ways of learning and interaction? If it is more, or less, is this good or bad?
- Can you ascertain the influence of the e-moderator and in what ways?

Resource 14

E-moderating for synchronous conferencing

E-moderating a synchronous session within a virtual classroom is similar to facilitating a face-to-face session, but without the direct eye contact and physical presence. Most virtual classrooms show the list of participants, so you know who is there. It's more difficult to know who is active, who is multi-tasking (common!) or has left their computers. It can also be difficult for participants to concentrate on listening through headphones and looking at a screen for long periods, no matter how interesting the presentation. It is essential to use participatory techniques in the design and delivery of the session.

If your group is meeting for the first time in a web-based virtual classroom, you need to take care of Stages 1 and 2 fast so that discussion can move quickly to more interesting things at Stages 3–5.

Designing the session

- Structure the virtual classroom session into 15–20 minute chunks followed by questions and discussions.
- Use polling or quizzes frequently to ensure that everyone understands the speaker, to ask for people's opinions and just to make sure that everyone is still actively taking part.

- In some virtual classrooms, the space on the screen used to display presentation materials can also be written on and viewed by participants, like a shared whiteboard, for brainstorms. Avert chaos by creating charts with spaces for people to write in, and showing participants how to resize and move their text.
- Collaborative writing tools (such Google Docs) can also be used in virtual classrooms via desktop sharing or alongside an online telephony service such as Skype. Participants will need to have two windows open on their computer screens – one for Skype and one for Google Docs.
- Some virtual classrooms have separate small group spaces usually called 'breakaway rooms'. Make sure there is at least one person who is confident with the technology and one person who is willing to lead or e-moderate the discussion, in each group. After a breakaway session, output from individual groups can be loaded onto the main screen.
- Consider whether you want your presentation materials to be made widely available after the session, for example on SlideShare. If so, check the copyright restrictions on any third-party material you use, and choose a licence (one of the Creative Commons licences).

Before the session starts

Send out an e-mail to participants giving them the following information:

- A link where they can test their computer setup (all the major webconferencing systems offer this support).
- The date and time of the session, with a link to a website which enables participants to convert time zones.
- The link to the session, and what time the session will be open.
- Advice regarding hardware: it is usually best to use a headset with a built-in microphone rather than external speakers, as external speakers can cause echoes and feedback.
- Who to contact with questions or technical difficulties.
- Invite participants to join 15–30 minutes before the start of the session, to check that their technology works and to have an informal chat with other participants. Introduce people to each other to make sure that the pre-session chat is inclusive.
- The pre-session chat time can also be used to develop important skills in participants new to the platform. Try: 'putting hands up', smiley faces, writing in the text box, resizing the windows, testing the microphone, responding to quizzes or polls and writing on the whiteboard.
- If participants are logging on from a less well-resourced location, groups of participants may be clustered around a single computer. Don't assume

that one name on the list of participants always equates to one participant. Check this out early!

During the session

- For larger groups (more than 12), it is helpful to have a team approach, with a main e-moderator, a co-moderator and a technical support person. The main e-moderator will welcome the participants, introduce the speaker, and carry out the weaving and summarizing. She or he should also seek permission before starting the recording and let participants know that the recording will be available for later viewing.
- The co-moderator will focus on following comments and questions in the chat box. The co-moderator can reply to questions in the chat box that can be answered by brief written messages, and should alert the first moderator to any questions or comments that need to be addressed during question times.
- The technical support person can be on standby to answer questions, do technical trouble shooting (there's usually something even if you've tested) for participants and support the presenter.
- People who join late will not be able to see any of the text chat that has gone before. E-moderators need to let latecomers know if they have missed any essential information.
- Invite participants to use video when they ask questions if they wish to, but no pressure!
- If the video becomes jerky or freezes (usually due to bandwidth) participants may wish to downgrade the resolution to black and white or turn the video off.
- Encourage the more technically proficient participants to support those less familiar to overcome any technology challenges.

After the session

- In addition to archiving the recording of the presentation, and the session materials, thanking the presenters and sending any follow-up messages to participants, you may want to publish the materials online as Open Educational Resources.

Many thanks to Gabi Witthaus of the Beyond Distance Research Alliance at the University of Leicester for developing this resource.

Resource 15

E-moderating for virtual worlds

- A virtual world offers a big choice of meeting venues, travel locations and activities.
- Maximize the benefits of the virtual world by organizing a virtual field trip, a virtual visit to the past, or creating an unusual or special setting for a group meeting.
- Avoid simply reproducing what you can do just as easily in real life.
- For a wide range of ways of deploying virtual worlds for pedagogical purposes see Salmon (2009).

Designing virtual world activities (VW-tivities): Some examples

In the Leicester Second Life island, we designed a vw-tivity that was effective for simulation and role play – activities too challenging to create in the real world! Occupational Psychology students worked together on an oil rig in a virtual work experience, getting a 'taste' of some of the hazards of oil rigs and their occupation-related challenges. The virtual oil rig is reusable and adaptable (Barklamb, 2010) (Stages 3–4).

A Sports Day in Second Life included obstacle-course ice skating, motorboat racing and skydiving. Participants as avatars from all over the world had fun together, trying out team-building activities they could not (or would not) undertake in real life. The activities only required a small amount of preparation (Learning Futures 10 workshops, 2010). These gave practice in virtual world movement and camera control and the start of socialization (Stages 1 and 2).

The Leicester online academic conferences conclude each day with a virtual world campfire meeting, in which delegates meet as avatars around a beach campfire complete with sunset and mugs of hot chocolate, to discuss the keynote, workshops and papers of the day. These socialization and reflection events require minimum design and technical preparation. (Learning Futures 10 workshops, 2010).

Plan your activity

- Virtual world activities need to be planned so that your main aims are achieved and contingencies are covered.
- Trial the vw-tivity yourself and with colleagues in advance in-world, to see how much time it takes and whether induction is needed for participants. Plan for groups no larger than about eight, at least until you gain experience.
- Test any equipment in advance and make sure you know how it works. Ask another avatar to test it as well.
- Plan in-world discussion time. You will find that many of the principles of using synchronous classrooms apply to virtual worlds (see Resource 14).
- Choose whether to use text chat or voice chat, and impose some light structure.
- It's sometimes hard to know which avatar is speaking as there is no direct 'eye' contact as in real life. More than four actively speaking avatars can become confusing. One solution is to take turns at standing up or moving to a particular position to speak.
- Using text has advantages with larger groups. Sometimes shyer avatars will ask questions by text where they would not wish to speak. Also it's easier to moderate since everything that has been typed remains available to view. Chat logs can be saved for later analysis and review.
- Some vw-moderators use voice for themselves and text for participant avatars.

Prepare participants for the activity

Participants' computers need to have good graphics cards and internet connection in order to provide a virtual world experience. If the virtual world environment appears to move in a sequence of jumps rather than smoothly, the access computer is probably not suitable.

You may be able to make your vw-tivity simple enough that you can quickly practise the required skills at the beginning of the session. Or hold an induction or training session prior to the event, if necessary to help participants to walk, fly, sit, chat and use the sound preferences.

VW-moderating

When working with participants who are still new to virtual worlds, be very encouraging and patient. New avatars often feel awkward and self-conscious about their movement skills.

Those new to virtual worlds are often eager to experiment with their appearance. Novice avatars should avoid changing their appearance or clothes when around other avatars to start with. Things don't always look how they intended!

With inexperienced avatars, try to work with a second vw-moderator whose role is to personally help individuals who are having difficulties in-world. This leaves the primary moderator free to guide the group as a whole toward the learning objectives.

In some vw-worlds, such as Second Life, there are many open areas and regions to explore. These can be helpful to encourage fun and research for an activity in-world. However, avatars sometimes have difficulty in finding their way back to the group. Decide in advance on a strategy to easily return them. For example, offer a teleport or send an Instant Message. Do regular head-counts to make sure everyone is still with you, especially if you are near "water", where it is easy for avatars to fall in and disappear from view! (Don't worry no avatars will drown.)

Familiarize yourself with the software's sound and voice chat settings. Make sure those who will use voice to communicate in-world are using headphones. The combination of speaking into a microphone and listening to the vw sounds through ordinary computer speakers would otherwise distort the sounds for other avatars.

Avatars and identities

Appearances: learners uniquely react to the opportunity to create new identities in virtual worlds. Give them space (and support if necessary) to choose their own in-world appearance and, whenever possible, accept individual's representations of themselves. Try to directly interact with the avatar when in-world (rather than to the real-life person), without challenging the differences between the two.

Culture: real-life people may maintain their cultural practices in-world or may take the opportunity to alter or discard them. The standard avatar identities offered by vws such as Second Life may not be acceptable to all participants. You may wish to consider discreetly offering further choices of clothing by informing participants how to find and wear them. One of our vw-tivities at Leicester featured a 'dressing-up box' dispensing free clothing and artefacts.

Ability and accessibility: participants with a disability may need to let you know if their use of the virtual world is affected. For example, someone with a hearing-impairment will need to use typed chat; participants with dyslexia may require more time for text. Consider the virtual world's potential to offer those with physical disabilities the chance to do things they may not be able to do in the real world.

Many thanks to Terese Bird, Paul Rudman, Gabi Witthaus, Alejandro Armellini and Palitha Edirisingha of the Beyond Distance Research Alliance at the University of Leicester for their avatars' input to this resource.

Resource 16

E-moderating for podcasting

Podcasts can be used within most VLEs and as externally accessible files from a website outside the VLE. Podcasts can be helpful to support the five-stage model. The voice of the e-moderator (rather than lengthy recording of lectures) coming through short well-worded podcasts but with an informal tone and style can add a new dimension to how discussion boards are used for collaborative learning activities.

1. Planning your podcasts

With some planning, you will be able to integrate podcasts more effectively into your e-moderation. I recommend the ten-factor design model in planning podcasts. The model is available online at www.podcastingforlearning.com as an interactive version, and in Salmon and Edirisingha (2008: 153–68).

1.1 *The purpose of podcasts*: think about which stage(s) of the five-stage model could be enhanced by voice.

Examples of podcasts for each of the five-stage model:

- Access and motivation: a podcast created by participants from previous cohorts describing their learning experience to motivate the current cohort.
- Socialization: ice-breaking podcasts created by each participant explaining something about themselves and/or their surroundings, sounds from the street where their office is located.

- Information exchange: an interview with someone relevant to the course material, for example, a head-teacher, police officer, or shop owner, with an audio commentary on the interview.
- Knowledge construction: a podcast with contradictory views from relevant people, related to the course material, as a spark to synchronous or asynchronous debate by participants.

1. *Development*: each participant selects one discussion topic and summarizes and weaves the threads and adds an audio critique demonstrating their own understanding of the course concepts.
2. *The medium*: you can choose audio only or audio and moving and/or still images (also known as vodcasts). The choice needs to be made on the purpose of podcasts and whether visuals are really necessary to convey the message. Creating audio podcasts is easier than creating video podcasts. And creating podcasts should not pose an additional technological and time barrier for participants, therefore, our advice is to stick to simplicity at least until participants become familiar with the technology. From our experience of research projects where both teachers and students created podcasts (IMPALA and DUCKLING projects (Nie et al., 2010; Edirisingha, Hawkridge and Fothergill, 2010)) we found that audio podcasts were sufficient to achieve the educational objectives identified.
3. *The convergence*: consider how much the podcasts are integrated with other e-learning or learning technologies (see the Engineering case study on page 97).
4. *The authors or contributors of content*: go for diversity of voices and interest! The contributors could be students, students from previous cohorts, relevant people from the general public, other staff from your organization (from the learning resource centre, disability support services, IT services) and yourself as the e-moderator. Students will love to hear your voice addressing them!
5. *The structure*: consider the frequency and timing of podcasts. Learning is enhanced if you create a regular pattern such as weekly or monthly.
6. *The reusability*: consider whether your podcasts, either as a whole or as sections, can be reused. The podcasts that your students have created can be re-used (with their permission) as exemplars for other students.
7. *The length*: the longer the podcast, the longer it takes to listen to. Keep the length of each podcast to five minutes or less.
8. *The style*: consider whether the podcasts take a presentation style, an interview, a dialogue, or other formats. Think 'radio show'! Because of the range of objectives (linked to the five stages), there is room for a variety of podcasting styles that can truly enrich your course.
9. *The framework of content organization*: in a text file, we can glance at the whole of it, skim read it and get a sense of its content to decide which

bits to focus our attention on. We can't do that with an audio file. We need to listen to the whole of the podcast. Therefore, it is important to have a common framework for your podcasts. This framework could be as simple as a 30 second introduction at the beginning that explains what the podcast is about and who the contributors are, a middle section with the main content, and a final 30 seconds which summarizes key points of the podcast and mention of further useful resources.

10. *The delivery and access systems*: podcasts can be made available via your VLE, a website or repository and through an internet-based feeder service such as Really Simple Syndication (RSS). Using a separate website or syndication and feeder system requires a little technical work, which we have discussed in some detail in pages 25–8 of our guide to creating podcasts (Salmon et al., 2008). Or to keep it simple, attach your sound file in the same way as you would a text file, in your VLE.

2. Training for creating educational podcasts

Some training for both e-moderator and the participants in the use of software and hardware for creation, distribution and management of podcast files is useful for the successful use of podcasts to support the five-stage model.

2.1 *Equipment and software for podcasting*. To create podcasts, you need a computer with a soundcard, and a headset which includes both a microphone and speakers. You can also record sound on a digital sound recorder which are easily sourced from high-street computer stores or from an online shop such as Amazon.

If you are using a computer to record podcasts, you need dedicated software designed for recording and editing sound files. There are a number of free and paid for software that can be downloaded from the internet. In our IMPALA research project (www.impala.co.uk), we used Audacity, free software, which we found adequate for creating pedagogical podcasts. You may have some software that comes freely with your computer, such as the GarageBand software that comes with Mac computers.

2.2 *Recording and editing a podcast*. You will need to carry out simple sound checks before you begin to record. This includes checking whether you have connected your microphone correctly and testing whether you have set the recording levels to the appropriate level.

The technical aspects of recording and editing sound files might look a bit daunting at first, but our experience with many students and teachers who took part in our IMPALA and DUCKLING projects suggest that learning the technical skills is easy. Pages 15–22 of our guide book (Salmon et al., 2008) provide step-by-step instructions with illustrations of screen shots.

2.3 *Publishing a podcast*. You can either upload the sound file in the same way you would upload a Word document, or you can use the VLE's podcast publishing tool to make your podcasts available on the VLE.

3. Guidelines for pedagogical podcasts

Listening to podcasts can be time consuming if there are too many, and if the messages are too long – keep them very short and focused.

The area within the VLE where podcasts are posted can be configured so that participants and their individual contributions can be identified. It is good practice to follow an agreed file naming convention and include meta data related to information on podcasts (e.g. name of creator and key words), so that contributions can be attributed to the creators of podcasts, and information contained in the podcasts become transparent.

You can ensure more effective use of podcasts by asking all participants to adhere to an agreed format and length of podcasts.

4. Weaving and summarizing podcasts

E-moderators and participants might find weaving and summarizing the thread of podcasts time consuming because it is not possible to copy, paste or edit as in the case with text-based environments. However, you can take notes while listening to podcasts, for weaving and summarizing later on. Participants can take responsibility for weaving in their small groups; the e-moderator can construct a final overarching summary.

Many thanks to the IMPALA (www.impala.com) and DUCKLING (www. le.ac.uk/duckling) research and development teams at the Beyond Distance Research Alliance at the University of Leicester (especially Dr Palitha Edirisingha) for their help in compiling this resource. Our books Salmon and Edirisingha (2008) and Salmon, Edirisingha, Mobbs, Mobbs and Dennett (2008) provide a guide for the e-moderator and participants and case studies. See also www.podcastingforlearning.com.

Resource 17

Monitoring e-moderating

You may find it useful to use something like the form below, if you decide to build up monitoring systems for quality assurance in e-moderating. Appoint monitors from experienced e-moderators who can take a collegiate and development approach to supporting and developing others and can themselves learn from the experience.

The form can be completed online by the monitor after a visit to a conference and shared, with discussion offered with the e-moderator visited.

E-Moderator's monitoring report

Name of e-moderator   Date: . . . .

Name of Monitor   Copied to: . . . .

I visited your VLE activity/conference(s) called *(names of conference(s))*

On *(dates and times)*

Here is my reaction to your online activities (as an eavesdropper). Please see my comments as a starting point for a debate. Please contact me by e-mail if you would like to discuss any of them.

Aspects of your e-moderating that seemed to be working well:

E.g.

I admired the structure of your e-tivity because
I noticed a clear scaffold for students in . . .
I observed that your opening questions were successful because . . .
I noticed that your activity ** went very well because . . .
I thought your review of (assignment, activity, technique) worked really well because . . .

Aspects that I'd like you to reflect on:

E.g.

Have you tried. . .
One technique I find helpful is. . .
I noticed that Participant X may need extra help because . . .
Maybe it's time to close off Conference Y because . . .
Here is my personal view on your online activities
Here is a resource you might find helpful . . .
Have you considered deploying other than text? E.g.:

Approach to:	Great	OK	Needs improvement	Comments
Design of e-tivities				
Content/resources				
Use of time				
Creativity/flexibility				
Housekeeping				
Diversity				
Participation				
Quality of contribution				
Your 'presence'				
Weaving & summarizing				

Best wishes (name of monitor)
E-Moderator's response to monitor:

Resource 18

Encouraging self-managing groups

E-moderating large groups can be time-consuming, and participants benefit from becoming self-managing, at least by Stage 4.

The basic framework for encouragement includes:

- *Describe the form and type of output (and of course by when) that the group should produce and where they should post it.* Aim to be prescriptive without being too restrictive. Indicate the main issues that must be addressed.
- *Set out the plenary process in the plenary thread.* This can be part of your welcoming message and will let them know that you'll be back later to help.
- Suggest that the first task of the groups is to decide what they have to do and who will do what to arrive at the sort of outcome to be produced. This can take some time for more complicated tasks! For new groups it would be better to suggest how they tackle the task. You could offer them this structure as a starting point.

  i) Agree what tasks are required. (A thread may be needed for each task.)
  ii) Who will lead for each task, who will contribute, when the task should be completed by.
  iii) Designate a thread to place the outcomes of each task.
  iv) One person to pull the outcomes together.
  v) All to agree or suggest changes to produce final outcome.
  vi) Post to the plenary thread.

- Invite larger groups into smaller work teams. Give them plenty of time to complete the e-tivity and then report back to the larger group in plenary.
- Offer clarification about the task, the timescale and the form of presentation if necessary.
- Leave them to get on with the task, only intervening if they fail to post their contribution to the plenary on time.
- Start a discussion on the results of the plenary contributions but do not dominate it. Summarize yourself or ask an experienced participant to do this.

There are some special characteristics that will help groups to self-manage online:

- *Ask individuals to confirm when they have joined in.* A simple joining activity in the thread will leave a trace to indicate that participants have arrived. A cross-check against a list of participants will reveal who is late. Designate a participant from each work team to follow up less visible contributors.
- *State the purpose of the task.* The task will motivate the participants. Offer clarification if necessary but allow opportunities for flexible interpretations.
- *Describe how groups will be formed.* An element of self-selection helps to maintain interest, but ensure that the method is simply described and incapable of being misunderstood.
- *Set up a thread for each group and let the group know where to locate the thread.* If you don't, they'll only ask you!
- *Ask the participants to review both content (their main focus) and the process.* Include setting up the group, the degree to which they found the task motivating, how they collaborated, their approach to feeding back as part of the learning points, so it becomes 'natural and normal' for them to reflect on not just their outputs but also on how they worked together.

Thanks to Naomi Lawless and David Shepherd for their input for this resource.

Resource 19

Supporting online novices

Many participants are novices at communicating in groups, teaching or learning online, even if they are familiar with computing or web-based social networking. If they are used to one type of online environment, they may be unused to another – for example, virtual worlds. In the early days, they need special attention.

Based on my research, e-moderators can expect three types of response. I call these swimming, waving and drowning online.

The swimmers:

- dive in early;
- have relevant experience – for example, Web 2.0;
- are usually willing to help others;
- may become disruptive if they think the learning activities are not demanding or interactive enough;
- are likely to claim they know of better systems than the one you've chosen to use.

The wavers:

- need considerable help and encouragement to get started;
- usually arrive after the main group;
- may need help in sifting through a mass of messages;
- feel there is too little time to do everything;

- do very well and become enthusiasts once they've got logged on, got going and are given support.

The drowners:

- find it very difficult indeed to log on;
- or promise to log on but do not;
- may be reluctant to ask for or accept help;
- may perceive working on line with others to be disruptive to their learning;
- have little motivation to succeed;
- complain at every opportunity that online work is irrelevant or too time consuming;
- find the relationship building and socializing online difficult, especially if they are used to taking a leading role in face-to-face groups;
- do better if a supportive *swimmer* is allocated to them as a mentor.

To convert wavers and drowners to swimmers:

- build 'scaffolding' – steps towards success and confidence – into your induction programme;
- provide social and test areas within the online environment where they can experiment and continue to build up their confidence;
- build on-screen displays that can be navigated fairly intuitively, without constantly reading instructions;
- address student expectations when providing online resources and activities;
- offer parallel ways of working where access is an issue, but only for the shortest possible time because you need to build up a critical mass online quickly;
- provide an effective e-mail helpline for resolving access and password problems;
- ask a naïve user (we call them 'reality checkers') to try out your e-tivities instructions before you put them on screen for everyone;
- provide an individual welcome to each participant in response to his/her first message and support each one in the early stages of learning conferencing;
- provide students with full encouragement to learn by doing, by experimenting and by making mistakes in a supportive environment;
- emphasize the purposeful and relevant nature of conferencing for future learning on the course;
- e-moderate conferences often, with archiving of messages so that newcomers have only a few to read.

Resource 20

Understanding lurking

There are many reasons for participants to log on but not contribute.

First, identify the types of lurkers you have. You will see that each challenge e-moderators in different kinds of ways:

- *Uncomfortable in 'public'*, a common reason is unfamiliarity with the use of language of the conference.
- *Learning about the group*, such as needing time before contributing.
- *Building an online identity*: common at Stage 2.
- *Fear of persistence of messages*: concern that postings become 'too permanent'.
- *Communication overload*: common at Stage 3.
- *Not necessary to post*: perhaps seeing others post what s/he might have contributed.
- *Group characteristics*: falling out with another individual or feeling the pace is too slow or fast.
- *Personal characteristics*, for example, introvert in a group of extroverts.

Adapted from Bax and Pegrum (2009). Bax and Pegrum's lurking study offers more research and understanding.

My taxonomy from experience is of three main kinds of lurkers:

- Those still trying to find out how to use the system, who lack access, skills or confidence to participate (i.e. those operating at Stages 1 and 2 in the five-stage model). Check whether they need help to log on, or simply greater motivation or encouragement through one-to-one contact with you, by e-mail or telephone, or perhaps some written instructions.

- The sponge – people who are needing a bit of time to come to terms with the environment, norms and ways of communicating online – that is, those at Stages 2 and 3 in the model. Give them time and support and they should start to take part.
- The silent thief/freeloader – people happy to use other people's contributions rather than feeling the need to contribute. These people need a reason – even a requirement – to take part.

Here are some strategies for text-based forums:

- Check that all participants know how to post and 'reply' to messages.
- Provide a test area and an arrivals area.
- Check that you have a free-flowing or social conferencing area.
- Give participants time to become used to the online environment before insisting that they post their responses.
- Check across all your conferences – your lurkers may be participating (and using their time and energy) in a different conference from where you were expecting them to be.
- Reduce the number of messages in each conference (by summarizing often) – there'll be less to read so they'll be more likely to reply.
- Check you have a critical mass for the purpose of a conference (less than six participants or more than 15 active participants is likely not to work well, depending on the online activity).
- Try to be proactive, perhaps use some humour rather than anger.
- Check whether one or two individuals are dominating the conference – and deal tactfully with them to create a more open and equal environment.
- Provide a structured evaluation questionnaire or an area for reflections and/or comments (some lurkers prefer safety in structure).
- Explain to active participants what you are trying to do.
- Allocate active participants to lurkers as mentors.
- Design for simple structured interaction where every participant plays a part (Salmon, 2002a).
- Summarize, plenarize and re-present.
- Change people's groups if that is really necessary.

Resource 21

Valuing online diversity

The skills of relating successfully to the many different kinds of people we encounter through online conferencing are not those any of us are born with! They are, however, those that we need to achieve quite quickly.

The challenge to all participants: typing the talk

Each conference will develop its own cultural norms. You can set the tone for this by making expectations abundantly clear from the beginning. E-moderators should clarify the conference's purpose and expectations, from the start, and if necessary remind participants from time to time.

When sitting at your keyboard, you may experience the illusion of isolation and safety, similar to what you may feel when driving your car. An e-mail message can then seem like an intrusion. If you are in a conference with others who are expressing views with which you cannot agree, that can be difficult too. The conference is a more public forum, like being in a train or a plane where you and the other travellers recognize some basic behavioural rules.

Views expressed in textual messages lack the non-verbal clues, such as facial expression, that add to our face-to-face conversations. This sometimes results in meanings being misinterpreted. You can see my piece about how sometimes voice works better (Resource 15). Take care therefore with using irony, sarcasm and humour in text in case they are taken literally. Take account of this when reading the messages of others.

- If someone accuses others of some incompetence or misdemeanour, there is a strong temptation to play the game of 'Yes! Me too!', 'Ain't it awful!' and 'What's more . . .!' without considering the impact of accumulative accusations. This can create electronic bandwagons. Avoid doing this yourself, and take action against it very fast if you are the e-moderator.
- Use a short period of 'reflection' before responding immediately to a message that disturbs or upsets you, or even those with which you agree particularly strongly.
- It's great to pursue minority interests, complaints or opportunities with others online, and if appropriate to enable data collection and take action. However, avoid doing this in the middle of wide interest, social or learning conferences. It's best to set up a conference for the purpose to which participants can migrate it they wish.
- It's rarely necessary to deprive someone of access to the conference because of inappropriate behaviour. However, this can happen if it's clearly in the interests of the majority.
- Try to use standard English wherever possible, so that slang or regional phrases are not misunderstood.
- Give all participants adequate time to reply, as they may be using a dictionary or assistive software prior to posting their comments.
- Your educational organization or learning and development centre will normally have clearly defined policies on all kinds of ways of ensuring the fairest possible access to learning such as bullying avoidance of harassment or discrimination on the grounds of race, gender and many others. All of these apply just as much when working together in any online environment.

Resource 22

What's going on?

You may find helpful my nine categories for analysing such conferences, because they make it easier to see what's happening in the debate. You could use these categories yourself in conferences that you e-moderate.

Individual thinking

1. Offering up ideas or resources and inviting a critique of them.
2. Asking challenging questions.
3. Articulating, explaining and supporting positions on issues.
4. Exploring and supporting issues by adding explanations and examples.
5. Reflecting on and re-evaluating personal opinions.

Interactive thinking

6. Offering a critique, challenging, discussing and expanding ideas of others.
7. Negotiating interpretations, definitions and meanings.
8. Summarizing and modelling previous contributions.
9. Proposing actions.

Resource 23

What will we call ourselves?

Many educators now talk about the 'Guide on the Side' rather than the 'Sage on the Stage' to indicate more facilitative approaches to teaching. For e-moderators, we need to update this image to reflect the changes in electronic conferencing. As you have seen throughout this book, e-moderators use different kinds of online environments. Now there are also avatar-moderators, who have virtual representations of themselves. I suggest you use this list for workshops and online discussion with e-moderators to explore the role in your own context.

E-moderator. I chose this term to refer to online teaching and facilitation roles. The term moderator has grown up with computer-mediated conferencing and has been used from the earliest days for online conference facilitators. Moderating used to mean to preside over a meeting or discussion. I have added the 'e' (short for electronic) to the front of it, borrowed from e-commerce and e-mail, to indicate the wider and special responsibilities that the online context adds to the role. I do not feel that otherwise, any one common word – for example, learning facilitator – quite embraces the role at all five stages of the e-moderation scaffold. Do you?

Zane Berge in North America and myself in Europe appear to have started using the term e-moderator at much the same time, as the millennium turned. Zane Berge and Mauri Collins maintain a useful e-moderators page, with lots of resources from the early days in the 1990s that can be found at: www.emoderators.com/moderators.shtml.

You will see that throughout this book I've persisted in using the term e-moderator to mean anyone who carries out these roles online. Though as we're finding out, in certain online environments there are special considerations –

hence the use of virtual worlds (VW) moderator and voice (V) boards moderators. If you really get going on the wonderful benefits of podcasted feedback, you might have a p-moderator.

1. *Online negotiator*: where knowledge construction online is desired, the key role for the e-moderator is one of negotiating the meaning of activities and information through online discussion and construction.
2. *Online host*: since the social role of online working is important, you may want to have a social host (or hostess) as well as e-moderators for the teaching and learning conferences. They do not need to run social events online as such (though they may) but ensure everyone is greeted and introduced to others with like-minded interests.
3. *Personal learning trainer*: this was a suggestion from Robin Mason. Learners may need a personal trainer to lead them through materials and networks, identify relevant materials and advisors and point out ways forward (Mason, 1998).
4. *Convenor*: this is a term that we adopted in the Open University Business School and used especially for online conferences and courses where there was a fairly wide audience. We also use e-convenor to mean a trainer of the trainers, e-moderator of the e-moderators in the All Things in Moderation (www.atimod.com) online training courses. Convenor means someone who invokes others to come together for a purpose.
5. *Online conductor*: this suggests the pulling together of a variety of resources whether as people (as in conducting an orchestra to produce a beautiful integrated sound) or perhaps as electrical current conductors – if your conferences are effective and flow along, there will be energy, excitement and power!
6. *Online concierge*: to provide support, advice and information on request (perhaps a map of the area. . .).
7. *Online manager*: much of e-moderating is also 'managing', especially in its up-to-date definition of coaching, supporting and leading. Managerial roles in conferencing include developing objectives, agendas, timetables, rules and group norms. Managing the interactions and capacity of a group is a key success factor in e-moderating, as in management.
8. *E-police*: I hope you will not call yourself this, nor find the need to make laws and enforce them. You will of course need a Code of Practice and protocols for e-moderators and participants.
9. *Online chair*: an e-chair would be useful if a structured meeting with clear action outcomes is needed. The skills of chairing online are similar to those of chairing a face-to-face meeting, with the added complexity and asynchronicity that should result in more democratic decision taking and hence more time than usual.

10. *Online leader*: this is a term I've not seen used. I expect this is because online tends to be a highly democratic medium and leadership may not be seen as quite appropriate. However, e-moderators are truly leaders – they need to set objectives and processes as well as provide and maintain optimum conditions online for the realization of these.

11. *E-teacher*: the terms 'teacher', 'trainer' and 'tutor' are generic and have the advantage of being in common use. Therefore adding 'e-' in front of them to indicate the electronic element probably makes them acceptable in most online courses and processes. I think the term then suggests a more facilitative and developmental role than traditional teaching.

12. *E-master*: the term 'master' has come into use in recent years as in 'web master' – someone who is responsible for the technical, design and perhaps the editorial content of a website. The notion of a 'moderating master', 'e-master' or 'master e-moderator' could be introduced like the sporting or chess term of 'master': someone who has previously won many important games.

13. *Faceless facilitator*: this was a suggestion from Tan Lay In of Ngee Ann Polytechnic, Singapore. She reminds us that instructors experienced in face-to-face facilitation have to learn many new skills in order to promote online collaboration (Tan, 1999).

14. *Tele-coach or tele-tutor*: from Germany came a reminder that learning free of space and time needs a tele-coach (as opposed to a 'presence' coach) able to support learners' entry into the new paradigms, in the way coaches used to be physically beside trainees (Mundemann, 1999).

15. *Online gardener*: this is an idea from the corporate training sector. E-moderators not only need to 'cultivate the garden' (by helping learners acquire knowledge) but also make the garden grow by increasing the store of knowledge available (Benque, 1999).

16. *Animateur*: this term has been used in the radical popular education movement. It originally came from the Greek and means to 'breathe life into' something. It was made popular by Augusto Boal (1988), the Brazilian theatre director and founder of 'Theatre of the Oppressed', building on the work of Paulo Freire (1972) and Freire and Shor (1987). It is sometimes used interchangeably with the term 'facilitator', but 'facilitator' is considered more politically neutral, whereas the animateur's role is more explicitly to support oppressed groups in recognizing and overcoming their oppression.

Try out these metaphors in discussion in your e-moderator development: e-ringmaster, online priest, agent provocateur, devil's advocate, whizzo on the gizmo, bod on the ipod, cybernaut, e-helmsman, e-coach, e-weaver, e-guide, e-captain, invent your own here. Perhaps take an online vote?

Resource 24

Communicating online

Good online communication cannot simply be directed or taught. Try using these ideas to discuss, change and build on. Eventually when there is some shared agreement, adopt your agreed approach to online communication as a protocol and inform newcomers of the approach from the start.
Use e-mail when:

- You have a message for one or several people that you don't want everyone else to see or they don't need to see.
- The convention is to address messages directly to people who need to take action or who need to reply to you and to copy the messages for information to people who you believe need to know about the content – but think first before sending an unnecessary message!

Use forums/conferencing when:

- the message is intended for everyone in a particular group;
- you expect that everyone will have the right to reply;
- there is benefit from everyone in the group seeing replies.

E-communication may be unsuitable when:

- Conveying something upsetting to someone else – choose face-to-face or other synchronous communications.

- To discredit someone by sending e-mail copies to people you consider 'should know' about some problem or misdemeanour. This reflects badly on the sender.
- To perpetuate 'recycling' of a problem or issue without closure or decision. E-mails and conferencing can be very good at exposing and exploring issues. However, someone needs to move to taking and articulating decisions or actions before long.

Online 'netiquette' for e-mails

E-mail conventions:

- Never copy an e-mail to anyone not on the original list, nor into a conference, without asking and receiving the permission of the originator of the message.
- If you do copy someone else in, delete earlier messages that may have become attached with everyone replying.
- Be very careful with titles. Choose a short effective title for your e-mail.
- If you reply to someone and change the subject, change the title too.
- Keep to one topic per e-mail with a relevant title. It's far better to send several short e-mails with different titles than one long one covering many subjects.
- If you need to make a number of points in an e-mail, label them 1, 2, 3 etc. This way, it's easy to reply.
- If you reply to just one part of someone else's e-mail, copy and paste their words into the start of your e-mail, so it's clear the sections to which you are referring.
- You can build 'groups' of people to e-mail for your convenience. Use these cautiously and only when your message truly concerns everyone in that group. If you have frequent messages of that kind, setting up a conference may work better.
- If you receive an e-mail message which has been addressed to a number of people, think carefully before replying to all of them when you may only need to make the comment to the originator of the message, or one or two other people. Some people get very annoyed about many minor e-mails circulating around large groups.
- If you receive a message that contains a 'reply all' to a large group including you, and which you consider irrelevant, simply delete it. Treat it as junk mail. Avoid replying to 'all' again in your anger and perpetuating the problem.
- Delete, before opening, all emails that are 'junk' or strange – they may be caused by, or conveying, a virus or attempting to get you to respond in

any way. You'll never be asked for your passwords or bank account this way.

Online 'netiquette' for group conferencing

Enter a CV (résumé) so that others know a little about you. Include:

- something about your background, jobs and interests;
- any particular expertise and support you can offer to others;
- your general geographical location.

About computer conferencing conventions

- Take advantage of training and support to get the most from the computer conferencing software. Then you'll be able to discuss issues rather than ask how to find conferences or send messages. However, you will find people on conferences very willing to help you with anything – just ask.
- The main principles of computer-mediated communication are the same as those of any conversation or dialogue but with a little more emphasis of coming to shared understandings.
- Wide participation without being able to see people offers distinct advantages of any time/any place. It means, however, that you need to be even more considerate than usual in the way you communicate and relate to others online because all communication is text based and displayed.
- There are delays before response, and with more than a few individuals joined to a conference, considerable complexity results, therefore you need to follow some protocols and conventions.

Communication principles

- Writing styles tend to be informal.
- Conferences are more open than e-mail, so you need to be careful what you say to or about others.
- Thank, acknowledge and support people freely.
- Acknowledge before differing.
- 'Speak' from your own (or an acknowledged) perspective.

Keeping online communication flowing

- Lift and quote from the messages of others before replying.
- Use 'emoticons' to convey emotions – for example, ☺ to convey a joke.

- Avoid putting words into capital letters – they are considered to be equivalent to shouting.
- Ensure that you place new messages in the appropriate conference.
- Put your test messages in a test conference.
- Put a short effective title for your message.
- When replying to someone else's message, use the same title if the subject remains the same as before, otherwise start a new thread with a new title.
- Keep all messages short – never more than one screenful.
- Use several messages for different topics (this aids replying).
- If you have something longer to say, attach it as a document.

Attaching documents to an e-mail or in a conference message

- To send or share anything longer than one screenful in a message, it is best to attach a document.
- Make sure the title is clear and there are one or two lines of description in the message so that your recipients can decide whether, and how soon, they need to download the document.
- Make sure that your recipients have suitable software to download and open your document (you may need to make an *.rtf version to be certain).
- Always check a document for viruses, using up-to-date virus checking software, before you send it to others.

See Crystal (2006) for more about text-based online communication.

References

Altbach, P G, Reisberg, L and L E Rumbley (2009) *Trends in Global Higher Education: Tracking an Academic Revolution*, UNESCO, Paris

Amirault, R J and Y L Visser (2009) The university in periods of technological change: a historically grounded perspective, *Journal of Computing in Higher Education*, 21 (1), pp 62–79

Armellini, A and O Aiyegbayo (2010) Learning design and assessment with e-tivities, *British Journal of Educational Technology*, 41 (6), pp 922–35

Armellini, A and S Jones (2008) Seizing each day to foster change in e-learning design, *Reflecting Education*, 4 (1), pp 17–29

Armellini, A, Salmon, G and D Hawkridge (2009) The carpe diem journey: designing for learning transformation, in T Hayes, D Morrison, H Mellar, P Bullen and M Oliver (eds), *Transforming Higher Education through Technology-enabled Learning*, The Higher Education Academy, York. Online: http://www.heacademy.ac.uk/assets/York/documents/ourwork/learningandtech/Transforming.pdf (accessed July 2010)

Aubert, B A and B L Kelsey (2003) Further understanding of trust performance in virtual teams, *Small Group Research*, 34 (5), pp 575–618

Aubusson, P, Schuck, S and K Burden (2009) Mobile learning for teacher professional learning: benefits, obstacles and issues, *ALT-J*, 17 (3), pp 233–47

Avila, R and N Léger (2005) *The Future of Higher Education: A Scenario Evaluation of Its Prospects and Challenges*, iUniverse, Lincoln

Axelsson, L E, Bodin, K, Norberg, R and T Person (2001) *Folkbildningnet: an anthology about folkbildning and flexible learning*, Swedish National Council of Adult Education, Stockholm

Azevedo, R (2002) Beyond intelligent tutoring systems: using computers as METAcognitive tools to enhance learning?, *Instructional Science*, 30, pp 41–45

Badge, J and J Scott (2009) Dealing with plagiarism in the digital age. Online: http://evidencenet pbworks com/Dealing-with-plagiarism-in-the-digital-age (accessed 24 September 2010)

Baptista Nunes, J M and M A McPherson (2002) Pedagogical and implementation models for e-learning continuing professional distance education (CPDE) emerging from action research, *International Journal of Management Education*, 2(3, Summer), pp 16–27

Barajas, M and G J Gannaway (2007) Implementing e-learning in the traditional higher education institutions, *Higher Education in Europe*, 32 (2), pp 111–19

Barker, P (2010) Implementation of Optical Fibre Communications Module in a Virtual Learning Environment HEA Engineering Subject Centre. Online: www.engsc.ac.uk/downloads/optical.pdf (accessed 12 August 2010)

Barklamb, K (2010) Using Second Life Simulations to Enhance and Develop the Learning Environment for Occupational Psychology Students, paper presented at The Division of Occupational Psychology Annual Conference, Brighton, UK, January

Bassis, M (2010) Changing the equation, *Inside Higher Education*, 25 March. Online: www.insidehighered.com/views/2010/03/25/bassis (accessed October 2010)

Bax, S (2010) Day 8 Keynote at Learning Futures Festival Online. Online: http://tinyurl.com/lff10-bax (accessed September 2010)

Bax, S and M Pegrum (2009) 'I wasn't invited to the party': Lurking in multicultural online educational forums, in A Ragusa (ed), *Interaction in Communication Technologies and Virtual Learning Environments: Human Factors*, IGA Global, Hershey, chapter 10, pp 145–59

Beck, U (2009) (version in English, translated by C Cronin) *World at Risk*, Polity Press, Cambridge and Malden

Behan, A and F Boylan (2009) Harnessing developments in technology and merging them with new approaches to teaching: a practical example of the effective use of wikis and social bookmarking sites in 3rd level professional education. Online: http://arrow.dit.ie/cgi/viewcontent.cgi?article=1002&context=beschspart (accessed April 2011)

Bennett, S and D Barp (2008) Peer observation – a case for doing it online, *Teaching in Higher Education*, 13 (5), pp 559–70

Bennett, S and S Marsh (2002) Are we expecting online tutors to run before they can walk?, *Innovations in Education and Teaching International*, 39 (1), pp 14–20

Bennett, S, Maton, K and L Kervin (2008) The 'digital natives' debate: a critical review of the evidence, *British Journal of Educational Technology* 39 (5), pp 775–86

Bennett, S and J Santy (2009) A window on our teaching practice: enhancing individual online teaching quality though online peer observation and support, *Nurse Education in Practice*, 9, 403–6

Benque, N (1999) *Online Training for Tutors*, proceedings of Online Educa Conference, December, Berlin

Berge, Z L (2007) Motivate and manage: key activities of online instructors, in J M Spector (ed), *Finding Your Online Voice: Stories Told By Experienced Online Educators*, Lawrence Erlbaum Associates, Inc, Mahwah, NJ, pp 73–82

Berge, Z L (2008) Changing instructor's roles in virtual worlds, *The Quarterly Review of Distance Education*, 9 (4), pp 407–11

Bevan, E (1999 and 2010) Personal e-mail communications

Biggs, J (2003) *Teaching for Quality Learning at University*, 2nd edn, Society for Research into Higher Education (SRHE) and Open University Press, Buckingham

Billett, S (2009a) Realising the educational worth of integrating work experiences in higher education, *Studies in Higher Education*, 34 (7) 827–43

Billett, S (2009b) Conceptualizing learning experiences: Contributions and mediations of the social, personal and brute, *Mind, Culture and Activity*, 16 (1) 32–47

Blumer, H (1969) *Symbolic Interaction*, Prentice-Hall, Englewood Cliffs, NJ

Boal, A (1988) *Theatre of the Oppressed*, Pluto, London

Bonk, C J (2009) *The World is Open,* Jossey-Bass, San Francisco

Bromby, M (2009) Virtual seminars: problem-based learning in healthcare law and ethics, *Journal of Information, Law and Technology*, 3 (December). Online: www2.warwick.ac.uk/fac/soc/law/elj/jilt/2009_3/bromby (accessed 24 September 2010)

Brown, A and S E Reushle (2009) The Power of Connection: Sharing Epistemological Approaches to Reach Beyond Knowledge and Skill Acquisition in an Australian Higher Education Context, paper presented at the 2nd International PBL Symposium: What are we learning about learning? Republic Polytechnic, Singapore, June 10–12

Brown, J Seely and P Duguid (2000) *The Social Life of Information*, Harvard Business School Press, Boston

Bruner, J (1986) The language of education, in J Bruner (ed), *Actual Minds, Possible Worlds*, Harvard University Press, Cambridge, MA

Bryson, J M, Ackermann, F, Eden, C and C B Fin (2004) *Visible Thinking – unlocking causal mapping for practical business results*, Wiley, London

Burn, J M and K D Loch (2003) The societal impact of the World Wide Web: key challenges for the 21st century, in M Khosrow-Pour (ed), *Advanced Topics in Information Resources Management*, IGI Publishing, Hershey, PA

Candy, P (2010) Reaffirming Core Academic Values in the Digital Era: Technology in the Context of Boyer's Four Scholarships, presentation at Beyond Distance Research Alliance, University of Leicester, July. Online: http://tinyurl com/mz-candy (accessed 24 September 2010)

Cann, A, Badge, J, Johnson, J and A Moseley (2009) Twittering the student experience, *ALT Online Newletter*, 17, 19th October

Carr, N (2010) *The Shallows: How the Internet is Changing the Way We Think, Read and Remember*, Atlantic Books, London

Carrington, S and S Gitta (2010) Critical social theory and transformative learning: evidence in pre-service teachers' service-learning reflection logs, *Higher Education Research and Development*, 29 (1), pp 45–57

Castelfranchi, C (2002) The social nature of information and the role of trust, *International Journal of Cooperative Information Systems*, 11 (3 and 4), pp 381–403

Cheung, W S and K F Hew (2010) Examining facilitators' habits of mind in an asynchronous online discussion environment: A two cases study, *Australasian Journal of Educational Technology*, 26 (1), pp 123–32

Chuang, S C, Hwang, F K and C C Tsai (2008) Students' perceptions of constructivist internet learning environments by a physics virtual laboratory: the gap between ideal and reality and gender differences, *CyberPsychology and Behavior*, 11 (2), pp 150–56

Collins, A and R Halverson (2010) The second educational revolution: rethinking education in the age of technology, *Journal of Computer Assisted Learning*, 26 (1), pp 18–27

Collis, B and J Moonen (2005) An On-going Journey: Technology as a Learning Workbench, monograph on occasion of their retirement from the University of Twente, Enschede, NL. Online: http://www.BettyCollisJefMoonen.nl/rb.htm (accessed August 2010)

Conole, G (2005) E-learning Research Methodological Issues, presentation at e-Learning Research Centre workshop, Manchester, 3 May. Online: http://www.slideshare.net/grainne/elearning-research-methodological-issues (accessed October 2010)

Creswell, J W and V L Clark (2007) *Designing and Conducting Mixed Methods Research*, Sage, Thousands Oaks, CA

Crystal, D (2006) *Language and the Internet*, 2nd edn, Cambridge University Press, Cambridge

Cuevas, H M, Fiore, S M, Bowers, C A and E Salas (2004) Fostering constructive cognitive and metacognitive activity in computer-based complex task training environments, *Computers in Human Behavior*, 20, pp 225–41

Cuevas, H M, Fiore, S M and R L Oser (2002) Scaffolding cognitive and metacognitive processes in low verbal ability learners: use of diagrams in computer-based training environments, *Instructional Science*, 30, pp 433–64

Cummings, J A and C J Bonk (2002) Facilitating interactions among students and faculty via web-based conferencing systems, *Journal of Technology in Human Services*, 20 (3/4), pp 245–65

Curşeu, P L, Schalk, R and S Schruijer (2010) The use of cognitive mapping in eliciting and evaluating group cognitions, *Journal of Applied Psychology*, 40 (5), pp 1258–91

Daniel, J, Kanwar, A and S Uvalić-Trumbić (2008) The right to education: a model for making higher education equally accessible to all on the basis of merit, *Asian Journal of Distance Education*, 6 (2), pp 5–11

Daniel, J, West, P and A Monaghan (2008) Course Development in Distance Education: Whose is the Content?, paper delivered to the Second CREAD Andes Congress/Second Virtual Educa Summit, Loja, Ecuador, April. Online: http://www.col.org/colweb/site/cache/bypass/pid/5285

Dawson, S (2010) Seeing the learning community: An exploration of the development of a resource for monitoring online student networking, *British Journal of Educational Technology*, 41 (5), pp 736–52

Design-based Research Collective (2003) Design-based research: an emerging paradigm for educational inquiry, *Educational Researcher*, 32 (1), pp 5–8

De Wever, B D, Van Keer, H, Schellens, T and M Valcke (2010) Roles as a structuring tool in online discussion groups: The differential impact of different roles on social knowledge construction, *Computers in Human Behavior*, 26 (4), pp 516–23

Dirckinck-Holmfeld, L (2002) Designing virtual learning environments based on problem orientated project pedagogy, in L Dirckinck-Holmfeld and B Fibiger (eds), *Learning in Virtual Environments*, Samsfundslitteratur, Frederiksberg

Downing, K J, Lam, T, Kwong, T, Downing, W and S Chan (2007) Creating interaction in online learning: a case study, *ALT-J*, 15 (3), pp 201–15

Duffy, T and J Kirkley (2004) *Learner-centered Theory and Practice in Distance Education: Cases from higher education*, Lawrence Erlbaum, Mahwah, NJ

Dulewicz, V and M Higgs (2002) Emotional intelligence and the development of managers and leaders, in M Pearn (ed), *Individual Differences and Development in Organizations*, Wiley, Chichester

Eden, C and J Ackermann (2004) Cognitive mapping expert views for policy analysis in the public sector, *European Journal of Operational Research*, 152, pp 615–30

Edirisingha, P and J Fothergill (2009) Balancing e-lectures with podcasts: a case study of an undergraduate engineering module, *Engineering Education*, 4 (2), pp 14–24

Edirisingha, P, Hawkridge, D and J Fothergill (2010) A renaissance of audio: podcasting approaches for learning on campus and beyond, *European Journal of Open, Distance and E-Learning*, 1. Online at http://www.eurodl.org/?article=393 (accessed March 2011)

Ellis, R A and P Goodyear (2010) *Students' Experiences of E-learning in Higher Education*, Routledge, New York and Abingdon

Ellis, R A, Goodyear, P, O'Hara, A and M Prosser (2007) The university student experience of face-to-face and online discussions: coherence, reflection and meaning, *ALT-J*, 15 (1), pp 83–97

Eshet-Alkalai, Y (2004) Digital literacy: a conceptual framework for survival skills in the digital era, *Journal of Educational Multimedia and Hypermedia*, 13, (1), pp 93–106

Feenberg, A (1989) The written word, in R D Mason and A R Kaye (eds), *Mindweave: Communication, computers and distance education*, Pergamon, Oxford

Fibiger, B (2002) Didactic design of virtual learning environments, in L Dirckinck-Holmfeld and B Fibiger (eds), *Learning in Virtual Environments*, Samfundslitteratur, Frederiksberg

Fisher, K (2003) Demystifying critical reflection: Defining criteria for assessment, *Higher Education Research and Development*, 22 (3), pp 314–25

Flood, R L (2010) The relationship of 'systems thinking' to action research, *Systemic Practice and Action Research*, 23, pp 269–84

Freire, P (1972) *Pedagogy of the Oppressed*, Penguin, Harmondsworth

Freire, P and I Shor (1987) *A Pedagogy for Liberation Dialogues on Transforming Education*, Macmillan, London

Friesen, N (2009) *Rethinking E-learning Research: Foundations, methods, and practices*, Peter Lang, New York

Fulantelli, G (2010) Blended learning, systems thinking and communities and practice, in L Dirckinck-Holmfeld, C Jones and B Lindstrom (eds), *Analysing Networked Learning Practices in Higher Education and Continuing Professional Development*, Sense Publishers, Rotterdam, Boston and Tapei

Goleman, D (1995) *Emotional Intelligence: Why it can matter more than IQ*, Bantam Books, New York

Goodfellow, P, Lea, M, Gonzalez, F and R Mason (2001) Opportunity and e-quality: intercultural and linguistic issues in global online learning, *Distance Education*, 22 (5), pp 65– 84

Gullifer, J and G A Tyson (2010) Exploring university students' perceptions of plagiarism: A focus group study, *Studies in Higher Education*, 35 (4), pp 463–81

Gunawardena, C N and R Zittle (1995) An examination of teaching and learning processes in distance education and implications for designing instruction, in M F Beaudoin (ed), *Distance Education Symposium 3: Instruction*, ACSDE Research Monograph, no 12, pp 51–63

Halliday, M A K and R Hasan (1989) *Language, Context and Text: Aspects of language in a social-semiotic perspective*, Oxford University Press, Oxford

Hamid, S, Chang, S and S Kurnia (2009) Identifying the use of online social networking in higher education, in *Same places, different spaces. Proceedings of Ascilite Auckland 2009*. Online: http://www.ascilite.org.au/conferences/auckland09/procs/hamid-poster.pdf (accessed September 2010)

Han, Y (2006) GROW: building a high-quality civil engineering learning object repository and portal, *ARIADNE*, 49. Online: http://www.ariadne.ac.uk/issue49/yan-han/#6 (accessed 18 August 2010)

Harris, E and R Woolley (2009) Facilitating innovation through cognitive mapping of uncertainty, *International Studies of Management and Organization*, 39 (1), pp 70–100

Harvey, L and P Knight (1996) *Transforming Higher Education*, SRHE and Open University Press, Buckingham

Hawkridge, D (2003) The human in the machine: reflections on mentoring in the British Open University, *Mentoring and Tutoring*, 11 (1), pp 15–24

Hawkridge, D, Armellini, A, Nikoi, S, Rowlett, T and G Witthaus (2010) Curriculum, intellectual property rights and open educational resources in British universities – and beyond (Special issue on Faculty Intellectual Property in the Digital Age), *Journal of Computing in Higher Education*, 22, pp 162–76

Hawkridge, D, Morgan, A and A Jelfs (1997) *H801 Students' and Tutors' Use of the Electronic Workbook and Electronic Mail 1997*, OU Report to the Electronic Tutoring Group, Milton Keynes, December

Helsper, E J and R Eynon (2010) Digital natives: where is the evidence? *British Educational Research Journal*, 36 (3), pp 503–520

Hendry, G (1996) Constructivism and educational practice, *Australian Journal of Education*, 40 (1), pp 19–45

Henri, F (1992) Computer conferencing and content analysis, in A Kaye (ed), *Collaborative Learning Through Computer Conferencing: The Najaden papers*, Springer-Verlag, Heidelberg

Hew, K F and W S Cheung (2010) Use of three-dimensional (3-D) immersive virtual worlds in K-12 and higher education settings: A review of the research, *British Journal of Educational Technology*, 41, pp 33–55. Online: http://www.ascilite.org.au/ajet/ajet26/cheung html (accessed March 2011)

Hmelo-Silver, C E, Duncan, R G and C A Chinn (2006) Scaffolding and achievement in problem-based and inquiry learning: a response to Kirschner, Sweller, and Clark (2006), *Educational Psychologist*, 42 (2), pp 99–107

Holsti, O R (1968) Content analysis, in G Lindzey and E Aronson (eds), *The Handbook of Social Psychology: Research methods*, Addison-Wesley, Reading, MA

Holton, D and D Clark (2006) Scaffolding and metacognition, *International Journal of Mathematical Education in Science and Technology*, 37, pp 127–43

Hookway, N (2008) Entering the blogosphere: some strategies for using blogs in social research, *Qualitative Research*, 8 (1), pp 91–113

Hopson, M H, Simms, R L and G A Knezek (2001–02) Using a technology-enriched environment to improve higher-order thinking skills, *Journal of Research on Technology in Education*, 34 (2), pp 109–19

Horizon (2002–10) http://www.nmc.org/horizon (accessed August 2010)

Hunt, C (2001) Shifting shadows: metaphors and maps for facilitating reflective practice, *Reflective Practice*, 2 (3), pp 275–87

Hunt, L, Bromage, A and B Tomkinson (2006) (eds) The *Realities of change in Higher Education*, Routledge, Oxford and New York

Jaques, D and G Salmon (2007) *Learning in Groups*, 4th edn, Routledge, London and New York

Johnson, M B and A J Onwuegbuzie (2004) Mixed methods research: A research paradigm whose time has come, *Educational Researcher*, 33 (7), pp 14–26

Jonassen, D, Davidson, M, Collins, M, Campbell, B and B Haag (1995) Constructivism and computer-mediated communication in distance education, *American Journal of Distance Education*, 9 (2), pp 7–25

Jones, C (2010) Networked learning and postgraduate professionals, in L Dirckinck-Holmfeld, C Jones and B Lindström (eds), *Higher Education and Continuing Professional Development*, Sense Publishers, Rotterdam, Boston and Taipei

Kanwar, A, Kodhandaraman, B and A Umar (2010) Toward sustainable open education resources: a perspective from the global South, *American Journal of Distance Education*, 24 (2), pp 65–80

Kelly, A E (2004) Design research in education: yes, but is it methodological?, *Journal of the Learning Sciences*, 13 (1), pp 5–8

Kelly, G A (1955) *The Psychology of Personal Constructs*, Norton, New York

Knight, P T (2002) *Being a Teacher in Higher Education*, SRHE and Open University Press, Buckingham

Kovacic, A, Bubas, C and Zlatovic, M (2008) E-tivities with a wiki: innovative teaching of English as a foreign language. Online: http://eunis.dk/papers/p87.pdf (accessed October 2010)

Leander, K M, Phillips, N C and K H Taylor (2010) The changing social spaces of learning: mapping new mobilities, *Review of Research in Education*, 34 (1), pp 329–94

Learning Futures 10 workshops (2010) http://tinyurl.com/lff10workshops (accessed August 2010)

Lippincott, K, Eco, U, Gombrich, E H et al. (2000) *The Story of Time*, Merrell Holberton, London

Littlejohn, A and C Pegler (2007) *Preparing for Blended E-learning*, Routledge, London and New York

Lopez-Fernandez, L and J Rodriguez-Illera (2008) Investigating university students' adaptation to a digital learner course portfolio, *Computers and Education*, 52 (3), pp 608–16

Loureiro-Koechlin, C and B Allan (2010) Time, space and structure in an e-learning e-mentoring project, *British Journal of Educational Technology*, 41(5), pp 721–35

Lowenthal, P R and N Leech (2010) Mixed research and online learning: Strategies for improvement, in T T Kidd (ed), *Online Education and Adult Learning: New frontiers for teaching practices*, IGI Global, Hershey, PA

Macdonald, J (2003) Assessing online collaborative learning: process and product, *Computers and Education*, 40 (4), pp 377–91

Macdonald, J (2004) Developing competent e-learners: the role of assessment, *Assessment and Evaluation in Higher Education*, 29 (2), pp 215–26

Macdonald, J, Weller, M and R Mason (2002) Meeting the assessment demands of networked courses, *International Journal on E-learning*, Jan–Mar, pp 9–18

Mann, B L (2006) *Selected Styles in Web-based Educational Research*, IGI Global, Hershey, PA

Mann, S J (2001) Alternative perspectives on the student experience: alienation and engagement, *Society for Research into Higher Education*, 26 (1), pp 7–19

Martell, C (2000) The age of information, the age of foolishness, *College and Research Libraries* (Jan), pp 10–27

Mason, R (1993) Written interactions, in R Mason (ed), *Computer Conferencing: The last word*, Beach Holme, Victoria, British Colombia, pp 3–19

Mason, R (1998) *Globalising Education: Trends and Applications*, Routledge, London

Mathiasen, H and P Rattleff (2002) The conditions of communication in computer-mediated, net-disseminated educational settings, in L Dirckinck-Holmfeld and B Fibiger (eds), *Learning in Virtual Environments*, Samsfundslitteratur, Frederiksberg

McDonald, J and G Postle (1999) Teaching Online: Challenge to a Reinterpretation of Traditional Instructional Models, paper presented at AusWeb99. Online: http://ausweb.scu.edu.au/aw99/papers/mcdonald/paper.htm (accessed October 2010)

McNaught, C (2003) Identifying the complexity of factors in the sharing and reuse of resources, in A Littlejohn (ed), *Reusing Online Resources*, Kogan Page, London

Meadows, M S (2008) *I, Avatar: the culture and consequences of having a second life*, New Riders, Berkeley, CA

Meyer, K A (2006) Cost-efficiencies of online learning, *ASHE Higher Education Report*, 32 (1), pp 1–123

Michinov, N, Brunot, S, Le Bohec, O, Juhel, J and M Delaval (2010) Procrastination, participation, and performance in online learning environments, *Computers and Education*, 56 (1), pp 243–52

Mitra, S (2010) The Future of Learning, keynote at ALT-C Conference 'Into something rich and strange', Nottingham, September. Online: http://www.alt.ac.uk/altc2010/ (accessed October 2010)

Morgan, D L (1988) *Focus Groups as Qualitative Research*, Sage, Beverley Hills, CA

Mundemann, F (1999) *Certified Training for Tele-coaches*, proceedings of Online Educa, Berlin

Ng'ambi, D and I Brown (2009) Intended and unintended consequences of student use of an online questioning environment, *British Journal of Educational Technology*, 40 (2), pp 316–28

Ng'ambi, D and S Goodman (2009) Bridging distance between actual and potential development: a case of using ICT mediated consultation tool, *Education and Information Technologies Journal*, 14, pp 89–102

Nicol, D (2007) Laying a foundation for lifelong learning: Case studies of e-assessment in large 1st-year classes, *British Journal of Educational Technology*, 38, pp 668–78

Nie, M, Armellini, A, Harrington, S, Barklamb, K and R Randall (2010) The role of podcasting in effective curriculum renewal, *ALT-J*, 18 (2), pp 105–18

Norman, D (2010) *Living with Complexity*, MIT Press, Cambridge, MA

Nussbaum, M, Alvarez, C, McFarlane, A, Florencia G, Claro, S and D Radovic, (2009) Technology as small group face-to-face, *Collaborative Scaffolding Computers and Education*, 52 (1), pp 147–53

OECD Committee for Economic Development Digital Connections Council (2009) Harnessing Openness to improve research teaching and learning in Higher Education, p 2. Online: http://www.ced.org/images/library/reports/digital_economy/dcc_opennessedu09.pdf (accessed August 2010)

Pettenati, M C and M E Cigognini (2009) Designing E-tivities to Increase Learning-to-learn Abilities, eLearning papers, University of Florence. Online: http://www.uh.cu/static/documents/RDA/Designing%20e-tivities%20increase.pdf (accessed October 2010)

Pidd, M (2003) *Tools for Thinking*, 2nd edn, Wiley, Chichester

Potter, J and M Wetherell (1989) *Discourse and Social Psychology*, Sage, London

Preece, J (2000) *Online Communities: Supporting sociability and designing usability*, John Wiley, Chichester

Redmond, P and J V Lock (2009) Authentic learning across international borders: a cross institutional online project for pre-service teachers, in Cleborne Maddux (ed), *Research Highlights in Technology and Teacher eduCation 2009*, Society for Information Technology and Teacher Education (SITE)/Association for the Advancement of Computing in Education (AACE), Chesapeake, VA, pp 265–73

Redmond, P and A Mander (2009) Constructing a Pre-service Teacher Online Learning Community, paper in 20th International Conference of the Society for Information Technology and Teacher Education (SITE 2009), 2–6 March 2009, Charleston, SC, USA

Reeves, T C, Herrington, J and R Oliver (2002) Authentic Activities and Online Learning, proceeding of 25th HERDSA annual conference, pp 567–62

Reiser, J (2004) Scaffolding complex learning: the mechanisms for structuring and problematising student work, *Journal of the Learning Sciences*, 13 (2) pp 273–304

Reushle, S E (2008) Virtual territories: researching and living transformative learning in online higher education contexts, in R Henderson and P Danaher (eds), *Troubling Terrains: Tactics for traversing and transforming contemporary educational research*, Teneriffe, Queensland

Reushle, S and M Mitchell (2009) Sharing the journey of facilitator and learner: online pedagogy in practice, *Journal of Learning Design*, 3 (1) pp 11–20

Rheingold, H (2002) *Smart Mobs*, Minerva, London

Roblyer, M D and J Edwards (2000) *Integrating Educational Technology into Teaching*, Merrill, Upper Saddle River, NJ

Rofe, J S (2011) The 'IR Model': a schema for pedagogic design and development in international relations, *European Political Science*, 10 (1), pp 103–17

Ross, S M, Morrison, G R and D L Lowther (2010) Educational technology research past and present: Balancing rigor and relevance to impact school learning, *Contemporary Educational Technology,* 1 (1), pp 17–35. Online: http://www.cedtech.net/articles/112.pdf

Rossi, D M (2010) Learning relationships in online contexts: a substantive theory constructed from the integrated analyses of learner-learner interaction and knowledge construction in an undergraduate communication course, unpublished PhD thesis, University of Southern Queensland

Rovai, A P (2002) Building a sense of community at a distance, *The International Review of Research of Open and Distance Learning*, 3 (1), pp 1–16

Rowntree, D (1995) Teaching and learning online: a correspondence education for the 21st century?, *British Journal of Educational Technology*, 26 (3), pp 205–15

Rudman, P, Lavelle, S, Salmon, G and A Cashmore (2010) SWIFT-ly enhancing laboratory learning: genetics in the virtual world, in L Creanor, D Hawkridge, K Ng and F Rennie (eds), Proceedings of 17th Association of Learning Technology (ALT-C) Conference 'Into something rich and strange – making sense of the sea-change', 7–9, Nottingham, pp 118–26

Ruey, S (2010) A case study of constructivist instructional strategies for adult online learning, *British Journal of Educational Technology*, 41 (5), pp 706–20

Rumble, G (2001) The costs and costing of networked learning, *Journal of Asynchronous Learning Networks*, 5 (2), pp 75–96

Rumble, G (2009) Talk on Costing Blended Learning to the Distance Learning Forum at the University of Leicester, UK, 28 April

Rumble, G (2010) Flexing costs and reflecting on methods, in E Burge, C Gibson and T Gibson (eds), *Flexibility in Higher Education: Promises, Ambiguities, Challenges*, Athabasca University Press, Athabasca, Alberta, pp 264–301

Russell, C (2009) A systemic framework for managing e-learning adoption in campus universities: individual strategies in context, *ALT-J*, 17 (1), pp 3–19

Salmon, G (2002a) *E-tivities: The key to active online learning*, Kogan Page, London

Salmon, G (2002b) Approaches to researching teaching and learning online, in C Steeples and C Jones (eds), *Networked Learning: Perspectives and issues*, Springer-Verlag, London

Salmon, G (2002c) Mirror, mirror, on my screen: exploring online reflections, *British Journal of Educational Technology*, 33 (4), pp 383–96

Salmon, G (2002d) Online networking and individual development, in M Pearn (ed), *Individual Differences and Development in Organizations, Wiley Handbooks in the Psychology of Management in Organizations*, Wiley, Chichester

Salmon, G (2005) Flying not flapping: a strategic framework for e-learning and pedagogical innovation in higher education institutions, *Association of Learning Technologies Journal (ALT-J)*, 13 (3), pp 201–18

Salmon, G (2006) 80:20 for e-moderators, in I Mac Labhrainn, C McDonald Legg, D Schneckenberg and J Wildt (eds), *The Challenge of eCompetence in Academic Staff Development*, CELT, Galway

Salmon, G (2009) The future for Second Life and learning, *British Journal of Educational Technology*, 40 (3), pp 526–38

Salmon, G and P Edirisingha (eds) (2008) *Podcasting for Learning in Universities*, Open University Press/McGraw Hill/Society for Research into Higher Education, Maidenhead and New York. Online: www.podcastingforlearning. com

Salmon, G, Edirisingha, P, Mobbs, M, Mobbs, R and D Dennett (2008) *How to create podcasts for education*, Open University Press/McGraw Hill/Society for Research into Higher Education, Maidenhead and New York. Also available as an iphone app

Salmon, G and D Hawkridge (2009) Editorial: out of this world, *British Journal of Educational Technology*, 40 (3), pp 401–13

Salmon, G, Jones, S and A Armellini (2008) Building institutional capability in e-learning design, *ALT-J*, 16 (2), pp 95–109

Salmon, G and N Lawless (2006) Management education for the twenty-first century, in C J Bonk and C R Graham (eds), *Handbook of Blended Learning: global perspectives, local designs,* Pfeiffer, San Francisco

Salmon, G, Nie, M and P Edirisingha (2010) Developing a five-stage model of learning in Second Life, *Educational Research* (Special issue: Virtual worlds and education), 52 (2), pp 169–82

Santoro, G P (1995) What is computer-mediated communication?, in Z L Berge and M P Collins (eds), *Computer-Mediated Communication and the Online Classroom*, Hampton Press, Cresskill NJ, pp 11–27

Schön, D (1983) *The Reflective Practitioner: How professionals think in action*, Basic Books, London

Schwan, S, Straub, D and F W Hesse (2002) Information management and learning in computer conferences: coping with irrelevant and unconnected messages, *Instructional Science*, 30, pp 269–89

Seel, N M (2001) Epistemology, situated cognition, and mental models: 'Like a bridge over troubled water', *Instructional Science*, 29 (29), pp 403–27

Sharma, P and M J Hannafin (2007) Scaffolding in technology-enhanced learning environments, *Interactive Learning Environments*, 15 (1), pp 27–46

Sharples, M, Arnedillo-Sánchez, I and G Vavoula (2009) Mobile learning small devices, big issues, in L Balacheff (ed), *Technology-enhanced Learning*, Part IV, Springer, Berlin, pp 233–49

Shen, K N and M Khalifa (2009) Facebook Usage Among Arabic College Students: Preliminary Findings on Gender Differences, 9th International Conference on Electronic Business, pp 1080–87

Simons, G F (2002) *Eurodiversity*, Butterworth-Heinemann, Elsevier Science, Woborn, MA

Skinner, E (2009) Using community development theory to improve student engagement in online discussion: a case study, *ALT-J*, 17 (2), pp 89–100

Slevin, J (2008) E-learning and the transformation of social interaction in higher education, *Learning, Media and Technology*, 33 (2), pp 115–26

Smet, M, van Keer, H and M Valcke (2008) Blending asynchronous discussion groups and peer tutoring in higher education: an exploratory study of online peer tutoring behaviour, *Computers and Education*, 50 (1), pp 207–23

Snavely, L (2008) Global educational goals, technology, and information literacy in higher education, *New Directions for Teaching and Learning* 114, pp 35–46

Sorensen, E K (2002) Distributed CSCL: a situated, collaborative tapestry, in L Dirckinck-Holmfeld and B Fibiger (eds), *Learning in Virtual Environments*, Samfundslitteratur, Frederiksberg

Stewart, D W, Shamdasani, P N and D W Rook (2007) *Focus Groups: Theory and Practice*, 2nd edn, Sage, London

Surowiecki, J (2005) *The Wisdom of Crowds: Why the many are smarter than the few*, Abacus, London

Sutton-Brady, C, Scott, K M, Taylor, L, Carabetta, G and S Clark (2009) The value of using short-format podcasts to enhance learning and teaching, *ALT-J*, 17 (3), pp 219–32

Swann, W B, Polzer, J T, Seyle, D C and S J Ko (2004) Finding value in diversity: Verification of personal and social self-views in diverse groups, *Academy of Management Review*, 29 (1), pp 9–27

Swindell, R (2002) U3A online: a virtual university of the third age for isolated older people, *International Journal of Lifelong Education*, 21 (5), 414–29

Tabak, I (2004) Synergy: a complement to emerging patterns of distributed scaffolding, *The Journal of Learning Sciences*, 13 (3) pp 305–35

Tan, L (1999) The 'Faceless Facilitator': An impossible learning approach?, proceedings of Online Educa, Berlin

Taylor, E W (2001) Transformative learning theory: a neurobiological perspective of the role of emotions and unconscious ways of knowing, *International Journal of Lifelong Education*, 20 (3), pp 218–36

Tochel, C, Haig, A, Hesketh, A, Cadzow, A, Beggs, K, Colthart, I and H Peacock (2009) The effectiveness of portfolios for post-graduate assessment and education, *Medical Teacher*, 31 (4), pp 299–318

Traxler, J (2010) Students and mobile devices, *ALT-J*, 18 (2), pp 149–60

Tsui, A B M and W W Ki (2002) Teacher participation in computer conferencing: socio-psychological dimensions, *Journal of Information Technology for Teacher Education*, 11 (1), pp 23–44

Tsui, L (2002) Fostering critical thinking through effective pedagogy, *Journal of Higher Education*, 73 (6), pp 740–63

Turney, C S M, Robinson, D, Lee, M and A Soutar (2009) *Active Learning in Higher Education*, 10 (1), pp. 71–83

Twining, P (2009) Exploring the educational potential of virtual worlds – some reflections from the SPP, *British Journal of Educational Technology*, 40 (3), 496–514

Underhill, J and J McDonald (2010) Collaborative tutor development: enabling a transformative paradigm in a South African University, *Mentoring and Tutoring: Partnership in Learning*, 18 (2), pp 91–106

Van den Akker, J, Gravemeijer, K, McKenney, S and N Nieveen (eds) (2007) *Educational Design Research*, Routledge, London

van Kouwen, K, Dieperink, C, Schot, P P and M J Wassen (2010) Computer-supported cognitive mapping for participatory problem structuring, *Environment and Planning 2009*, 41, pp 63–81

Wang, F and M J Hannafin (2005) Design-based research and technology-enhanced learning environments, *Educational Technology Research Development*, 53 (4), pp 5–23

Warburton, S (2009) Second Life in higher education: assessing the potential for and the barriers to deploying virtual worlds in learning and teaching, *British Journal of Educational Technology*, 40 (3), 414–26

Warren, C M J (2008) The Use of Online Asynchronous Discussion Forums in the Development of Deep Learning Among Postgraduate Real Estate Students, *CIB International Conference on Building Education and Research*, Kandalama, Sri Lanka, 11–15 February, pp 1698–1708

Weller, M (2002a) *Delivering Learning on the Net: The why, what and how of online education*, Kogan Page, London

Weller, M J (2002b) Assessment issues on a web-based course, *Assessment and Evaluation in Higher Education*, 27 (2), pp 109–16

Weller, M and L Robinson (2001) Scaling up an online course to deal with 12,000 students, *Education, Communication and Information*, 1 (3), pp 307–22

Wenger, E, McDermott, R and W M Snyder (eds) (2002) *Cultivating Communities of Practice*, Harvard Business School Press, Boston MA

Wheeler, M and G Salmon (2008) *Second Life: guide for learning group participants*, University of Leicester, Leicester

Wheeler, S (2007) The influence of communication technologies and approaches to study on transactional distance in blended learning, *ALT-J*, 15 (2), pp 103–17

Woo, Y and T C Reeves (2007) Meaningful interaction in web-based learning: a social constructivist interpretation, *Internet and Higher Education*, 10, pp 15–25

Index